MEMOIRS OF A MILITIA SERGEANT

D0059230

MEMOIRS OF A MILITIA SERGEANT

A Novel by
MANUEL ANTÔNIO DE ALMEIDA

Translated from the Portuguese by
RONALD W. SOUSA

WITH A FOREWORD BY THOMAS H. HOLLOWAY
AND AN AFTERWORD BY FLORA SÜSSEKIND

New York   Oxford
Oxford University Press
1999

Oxford University Press

Oxford New York
Athens Auckland Bangkok Bogotá Bombay
Buenos Aires Calcutta Cape Town Dar es Salaam
Delhi Florence Hong Kong Istanbul Karachi
Kuala Lumpur Madras Madrid Melbourne
Mexico City Nairobi Paris Singapore
Taipei Tokyo Toronto Warsaw

and associated companies in
Berlin Ibadan

Copyright © 1999 by Oxford University Press, Inc.

Published by Oxford University Press, Inc.
198 Madison Avenue, New York, New York 10016

Oxford is a registered trademark of Oxford University Press, Inc.

Library of Congress Cataloging-in-Publication Data
Almeida, Manuel Antônio de, 1831–1861.
[Memórias de um sargento de milícias. English]
Memoirs of a militia sergeant : a novel / by Manuel Antônio de Almeida;
translated from the Portuguese by Ronald W. Sousa;
with a foreword by Thomas H. Holloway;
and an afterword by Flora Süssekind.
p. cm. — (Library of Latin America)
Includes bibliographical references
ISBN 0-19-511549-X
1. Sousa, Ronald W., 1943–   .
II. Title.   III. Series.
PQ9697.A6M413   1999
869.3—dc21   98–48751

1 3 5 7 9 8 6 4 2

Printed in the United States of America
on acid-free paper

Contents

Series Editors'
General Introduction

(e u

The Library of Latin America series makes available in translation major nineteenth-century authors whose work has been neglected in the English-speaking world. The titles for the translations from the Spanish and Portuguese were suggested by an editorial committee that included Jean Franco (general editor responsible for works in Spanish), Richard Graham (series editor responsible for works in Portuguese), Tulio Halperín Donghi (at the University of California, Berkeley), Iván Jaksić (at the University of Notre Dame), Naomi Lindstrom (at the University of Texas at Austin), Francine Masiello (at the University of California, Berkeley), and Eduardo Lozano of the Library at the University of Pittsburgh. The late Antonio Cornejo Polar of the University of California, Berkeley, was also one of the founding members of the committee. The translations have been funded thanks to the generosity of the Lampadia Foundation and the Andrew W. Mellon Foundation.

During the period of national formation between 1810 and into the early years of the twentieth century, the new nations of Latin America fashioned their identities, drew up constitutions, engaged in bitter struggles over territory, and debated questions of education, government, ethnicity, and culture. This was a unique period unlike the process of nation formation in Europe and one which should be more familiar than it is to students of comparative politics, history, and literature.

The image of the nation was envisioned by the lettered classes—a minority in countries in which indigenous, mestizo, black, or mulatto peasants and slaves predominated—although there were also alternative nationalisms at the grassroots level. The cultural elite were well educated in European thought and letters, but as statesmen, journalists, poets, and academics, they confronted the problem of the racial and linguistic heterogeneity of the continent and the difficulties of integrating the population into a modern nation-state. Some of the writers whose works will be translated in the Library of Latin America series played leading roles in politics. Fray Servando Teresa de Mier, a friar who translated Rousseau's *The Social Contract* and was one of the most colorful characters of the independence period, was faced with imprisonment and expulsion from Mexico for his heterodox beliefs; on his return, after independence, he was elected to the congress. Domingo Faustino Sarmiento, exiled from his native Argentina under the presidency of Rosas, wrote *Facundo: Civilización y barbarie,* a stinging denunciation of that government. He returned after Rosas' overthrow and was elected president in 1868. Andrés Bello was born in Venezuela, lived in London where he published poetry during the independence period, settled in Chile where he founded the University, wrote his grammar of the Spanish language, and drew up the country's legal code.

These post-independence intelligentsia were not simply dreaming castles in the air, but vitally contributed to the founding of nations and the shaping of culture. The advantage of hindsight may make us aware of problems they themselves did not foresee, but this should not affect our assessment of their truly astonishing energies and achievements. It is still surprising that the writing of Andrés Bello, who contributed fundamental works to so many different fields, has never been translated into English. Although there is a recent translation of Sarmiento's celebrated *Facundo,* there is no translation of his memoirs, *Recuerdos de provincia (Provincial Recollections).* The predominance of memoirs in the Library of Latin America series is no accident—many of these offer entertaining insights into a vast and complex continent.

Nor have we neglected the novel. The series includes new translations of the outstanding Brazilian writer Joaquim Maria Machado de Assis' work, including *Dom Casmurro* and *The Posthumous Memoirs of Brás Cubas.* There is no reason why other novels and writers who are not so well known outside Latin America—the Peruvian novelist Clorinda Matto de Turner's *Aves sin nido,* Nataniel Aguirre's *Juan de la Rosa,* José de Alencar's *Iracema,* Juana Manuela Gorriti's short stories—should not be read with as much interest as the political novels of Anthony Trollope.

A series on nineteenth-century Latin America cannot, however, be limited to literary genres such as the novel, the poem, and the short story. The literature of independent Latin America was eclectic and strongly influenced by the periodical press newly liberated from scrutiny by colonial authorities and the Inquisition. Newspapers were miscellanies of fiction, essays, poems, and translations from all manner of European writing. The novels written on the eve of Mexican Independence by José Joaquín Fernández de Lizardi included disquisitions on secular education and law, and denunciations of the evils of gaming and idleness. Other works, such as a well-known poem by Andrés Bello, "Ode to Tropical Agriculture," and novels such as *Amalia* by José Mármol and the Bolivian Nataniel Aguirre's *Juan de la Rosa,* were openly partisan. By the end of the century, sophisticated scholars were beginning to address the history of their countries, as did João Capistrano de Abreu in his *Capítulos de história colonial.*

It is often in memoirs such as those by Fray Servando Teresa de Mier or Sarmiento that we find the descriptions of everyday life that in Europe were incorporated into the realist novel. Latin American literature at this time was seen largely as a pedagogical tool, a "light" alternative to speeches, sermons, and philosophical tracts—though, in fact, especially in the early part of the century, even the readership for novels was quite small because of the high rate of illiteracy. Nevertheless, the vigorous orally transmitted culture of the gaucho and the urban underclasses became the linguistic repertoire of some of the most interesting nineteenth-century writers—most notably José Hernández, author of the "gauchesque" poem "Martín Fierro," which enjoyed an unparalleled popularity. But for many writers the task was not to appropriate popular language but to civilize, and their literary works were strongly influenced by the high style of political oratory.

The editorial committee has not attempted to limit its selection to the better-known writers such as Machado de Assis; it has also selected many works that have never appeared in translation or writers whose work has not been translated recently. The series now makes these works available to the English-speaking public.

Because of the preferences of funding organizations, the series initially focuses on writing from Brazil, the Southern Cone, the Andean region, and Mexico. Each of our editions will have an introduction that places the work in its appropriate context and includes explanatory notes.

We owe special thanks to Robert Glynn of the Lampadia Foundation, whose initiative gave the project a jump start, and to Richard Ekman of the Andrew W. Mellon Foundation, which also generously supported the project. We also thank the Rockefeller Foundation for funding the 1996 symposium "Culture and Nation in Iberoamerica," organized by the editorial board of the Library of Latin America. We received substantial institutional support and personal encouragement from the Institute of Latin American Studies of the University of Texas at Austin. The support of Edward Barry of Oxford University Press has been crucial, as has the advice and help of Ellen Chodosh of Oxford University Press. The first volumes of the series were published after the untimely death, on July 3, 1997, of Maria C. Bulle, who, as an associate of the Lampadia Foundation, supported the idea from its beginning. We received substantial institutional support and personal encouragement from the Institute of Latin American Studies of the University of Texas at Austin.

—*Jean Franco*
—*Richard Graham*

Historical Context and Social Topography *of* Memoirs of a Militia Sergeant

M *emoirs of a Militia Sergeant*, which literary scholars usually do not call a major novel in a grand tradition, is an important literary and historical document in the development of Brazilian culture. Since its first appearance in weekly installments in the *Correio Mercantil* newspaper over a period of a year beginning in June 1852, later published in two volumes in 1854–55, literary taxonomists have puzzled over which category fits a work that in many ways is a literary anomaly—the one major product of a brief but varied career of an author who was barely past adolescence when the work first appeared in print. In chronological terms it fits in the period of romantic literature, yet *Memoirs* shares few characteristics with that genre. It exhibits some traits of naturalism, but predates the emergence of that genre. It also shares some features associated with the picaresque novel of the Golden Age of Spanish literature, and is sometimes called a novel of manners, a loosely connected series of vignettes held together by the adventures and misfortunes of the two main characters, father and son, both named Leonardo. It seems likely that Almeida himself was little concerned with how his modest efforts would fare in cultural history as he produced this work in weekly bits and pieces, maintaining a familiar dialogue with the reader and telling the story in everyday language with a minimum of stylistic artifice and literary pretension, but rich in detail of life on the streets of Brazil's capital city. It further seems likely that at the time the installments began to appear Almeida had not thought through the plot line, much less pondered the moral and ethical and many other implications that later analysts would read into his character sketches, satirical fun-poking, and the escapades of characters seemingly always close to the brink of some personal crisis or social misstep, yet who manage to pull through by hook or by crook.[1] In this regard, the novel shares some features of the serial films of the mid-twentieth century, or the television situation comedies and serial *novelas* of more recent times.

However students of literature might decide to place it among styles and genres, *Memoirs* provides the historian with a window on a world that is difficult to reconstitute through the sorts of archival and documentary records normally available. Two aspects of the historical setting deserve some mention here. One might be called the institutional matrix in which the characters of the story are enmeshed in various ways, particularly the judicial and police systems. Related to that institutional environment is the social landscape of the city, particularly with regard to the free lower classes from which most characters are drawn. The political chronology of Brazil in this era is, of course, well known,[2] and much has been recovered regarding the slaves of Rio de Janeiro in the period, a social category which barely figures in *Memoirs*.[3] But the experience of the free lower classes, existing on the margins of the power hierarchy and occupying interstices of the social structure, is difficult to recover. We must assume that Manuel Antônio de Almeida, perceptively circulating in that environment from the time his father died in 1840, when the boy was nine years old, through his student days and beginnings of a career in journalism, was able to learn much about life and customs in the city in his own and in earlier times, a familiarity which he drew upon for the *Memoirs of a Militia Sergeant*.

The best known phrase of the novel is probably the very first: "It was back in the time of the king," the period bracketed by the arrival of the Portuguese royal court in 1808 and the return of King João VI to Portugal in 1821, an era still in the living memory of the older generation of readers in the early 1850s. At the time the royal entourage arrived, having fled Lisbon to escape the advancing armies of Napoleon, João was still Prince Regent, ruling in the name of his mentally incapacitated mother, Queen Maria I. Only upon Maria's death in 1816 did her son ascend the throne as King João VI, so "the time of the king" might be further narrowed to the period 1816–21. (This of course reminds us that the novel is a work of fiction, and the time period something of a literary abstraction, because the period its plot encompasses, from the birth of the second Leonardo through his young adulthood, is considerably longer than the 13 years the royal entourage spent in Brazil.) Much had happened in the political history of Brazil between "the time of the king" and Almeida's adolescence in the 1840s. Briefly, late in 1815 João VI elevated Brazil to the formal status of co-kingdom with Portugal, and upon his return to Europe João left his son Pedro as Regent of Brazil. When the Portuguese parliament demanded that Pedro also return to Europe, the latter refused that order, and then on September 7, 1822, declared Brazilian independence from Portugal and was subsequently crowned Emperor Pedro I. Pedro decreed a constitution for the Brazilian Empire in 1824, based on the liberal Portuguese constitution of 1821, but Pedro I himself was pressured to abdicate the throne and return to Portugal in April 1831. There followed an unsettled regency, which ended in 1840 when the parliament prematurely declared Pedro's Brazilian-born son, also named Pedro, to be of age to assume the imperial throne, which he occupied as Emperor Pedro II from 1840 to 1889.

For Almeida himself, born in 1831 and not yet 21 years of age when publication of *Memoirs* began, the time of João VI's residence in Rio must have seemed remote. Despite continuity in the physical environment of Rio that Almeida's readers would have found familiar, the institutional context and its operation had changed considerably in the intervening generation. In the process of independence and state formation from 1821 to 1840, most of the administrative structures of the colonial regime, including those installed by João VI in "the time of the king," were replaced in Rio de Janeiro by new institutions based on liberal precepts and modern notions of bureaucratic efficiency. Thus by the time Almeida was approaching maturity, the office of *meirinho* (bailiff), so important in positioning Leonardo-Pataca in the social and political hierarchy of Rio, had been eliminated, as was the *Guarda Real de Polícia*, the informally styled "militia" in which the historical Major Vidigal, principal representative of the authority of the state in the streets of the city, had served from its founding in 1809 until his retirement in 1824. At this remove, in order to frame the institutional setting and the authority hierarchy in which the novel's characters operate, it is appropriate to lay out the main features of the legal and police structures of "the time of the king."

One of the institutions transferred from Portugal along with the royal family was the Intendancy of Police, instituted in Rio by royal decree on 10 May 1808.[4] This police intendancy was based on the French model of enlightened despotism, introduced into Portugal in 1760, with responsibility for a variety of urban services, in addition to personal and collective security. These responsibilities included public order, surveillance of the population, the investigation of crimes, and apprehension of criminals. In the tradition of royal absolutism, the intendant as the king's agent had the power to decide what behavior was to be declared criminal, establish the punishment he thought appropriate, and then to arrest, prosecute, pass judgment, and supervise the sentence of individual perpetrators. In Brazil the intendant became part of a local judicial system that had been built up through the colonial era by the accumulation of edicts and decrees, and which in the colonial capital was supervised by the judges of the High Court of Appeals (the *Relação*), which in turn supervised a variety of lesser judges and judicial officers.[5]

One of the latter positions was that of *meirinho* (bailiff), the post held by Leonardo-Pataca, the satirical description of which opens the novel and frames subsequent action and relationships. The title, one of many linguistic traces of Moslem rule of medieval Iberia, derives from the same word as the Arabic *emir* (governor or commander), with the addition of the Portuguese diminutive *-inho* denoting the petty nature of the position. Another legacy of the old regime is that the *meirinho* of the time in which *Memoirs* is set was not a public employee in the modern, bureaucratic sense. Although he was formally an officer of the law, the *meirinho* was a private individual who had obtained, probably through personal connections or in return for some favor or in response to a petition, an appointment authorizing him to exercise the profession in question. Like most state officials in the late colonial and early independence era, he received no salary. In return for a fee for services rendered, *meirinhos* were called upon by magistrates or by private individuals or their agents to serve writs and citations and deliver legal papers, including orders of arrest in certain circumstances. Such bailiffs hung out on the street corner where the novel opens, to be available when called upon by lawyers or higher judicial authorities. Upon completing an assignment, they would be paid the fee that gave Leonardo-Pataca his nickname. They were not expected to have any legal training, and had no authority or responsibilities independent of the commissions they took on. In practice, despite the pretensions to status and authority to which Almeida alludes in opening the novel, the bailiffs of "the time of the king" were little more than officially sanctioned errand runners.

In one of many ironies and satirical thrusts of the novel, Leonardo-Pataca was professionally connected to the same judicial system in which served Major Vidigal, the ominous and omnipresent representative of state authority and nemesis of both Leonardo-Pataca and his son, who in the last pages of the novel enters the ranks of the corps commanded by the same Vidigal. Informal usage still referred to that body as the "Militia," a popular holdover from the terminology of colonial times—the militia of the novel's title. But by making Vidigal a principal character Almeida was fixing in the mind of the reading public and successive generations the popular image of a historical figure well known in "the time of the king," whose career is well documented. The historical Vidigal was still remembered in the Rio de Janeiro in which Almeida grew up, and his legacy was ideal material for the tensions the author sets up between state authority and repression on the one hand, and the spontaneous exercise of popular will on the other. Since the publication of *Memoirs*, in fact, the historical Vidigal and the fictional character based explicitly on him have become intertwined. In view of the central role in the novel of the fictional major and the corps in which he served, a brief exploration of the historical Vidigal and the *Guarda Real de Polícia* helps flesh out the context with which Almeida and his readers were familiar.

Another innovation following the transfer of the Portuguese royal family to Brazil was the creation of a full-time police force, organized along military lines and given broad authority to maintain order and pursue criminals. This was the *Guarda Real de Polícia*, established in May 1809. Like the Intendancy of Police, to which it was subordinate, the *Guarda Real* replicated in Rio de Janeiro an institution already existing in Lisbon. Members of the *Guarda Real* became notorious as the ruthless agents of the Intendant of Police. Miguel Nunes Vidigal was the most famous among them, celebrated or reviled by contemporaries and later historians on both sides of these issues. Vidigal transferred to the new unit from the colonial militia, which he had entered as a cadet in 1770, and subsequently became the terror of the vagrants and idlers who might meet him coming around a corner or see him suddenly appear at a late-night social gathering. Without so much as *pro forma* deference to legal procedures, Vidigal and his soldiers, handpicked for their size and strength, proceeded to beat any participant, miscreant, or vagrant they could capture. These brutal attacks became known in the folklore of the city as "shrimp dinners" (*ceias de camarão*) recalling the flaying necessary to get at the pink flesh of those crustaceans. Instead of the usual military sword, the normal equipment of Vidigal and his grenadiers was a whip with a long heavy shaft tipped by rawhide strips, used as both club and lash. Following the beating viciously and indiscriminately administered at the time of arrest, slaves were returned to their owner's custody or submitted to the intendant or his assistants, the criminal magistrates, for judgment of their offense. Nonslave detainees were kept in the short-term lock-up, the *casa de guarda* on the Palace square (now Praça XV de Novembro), from where some went to a longer term in the city jail, and others among the able-bodied were selected as conscripts for the army or navy. Some of the latter, as is eventually the situation of the title character of the novel, might find themselves serving in the corps under Vidigal's command. Thus what to later readers might seem like an unlikely plot development, in view of the recurring antagonism between Vidigal and the other characters and Leonardo in particular, was in fact well within the realm of historical possibility.

The real Vidigal retired with honors in 1824, lived to a ripe old age, and died in Rio in 1843.[6] By placing a figure based closely on the historical Vidigal in close relation to purely fictitious characters, Almeida provided readers with a sense of verisimilitude—because his fictional Vidigal was so much like the memory of the real one, the other characters seemed more realistic. At the same time, Almeida avoided any direct connection with existing people and institutions. Like the office of *meirinho*, the militia of the book's title, the *Guarda Real de Polícia*, no longer existed at the time the novel began to appear in serial form. In 1831 the troops of the *Guarda Real* had mutinied and the corps was subsequently disbanded, replaced by a new uniformed police force called the *Corpo Municipal de Permanentes*. Thus Almeida's satirical jabs at the judicial and police systems mentioned only offices and institutions no longer in official existence, even though popular memory of them persisted. Similarly, the identity of the author himself was left formally anonymous, not only in the first appearance as weekly installments but also in the subsequent publication in book form, when its author was designated as only "A Brazilian." Not until the edition of 1863, two years after the untimely death of the author, at age 30 (in the shipwreck of a coastal steamer near Rio), was his name placed on the title page.

The Vidigal of history was delegated authority by the king, through the intendant, and personified the powerful presence of the legally constituted authority of the state. But as portrayed by Almeida, the notorious major Vidigal of the novel also operates in what might be termed the relational social universe central to Brazilian culture, in which individual members of society are in personal, hierarchical, dyadic relationships with every other member with whom they interact.[7] The novelistic Vidigal exercises his considerable authority in personalistic and arbitrary ways, depending on the circumstances and individuals involved. Each person in the relational system brings to the arena of social contact their individual qualities, but also brings relative status based on economic and social standing, professional activity, gender, kinship both biological and fictive, age, race and ethnicity, nationality, and legal condition.

The latter characteristic refers to slave status versus free, and an aspect of *Memoirs* that touches modern sensibilities is that slaves and slavery are not so much ignored, as simply taken for granted. Despite the fact that more than 40 percent of the population of Rio de Janeiro was enslaved (both in the era of João VI and still at midcentury), and a large but indeterminate proportion of the free population were of some degree of African descent, neither slaves nor free people of color occupy significant positions in the cast of characters of this story of life on the city's streets. The Afro-Brazilian presence in the novel can be summed up quickly: Unnamed house slaves are called upon to report gossip; Leonardo's barber/godfather talks his way into a berth as a ship's doctor on a slave ship to Africa; *Bahianas*, the street vendors so-called because of their association with the city of Salvador, Bahia, appear in a procession; and the street tough Chico-Juca, apparently a free man of color, is commissioned to start a fight at a social gathering. Even when Leonardo-Pataca seeks out a necromancer to win the affections of a Gypsy girl, the sorcerer is an aging *caboclo* (native Indian or mixed Indian/Portuguese), rather than a practitioner of Afro-Brazilian ritual. Although there are occasional hints at distinctions between native Brazilians and recent arrivals from Portugal, all other characters are apparently of Portuguese or Euro-Brazilian racial and ethnic stock. Gypsies, in fact, play a more central role than do Africans or Afro-Brazilians of whatever legal status. Despite their virtual absence in the novel, the role of slaves in Rio de Janeiro created a situation for the free lower classes that is significant for the social environment in which the plot develops. Most centrally, no one in the book works. Some characters hold positions of professional status such as policeman or bailiff, and others exercise such trades as barbering and midwifery, but no one engages in physical labor, much less productive activity.

Turning to the social types and relationships that are in the novel rather than what is absent, the action is focused on the ways the central characters make it through life by cultivating connections in the relational social universe, taking advantage where possible and making the best of the situation when no advantage is to be gained or a loss must be sustained. One develops a sense of the individual characters behaving like social atoms bouncing against one another, or that the characters play the game of life as if it were a game of cards, depending on an uncertain combination of the luck of the draw and the strategies of the play, doing the best one can with the hand one is dealt. Some of the players are stronger and some are weaker, based on professional status and derived authority, or on such personal qualities as bluster or reticence. Some have properties specific to females and others those of males. Some are young and naive, and others have the wisdom of experience and deference given to age. Some are simply more crafty and calculating than others. Their actions and interactions are based on perceived self-interest, however misinformed or miscalculated, or doomed to failure in the face of forces arrayed in opposition to them.

Moral and ethical considerations, concern for whose interests might be hurt even as others benefit, pangs of conscience, or issues of a deeper or higher nature are largely absent here. Points are scored in this game, in fact, for successfully damaging the interests of others, whether as revenge for real or perceived injury (as when Leonardo-Pataca seeks vengeance on the Gypsy girl and her new beau, who is also a priest), or as a way to demonstrate relative power (as when Vidigal doggedly pursues the young Leonardo until the latter becomes a protected subordinate in the militia under Vidigal's own command). Even affairs of the heart are conducted in an atmosphere of self-interested calculation (as in the machinations of matchmaking older ladies, or Leonardo's movement between Vidinha and Luisinha). As a final example, one of the more sympathetic actions in the novel is the barber's kind persistence in providing a home and upbringing for his ungrateful and unregenerate godson. The same barber got his start in life when he took the wages of a physician by signing up on the crew of slave ship under false pretenses. And when the ship's captain died under his care, the barber made a deathbed promise to deliver an inheritance to the captain's daughter, but kept it for himself instead—who would be the wiser?

One of the best known of modern critical assessments of *Memoirs of a Militia Sergeant* is that of Antônio Cândido, one of Brazil's renowned intellectual figures of the recent era, in a 1970 essay entitled "Dialética da malandragem," or The Dialectic of Roguery.[8] Cândido's analysis is organized around the oppositional play between the forces of order and disorder, as displayed by the relative positions of the characters in the novel as the action develops. It is worthwhile in introducing the present edition to convey to the English-language audience some of Cândido's general conclusions, as the insights of a perceptive Brazilian student of both society and literature. The character Vidigal is a prime representative of the world of order, yet his actios bring problems and pain to inhabitants of the world of disorder for little apparent reason and less permanent result. Leonardo the ne'er-do-well spends most of his young life in the world of disorder, even though his pranks and transgressions seem fairly harmless, and he ends up as the eponymous sergeant in Vidigal's own militia, representing order. As Cândido explains such apparent flip-flops, "the special feature of the book is the absence of moral judgment, and in the acceptance of human nature 'as is,' a mixture of cynicism and bonhomie that shows the reader a certain equivalence between the universes of order and disorder, or what might more conventionally be called good and evil." The world of Leonardo and Vidigal is "a universe without blame or guilt, and even without internally produced restraint on behavior, other than the exterior repression that is constantly present in the figure of Vidigal—who himself appears stripped of the authority symbolized by his uniform and rank when people visit his house and find him clad in pajamas."[9]

Cândido characterizes the more general role of a work like *Memoirs* in the following terms:

> One of the greatest endeavors of societies, through their organizational structures and the ideologies that serve to legitimize them, is to assume the objective existence and the real value of antithetical pairs, between which people must choose. These pairs include behavior that is permitted and forbidden, what is true and the false, moral and immoral, just and unjust, political left and right, and so forth. The more rigid a society is, the more clearly defined is each choice, and more narrow the options. In this situation there develop parallel accommodations of a casuistic nature, which make hypocrisy a pillar of civilization. One of the great functions of satirical literature, of demystifying candor, and of psychological analysis is that they show, each in its own way, that the pairs are reversible, not fixed, and that beyond the realm of ideological rationalization the contradictions coexist in a curious twilight.[10]

Cândido thus takes issue with those who read this novel as a sort of documentary record of what life was like in Rio de Janeiro in "the time of the king." He suggests instead that the work of Antônio de Almeida, despite the author's modestly expressed intent and his relative youth and inexperience at the time the story was published, and beyond the problems of continuity, chronological possibility, and unlikely twists of plot, is "perhaps unique in Brazilian literature of the nineteenth century for not taking the point of view nor expressing the vision of the sociopolitical elite." He suggests that "In the transparent clarity of this society without culpability, we can perceive the contours of a land without definitive and unresolvable problems, governed by an enchanting moral neutrality. In this land no one works, no one is needy, everything is taken care of."[11]

Rather than realistically depicting life as it was, Manuel Antônio de Almeida put together a cast of characters who, by their narrow and superficial approach to their interaction with others, made a subtle and incisive comment on Brazilian society and culture of the nineteenth century. With its demystifying candor, *Memoirs of a Militia Sergeant* rightfully occupies an important position in the satirical literature of Brazil and the world.

—*Thomas H. Holloway*

Notes

1. The first installment, published on 27 June 1852, included a few lines of introduction suggesting that the story would be a little long, because it begins in the time of the king, and goes to the present day. At its conclusion the historical moment has been, in effect, suspended still in the time of the king, and the same major Vidigal (of whom more below) who roamed the streets in the opening chapter still occupies the same position of authority.

2. For detailed accounts see Neill Macaulay, *Dom Pedro: The Struggle for Liberty in Brazil and Portugal, 1798-1834* (Durham, N.C.: Duke University Press, 1986); and Roderick Barman, *Brazil: The Forging of a Nation, 1798–1852* (Stanford, Calif.: Stanford University Press, 1988).

3. See especially Mary Karasch, *Slave Life in Rio de Janeiro, 1808–1850* (Princeton, N.J.: Princeton University Press, 1987).

4. For more on these institutions, their legal bases, and ideological origins, see Thomas H. Holloway, *Policing Rio de Janeiro: Repression and Resistance in a Nineteenth-Century City* (Stanford, Calif.: Stanford University Press, 1993), pp. 28–38 and passim.

5. For an overview of Brazil's judicial system on the eve of independence, see Thomas Flory, *Judge and Jury in Imperial Brazil, 1808–1871* (Austin: University of Texas Press, 1981), pp. 31–43.

6. José Viera Fazenda, "Vidigal," in *Antiqualhas e memorias do Rio de Janeiro*, 5 vols. (Rio de Janeiro: Tipografia Nacional, 1923–28), 4:87–90; J.C. Fernandes Pinheiro, "Paulo Fernandes e a polícia de seu tempo," *Revista do Instituto Histórico e Geográfico Brasileiro*, 39 (1876), pp. 65–76; and Mello Barreto Filho and Hermeto Lima, *História da Polícia do Rio de Janeiro*, 3 vols. (Rio de Janeiro: A Noite, 1939–43), 1:202–208.

7. Roberto da Matta treats this theme in "The Quest for Citizenship in a Relational Universe" in John Wirth, Edson de Oliveira Nunes, and Thomas Bogenschild, eds., *State and Society in Brazil* (Stanford, Calif.: Stanford University Press, 1987), pp. 307–335; and in *Carnivals, Rogues, and Heroes: An Interpretation of the Brazilian Dilemma* (Notre Dame, Ind.: Notre Dame University Press, 1991), especially in the essay 'Do You Know Who You're Talking To?' The Distinction between Individual and Person in Brazil," pp. 137–197.

8. Antonio Cândido, "Dialética da malandragem" in Cecilia Lara, ed., *Memórias de um sargento de milícias: Edição crítica* (Rio de Janeiro: Livros Técnicos e Científicos, 1978). Cândido's influential essay was originally published in *Revista do Instituto de Estudos Brasileiros*, 8 (1970), pp. 67–89. In turn, it has led to further examinations of the theme, including Roberto Schwarz, "Pressupostos, salvo engano, de 'Dialética da malandragem,' " in Celso Lafer, ed., *Esboço de figura* (São Paulo: Duas Cidades, 1979), reprinted in Roberto Schwarz, *Que horas são?* (São Paulo: Companhia das Letras, 1987), pp. 129–155; and Roberto Goto,

Malandragem revisitada: Uma leitura ideológica de "Dialética da malandragem" (Campinas: Pontes, 1988).

9. Cândido, "Dialética," pp. 322, 337.

10. Ibid., p. 338

11. Ibid., p. 341, 342.

MEMOIRS OF
A MILITIA
SERGEANT

Contents

Volume II

VOLUME I

I

Origins, Birth, and Baptism

I t was back in the time of the king. In those days, one of the four
corners at the intersection of Ouvidor and Quitanda streets was referred to as "Bailiffs' Corner." And an apt name it was, for that corner
was the favorite meeting place of all the individuals exercising that office, which was then held in no inconsiderable esteem. The bailiffs of
today are but meager shadows of bailiffs in the time of the king, which
were figures fearsome and feared, respectable and respected. They represented one end of a formidable judicial chain that embraced all of Rio
de Janeiro back when, amongst us, legal proceedings constituted one of
the staples of life. At the other end were the appeals court judges. Now,
ends can, after all, meet, and those ends, when they met, formed a circle
inside of which there was fought out a terrible combat of summonses,
bills of indictment, principal and final arguments, and all the judicial
maneuverings that go into a court case. Hence the moral influence the
bailiffs exercised.

But they had another influence as well, one that is precisely lacking
in their modern-day counterparts. That was the influence deriving from

their physical appearance. The bailiffs of today are men just like any others; there is nothing particularly imposing about them, either in countenance or in dress. They might be taken for a solicitor, a law clerk, or an office underling. The bailiffs of that fine time would never, ever be taken for anything other than what they were: originals, character types whose countenance reflected a certain air of forensic majesty, whose sharp, knowing look bespoke cunning. They dressed in sober black dress coats, breeches and stockings of that same color, and shoes with buckles; an aristocratic smallsword hung at their left side and at the right a white circle whose significance we no longer understand. They topped it all off with a severe cocked hat. Defined by the imposing presence of such features, the bailiff used and abused his position. It was a terrifying occurrence when, as a citizen turned a city corner or stepped out of his house in the morning, he came across one of those solemn figures who, unfolding a piece of paper in front of him, began reading it in a confidential tone of voice. No matter what he might think of doing, there was no alternative but to let escape from between his lips the doleful phrase: "I accept the summons." No one now can understand the fateful and cruel significance that those few words contained! They constituted a sentence to eternal pilgrimage pronounced upon oneself; they meant that a long, wearying journey was being begun whose remote destination was the clerk of the appeals court. On that journey, toll had to be paid at an endless number of checkpoints: lawyer, solicitor, investigator, notary, judge, inexorable Charons all, standing in doorways with hands outstretched. And no one could pass through without depositing not an obol but the entire contents of his pockets and the last ounce of his patience.

But let us return to the corner. Whosoever passed by on a weekday in that blessed age would see seated there on low, worn leather seats, called "campaign chairs," a more or less numerous group of those worthies peacefully conversing about anything and everything that was considered a legitimate topic of conversation: the lives of the nobles, the news of the kingdom, and the wily police exploits of Major Vidigal. Among the terms that made up the bailiff equation affixed to this corner was one constant quantity: Leonardo-Pataca. For such was the name commonly applied to a rotund and extremely fat personage with white hair and a florid complexion who was the dean of this corporation, the eldest of the bailiffs living at that time. Old age had made him soft and sluggish; his slowness delayed clients' business, so he was little utilized and therefore never departed from the corner. He spent his days seated upon his chair with his legs stretched out before him and his chin propped on a thick cane that, after he turned fifty, had become his constant companion. From the habit that he had of incessantly complaining that his services brought but the meager sum of 320 réis, one pataca, came the tag that had been appended to his name.

Leonardo's story has about it very little worthy of remark. He had been a used-clothes hawker in his native Lisbon, but he grew tired of that trade and moved to Brazil. When he got here, through whose intercession no one seems to know, he came into the position in which we now see him — in which, as we have said, he had been engaged for a great many years. Moreover, there came with him on the same ship, for what purpose it is hard to say, one Maria da Hortaliça, former produce vendor in the squares of Lisbon, a roundish, quite pretty native of the rural environs of the capital city. To do him justice, Leonardo was not all that unattractive in that time of his youth either; most of all, however, he was a rogue. Before they even got out of the Tagus, as Maria was leaning on the ship's rail, Leonardo pretended to push innocently past her and trod heavily on her right foot with his iron-toed boot. As if she had been awaiting some such ruse, Maria smiled as though disconcerted and then, under the cover of that indirection, gave him a ferocious pinch on the back of his left hand. This, according to the customs of the land, constituted a formal declaration. They spent the rest of that day in the closest of courtship, and that night the scene of foot tromping and hand pinching was repeated, only this time more definitively. On the following day the two lovers had grown so ardent and so familiar that it seemed they had shared the relationship for years.

By the time they set foot back on land, Maria had begun feeling touches of nausea. They set up house together, and not more than a month later the effects of the tromping and the pinching became clearly evident. Seven months after that Maria gave birth to a son, a formidable youngster nearly three palms long, chubby and red, hairy, flailing his legs and yowling. Scarcely was he born when he nursed for two hours straight without relinquishing his mother's breast. Of everything heretofore observed, this birth is what most interests us, for the child of whom we speak is the hero of this story.

There arrived the day on which the boy was to be baptized. The midwife was the godmother, but there was some debate about who should be the godfather. Leonardo wanted it to be the judge; ultimately, how-

---

* In Portuguese there are two sets of terms to refer to godparents. The first, *padrinho*, 'godfather' and *madrinha*, 'godmother' are used to refer to the godparent in respect to his or her relationship to the godchild. The second, *compadre*, 'godfather' and *comadre*, 'godmother' refer to the godparents in respect to their

ever, he had to give in to Maria's insistence, and the midwife's, that it be the barber from across the street. There was, needless to say, a party that day. The invitees of the master of the house, all of whom were likewise from the old country, sang *ao desafio*, as was their custom. The *comadre*'s guests, all of whom were native, danced the fado. The *compadre** brought his fiddle with him, which, as everyone knows, is the preferred instrument of the people of his trade. At the outset Leonardo, wanting to impart an aristocratic air to the celebration, proposed they dance the courtly minuet. The idea won general acceptance, but they had some difficulty in creating partners. Finally, a short, heavy matron, wife of one of the invitees, got up, along with a woman friend of hers whose figure was her complete opposite; likewise, both a colleague of Leonardo's, a tiny little man a waggish air about him, and the sacristan of the Sé.* The godfather played the minuet on his fiddle, and the godson, lying in Maria's lap, accompanied each and every pass of the bow with a squall and a kick. That caused the godfather to lose the beat over and over again and have to start in anew each time.

After they had finished the minuet, the formality gradually waned, and the party "came to a boil" as they used to say back then. Some young men arrived with guitars and *machetes*.** Leonardo, urged on by the ladies, decided to launch into a lyric portion of the program. He seated himself on a stool in an empty part of the room and took up a guitar. It produced a wonderful comic effect to see him there, in his bailiff's dress with the coat, breeches, and smallsword, accompanying his own toneless warbling of an old-world *modinha* with a monotonous strumming on the instrument's strings. He found in the nostalgia for his native land the inspiration for his song, which was natural in a good Portuguese such as he was. The *modinha* went like this:

> When I lived in my native land,
> Whether in company or on my own,
> A glass of wine in my hand,
> I'd sing the night and daytime long!

relationship to each other and to the natural parents, all of whom may refer to each other as "*comadre*" or "*compadre*" respectively. Also, by extension, other adults may use the terms *comadre* and *compadre* to refer to godparents in respect to their role as such. In this text, with some exceptions owing to context, the former set of terms will be translated into English while the latter will be reproduced in the original Portuguese.

*   In Portuguese, the Sé is the principal church of a diocese.

**   A small-sized guitar.

The song was painstakingly executed and enthusiastically applauded; the only person who did not seem to accord it great appreciation was the boy, who rewarded his father as he had rewarded his godfather, keeping the beat with squalls and kicks. Maria's eyes grew red and she sighed.

Leonardo's song was the last call to arms needed for the party to take off—the farewell to formality. Thereafter, it turned into an uproar, which soon gave way to a din and then went on to become a riot, which progressed no further only because now and again there could be seen through the door and window shutters certain passing figures that suggested that Vidigal was somewhere in the vicinity.

The party did not end until late; the godmother was the last to leave, bestowing a blessing upon her godson and placing on his bellyband a sprig of rue.

I I

Early Misfortunes

Let us leap over the years that elapsed immediately after the birth and baptism of the subject of these memoirs and meet him now at the age of seven. We shall say only that during all that time the youngster did not belie all that he portended at birth: He tormented the neighborhood with a squall always squalled at the highest of registers; he was ill-tempered; his bad humor was directed particularly toward his godmother, whom he could not abide; and he was intractable in the extreme.

As soon as he could walk and talk, he became a scourge. He ripped or broke everything that came into his hands. And he conceived a particular passion for Leonardo's cocked hat. Should the latter forget it in a place within his reach, he would immediately snatch it up, dust all the furniture with it, put everything he could find inside it, rub it across a wall, and end up sweeping the house with it, until Maria, upset at what those actions were about to cost her ears, and perhaps her back, could tear the unfortunate victim from his hands. Besides being incorrigible, he was also a glutton; when he was not engaged in some devilment or other, he was eating. Maria did not spare him; she kept one area of his body well worked over all of the time. But that did nothing to improve his behavior, for he was also strong-willed, and the devilment would begin anew even before the pain of the spankings wore off.

It was in this state that he reached the age of seven.

Maria was, after all, just a rustic, and Leonardo was beginning to regret seriously all that he done for her and with her. And he was right, for—let us say it plainly and quickly—he had for some time harbored quite plausible suspicions that he was being played for a fool. Several months ago he had noticed that a certain sergeant often walked by his door and peered with curiosity through the shutters. One time when he was going into the house he thought he caught a glimpse of that same sergeant leaning next to the window. This, however, passed with no further incident.

Then he began to find it curious that a certain colleague of his would come to his house to talk over business, always at hours when he was not there. This too soon came to an end. Finally it happened that on three or four occasions he ran across in the vicinity of the house the captain of the ship in which he had voyaged from Lisbon; this caused him some serious concern. One morning he came in unexpectedly through the back way; someone in the living room raced over, threw open the window, leaped through it out onto the street, and vanished.

In the light of this, there was no further room for doubt; and the poor man, as they say, slipped his tether: He went blind with jealousy. Hastily dropping on a bench the legal papers that he was carrying under his arm, he aimed himself in Maria's direction with fists clenched, "You big . . . !"

The insult that he was going to utter was so great that he choked on it . . . and began shaking all over.

Maria retreated a couple of steps and prepared to defend herself, for she was not the sort of person to let much of anything intimidate her. "Lay off, Leonardo."

"Don't you ever use my name again, ever, or I'll shut your mouth with my fists."

"You stay away from me! Who asked to get involved with you on that boat anyhow?"

That exasperated Leonardo; the reference to their romance exacerbated the pain he felt in her treachery, and the jealousy and anger inside him poured out in a rain of blows that fell on Maria, who after a failed attempt at resistance broke into flight, crying and screaming, "Ow, ow . . . help *compadre*, help . . ."

At that moment, however, the *compadre* was spreading shaving lather on a customer's face and could not just up and leave. So Maria receipted for all her misdeeds at one and the same time—and at a very high price. She ended up huddled in a corner, sobbing.

The child had witnessed the whole scene with imperturbable equanimity: As Maria caught what Leonardo's fury dished out, he calmly occupied himself in ripping up the legal papers that his father had set down when he came in and in creating a huge cache of paperwads with the results.

When his fury subsided and Leonardo could see something beyond his jealousy, he became aware of that meritorious labor to which the youngster had dedicated himself. He hit the ceiling again and jerked the boy off the ground by his ears, spun him a half-turn in midair, lifted his right foot, and brought it fully to bear against the boy's backside, launching him a distance of several yards, where he came back to earth in a sitting position.

"You are the product of a foot-tromp and a pinch; you needed a good swift kick to round out your pedigree."

The boy took it all with the courage of a martyr, merely opening his mouth a bit as he was being hoisted by the ears. No sooner had he landed, however, than he was back on his feet and out the door, and in three shakes he was in the door of the barbershop clutching his godfather by the legs. The barber was, at that moment, lifting his basin up over the customer's head, having just removed it from under his chin, and the sudden jolt caused the basin to tip, with the result that the customer received a baptism of soapy water.

"Hey, master, what's the idea?"

"Sir," he stammered, " . . . it's this little devil's fault. What is the matter, boy?"

The youngster did not answer. He merely directed his eyes back across the street, pointing in that same direction with a trembling hand.

The *compadre* looked, concentrated his attention, and then heard Maria sobbing. "Oh," he muttered. "I'll bet I know what that's about . . . I've been expecting it, and now here it is." And apologizing to his customer, he headed out of his shop and across the street to see what was happening. His words suggest that he had suspected something. And let the reader be assured that what had happened was what he suspected.

Back then, mounting vigil upon others' lives, questioning the slaves about goings-on inside the house, was so common, so rooted in custom that even today, after the passage of all the years, vestiges of that honored practice are still to be found. Sitting in the back of his shop going through the motions of sharpening the instruments of his trade, the godfather had watched the sergeant repeatedly pass by, the colleague come on his extemporaneous visits, and finally the sea captain come and go. Hence his conclusion that before too much longer what had now came to pass would in fact occur.

Gaining the other side of the street, he pushed open the shutters that the boy had closed upon his escape and went in. He addressed himself to Leonardo, whose attitude was still a hostile one. "*Compadre*," he asked, "have you lost your senses?"

"Not my senses," retorted Leonardo in a dramatic tone of voice. "It's my honor I've lost!"

Maria, seeing the *compadre*'s presence as protection, took heart anew and, getting to her feet, shot back in a mocking tone, "Honor? . . . Honor in a bailiff? Ha!"

At that insult, attacking as it did not merely one man but an entire institution, the volcano of resentment that Maria's tears had somewhat allayed erupted all over again! A mix of imprecations and buffets descended anew upon her from Leonardo's fists and lips. The *compadre*, who had stepped in between them, accidentally caught a few of the blows himself and as a consequence withdrew to a safe distance, grumbling in frustration at the failure of his efforts as peacemaker.

"A bailiff's honor is like a Lisbon rustic's faithfulness."

The storm finally blew itself out: Maria sat down in a corner to cry and curse the day she was born, the moment she first saw Leonardo, the foot-tromping, the pinch with which she had initiated their shipboard romance, and everything else that the pain from the beating she had taken led her to bring to mind.

After a short period of calm, Leonardo underwent a moment of exasperation: His eyes and face turned red, he clenched his teeth, he thrust his hands in his breeches pockets, puffed out his cheeks, and began to swing his right leg violently back and forth. Then, as if arriving at a definitive resolution, he gathered the scattered sheets of paper that the boy had torn up, jammed his cocked hat down sideways on his head, snatched up his cane, and stalked out slamming the shutter and shouting "To Hell with the whole thing!"

"Go on, leave," the emboldened Maria exclaimed, putting her hands on her hips. "You haven't seen the end of this business yet—hitting me like this. You'll see. I'm going to the authorities."

"Young lady."

"No, *compadre*, you can't talk me out of it—I'm going to the authorities, and even if he is a scoundrelly stupid old bailiff, he's going to have to answer to me."

"You'd be better off not opening that up, young lady—it'll get you involved with the law, after all. He's an officer of the law, and it'll take care of him in its own way."

Maria's threats were no more than bravado serving to vent her spite, and so after a few more of the *compadre*'s arguments she gave in, and peace was restored to the house. There then ensued a long conference between the two, at the end of which the *compadre* took his leave saying, "He'll most likely be back. It's just his temper talking. The whole thing'll blow over. But if it doesn't, I'll do as I've said. I'll take the boy."

Maria manifested satisfaction. She had made up her mind—either then or perhaps even previously—and therefore during the aforementioned conference had been trying to lure in the *compadre* so as to elicit from him the promise that should the relationship break up he would take the child and look after him. She proclaimed that such a breakup would come only from Leonardo, and the *compadre* believed that contention. Nevertheless, the reader will soon see that the poor man was overly generous in his judgment and that Maria was absolutely correct when she spoke sarcastically about the honor of a bailiff.

The whole scene that we have just described took place in the morning. That afternoon Leonardo walked into the barbershop, sad and downcast. On the bench where he had been sitting, the boy shrank back in recollection of the airborne turn that his father's foot had caused him to take that morning. The *compadre* stepped forward and said, with a conciliatory smile, "What's past is past; come on—she is sorry. A young girl's foolishness. But she won't do it again."

Leonardo did not answer. He started walking back and forth in the shop, his hands crossed behind his back under his coat skirts. You could see from his expression, however, that he was appreciative of the barber's words and would have uttered them himself if the other man had not done so first.

"Let's go over there," suggested the *compadre*, "and get it all resolved. Poor girl . . . she has been crying all day."

"Let's," said Leonardo.

When they got to the door, he slowed to a halt, like one who had resolved never to pass that way again. All he was waiting for, however, were a few entreaties from the *compadre* uttered in such a way that Maria could hear and believe that he had had to be dragged back against his better judgment. The *compadre* understood and he followed Leonardo's lead by saying "Go on in, man. Put an end to this childish behavior. What's past is past."

So they went in. The living room was empty. Leonardo sat down at a table and rested his face in one of his hands, keeping his hat jammed down sideways on his head, which gave him a half-comic, half-melancholy appearance.

"Young lady," called the agent of reconciliation. "It's all over. Come on out . . ."

No answer came.

"She's probably somewhere around here crying," the *compadre* ventured. And he started a housewide search.

Now, it wasn't a very large house, and he went over all of it in short order. He registered the cruelest of disappointments at not finding Maria anywhere there. He then returned to the living room in a state somewhere between consternation and alarm.

Leonardo, presuming that the barber had found Maria and was leading her, humble and contrite, back by the hand, tried to put himself in the position of advantage: He got to his feet, put his hands in his pockets, and located himself with his back turned toward the direction from which the *compadre* was coming.

"Oh, Leonardo," said the latter as he approached.

"It's no good," cut in the other without turning around. "I can't go through with it. I've changed my mind."

"Look, man."

"No, no. It's over." As Leonardo was saying this, he kept his back resolutely turned to the *compadre*, while the latter kept trying to get in front of him.

"Listen, man, listen. She—"

"I don't want anything more to do with her. It's over. And I've already said—"

"She's gone, man. Gone," shouted the *compadre*, growing impatient.

Leonardo was thunderstruck by the words. Now he turned around, trembling all over. When he didn't see Maria, he dissolved into tears.

"Well," he said amid sobs, "it really is over. Good-bye, *compadre*."

"But the boy . . ." shot back the other.

Leonardo gave no answer; he simply left the house hurriedly.

Then the *compadre* saw it all: He saw that Leonardo was abandoning his son now that the mother had done the same before him. He made a gesture as if to say "That's right, go off and leave me with the burden on my back."

By the next day the whole neighborhood had heard that Leonardo's young lady had run off to Portugal with the captain of a ship that had set sail the prior evening.

Upon hearing the news, the *compadre* commented with a malevolent smile, "Ah, it was homesickness for her own country! . . ."

Farewell to Deviltry

Leonardo had abandoned once and for all that fateful house in which he had experienced such unhappiness. In fact, he was never again seen in that neighborhood, with the result that the *compadre* did not lay eyes upon him again for a very long time.

The boy, while he was new in his godfather's house, comported himself with the utmost circumspection and gravity. As soon as he started feeling at home, however, the gloves came back off. He nonetheless gained his godfather's great affection, which grew day in and day out until it reached a state of emotion-filled, blind devotion. Even the boy's misdeeds, which more often than not were quite vicious, the good man usually considered funny. To his mind, no other boy in the entire neighborhood could compare with his godson, and he never tired of talking about everything the youngster said and did. Sometimes what went on was obviously the behavior of a spoiled child, but he found it the manifestation of liveliness and spirit. Other times it involved language that bespoke a highly developed reprobacy in someone so young, but he judged it the most ingenuous language in the world.

This was natural in a man who had lived a life such as he had lived: He was fifty years old and had never had an emotional relationship; he had always got along by himself, alone; he was a genuine practitioner of the most resolute celibacy. As a result, with the first emotional attachment he had ever formed, his heart expanded fully, and his love for the boy grew to the proportions of complete blindness, while the latter, availing himself of the immunity provided him by this state of affairs, simply did anything that came into his head.

Sometimes, while sitting in the barber shop, he would amuse himself by making faces at the customers as they were getting their shave. Some of them reacted angrily, others laughed despite themselves. A consequence of either was that they usually left the shop with their faces nicked up—to the boy's great amusement and the barber's discredit. Other times he would secret his godfather's sharpest razor away in some corner or other, so that the customer would have to sit there for a long while with his face lathered up, biting his lip with impatience, as the barber searched the place over. All the while he would be laughing nastily to himself. Nothing that came into the house stayed in one piece for long; and he kept everything in a dither. In the backyards he would throw stones at the neighbors' roofs; from the street door he would pick a quarrel with every passerby and anyone who came to a window, with the result that no one around had a good word to say about him. The godfather, however, took no heed and continued to lavish affection upon him. In fact, he devoted a great deal of effort to planning for his future. He sometimes spent his nights building castles in the air: He dreamed of great fortune and elevated position for his godson and tried to plan ways leading to such ends. Here, more or less, is the thread of his thinking: "It is true (he reasoned) that in the office that his father practices you can earn good money, if you're good at the job. But there will always be someone who'll say 'Oh, he's just a bailiff.' No, that won't do. Now in my own trade it's true that I've done pretty well (there is a whole story in that 'I've done pretty well' that will have to be told), but I don't want him to end up a slave to customers' small change. Maybe it would be good to send him to school, but where would school get him? It's true that he does seem to have a good memory, and after a few years I could send him on to Coimbra. Yes, I could do that, since I've saved up all that small change. And I'm old; I have no children or other relatives. But what the devil will he take up at Coimbra? Lawyer? No . . . that's a bad profession. Solicitor? That would be good. Yes, a solicitor. But . . . no, no; I hate people who bother me with papers and lawsuits. Clergyman? A gentleman cleric would be nice . . . very dignified; you make a lot of money; you could get to be a parish priest. So it's decided; he's going to be a clergyman, that's what. I'll have the pleasure of seeing him say Mass, of seeing him preach in the Sé. I'll show all these lowlifes here in the neighborhood who don't like him now how right I have been in loving him. He's still pretty young, but I'm going to start trying to get him straightened out right here at home, and when he gets to be twelve or fourteen he'll start school."

Having ruminated this idea over for a considerable period of time, one day he called the boy to him and said, "Young man, look here; you're getting bigger all the time (he was then nine years of age). You will have to learn a calling so you can be somebody someday. From next Monday on (it was then Wednesday) I'm going to start teaching you your ABC's. Get your fill of rascality the rest of this week."

The youngster listened to this speech with a mixture of astonishment and disgust, and asked in return, "You mean I'm not going to be able to play in the backyard anymore, or in the doorway?"

"Only on Sundays after we get back from Mass—"

"But I don't even care for Mass."

The godfather did not like that answer; it did not augur well in one destined for the priesthood. But it wasn't enough to make him lose hope.

The child took to heart the words "Get your fill of rascality the rest of this week," seeing them as an open license to do anything, be it good or bad, that might come into his head in the free time he had remaining. He spent the days in a frightening licentiousness. Two or three times the godfather found him astride the wall that separated their backyard from the neighbor's, at great risk of falling.

That evening as he was seated in the barbershop door, he saw down at the end of the street a procession illuminated by the light of lanterns and candles and heard the voices of priests praying. He quivered with delight and leaped to his feet. It was the Procession of the Bom-Jesus.

Up until not too long ago some city streets still had black crosses nailed up at intervals along their walls. On Wednesdays, and some other days of the week as well, there would set out from the Church of the Bom-Jesus and other churches a kind of procession made up of priests carrying crosses, members of some of the brotherhoods with lanterns, and people in great numbers. The priests would pray aloud, and the people would intone the prayer along with them. At each of the affixed crosses the procession would stop, everyone would kneel, and they would pray for an extended period. This act, which satisfied the sensibilities of the pious, provided means and occasion for every kind of mockery and immorality that the youth of the time could dream up—they who are the elders of our time and constantly complain about the irreverence of the youth of today. They would walk along in a jeering mass behind the procession and interrupt the chanting with proclamations of their own, some merely amusing, others outright indecent. They carried with them lengths of string with heavy balls of wax fastened to one end. If some unfortunate man whose head the passing years had deprived of hair should come close enough, they would work their way into range and, hiding behind their fellows, throw the projectile so that it hit full upon that devotee's bald pate. Then they would quickly wind in the string, and no one would be able to tell where the attack had come from. These and other scenes further excited mockery and hilarity from the crowd.

This is what, in those times of devotion, was referred to as "running the Via-Sacra."

Now as we said, the boy fairly quivered with pleasure as he saw the procession approach. He surreptitiously dropped down to threshold level and then, without the barber seeing, flattened himself against the wall between the shop's two doors, getting up on his tiptoes so he could see as much as possible.

The procession got closer and closer, and the youngster palpitated with pleasure. It reached their very door. Then a thought occurred to him that made him absolutely shiver; he remembered the godfather's words: "Get your fill of rascality . . . ." He peeked inside the shop, saw his godfather busy, leaped out from where he had stationed himself, mixed in with the crowd, and chimed right in with his own jeers and shouts, adding to the level of the hubbub. It was a feverish pleasure he felt. He lost track of everything; he leaped about, he jumped, he shouted, he prayed, he sang. The only things he failed to do were those that were beyond his ability to accomplish. He got in league with two other boys his size who were also in the crowd. And when he finally realized where he was, he was all the way back at the Church of the Bom-Jesus with the Via-Sacra procession.

I V

Fortune

While the *compadre*, in a panic, is hunting high and low for the boy without so much as a scrap of information from anyone as to his whereabouts, let us look into what has happened with Leonardo and what new predicaments he has gotten himself into.

At the edge of the mangrove swamp in the Cidade Nova, next to a pond, there stood an ugly-looking straw-roofed house whose dirty exterior and muddy streetfront clearly indicated that its interior cleanliness would be no better. It comprised a small living room and a bedroom; its furniture consisted of two or three seats made of wood, some mats in one corner, and a large wooden box that served several functions: it was dinner table, bed, wardrobe, and cupboard. The house was almost always shut up tight, which cast a certain air of mystery upon it. This sinister dwelling was inhabited by a figure cut from the most detestable of molds: an aged half-breed with a foul, dirty face who dressed in rags. Nevertheless, the reader should know, for his amazement, that this man's trade was that of necromancy!

Back then considerable credence was given to such things, and those who practiced that calling were held in superstitious respect. You can imagine the inexhaustible mine that the slick operators found in this!

And it wasn't just the common folk who believed in the black arts; it is said that many people from the high society of the time would go buy fortune and felicity for the modest price of practicing a bit of immorality and superstition.

Now our friend Leonardo had taken it into his head to work on his fortune; this had as its cause the fact that he was involved in a new romance that was making his head veritably spin.

It had to do with a gypsy girl. Leonardo had seen her shortly after Maria left, and from the still-warm ashes of an ill-requited love was born another that was in that same respect no better at all. But the man was a romantic as they say nowadays, or a "stammerer" as they used to say back then; he couldn't get along without an involvement of some sort. As his work paid well and he always had coins jingling in his pockets, it had not been hard for him to attain the object of his affections; faithfulness, exclusivity in enjoyment, which were what his heart desired, had, however, proved more difficult. The gypsy had been cast in just about the same mold as the Lisbon produce-vendor, and there are, after all, sergeants, colleagues, and ship captains all over the place. The girl had done him more than once and then ended up running away from his house. This time, however, since the flight had not been occasioned by any homesickness, Leonardo decided to regain possession of his love by whatever means necessary. He located her easily enough, and after trying tears, entreaties, and threats, all in vain, he decided to seek through supernatural means what human means had not been able to achieve.

He therefore turned himself over body and soul to the half-breed in the house by the swamp, the most famous of all then plying the trade. He had already submitted to a huge number of tests—all of which began with a monetary contribution—to no result. He had undergone fumigation with suffocating herbs, drunk nauseating potions, learned by heart thousands of mysterious prayers, which he had to repeat many times every day, and gone off almost every night to leave objects and sums of money in specified locations with the goal of securing the intervention—or so the half-breed said—of their respective divinities. Despite all this, the gypsy resisted the sorcery. At last he decided to submit to the final ritual, which was set for that house with which we are now familiar, at midnight on the dot.

At the appointed hour Leonardo appeared; at the door he found the hideous necromancer, who would not let him in as he was but first ordered him to array himself in the dress Adam wore in Paradise and then covered him with a dirty cloak that he brought along. Only then was entry permitted.

The front room was arranged in a sinister manner that we shall not exhaust ourselves with describing. Among other things, whose significance was known only to those initiated into the half-breed's mysteries, was a small fire ablaze in the center of the space.

To begin the ceremony, Leonardo was ordered to kneel before all of the corners of the house and there to recite some of the prayers he already knew plus other ones taught him for this occasion; afterward he went to pray at the fire. At that moment there entered from the bedroom three new figures who had come to take part in the ceremony. Along with the head priest, they began a sinister dance around Leonardo. Suddenly they heard a light knock upon the outside door and a slow voice call, "Open the door!"

"Vidigal!" they all said in unison, transfixed by the greatest fright.

V

Vidigal

As we have said, the sound of that voice that had called out "Open the door!" sent a wave of fear and trepidation through the participants. And not without reason; it was the announcement of a predicament from which there was no escape whatsoever. At that time the city police was not yet organized—or, rather, it was organized in a way consonant with the trends and ideas of the time itself. The absolute monarch, supreme arbiter of all that had to do with that branch of the administration, was Major Vidigal; he was the magistrate who judged and meted out punishment and at the same time the police officer who hunted down the criminals. In the cases that fell under the wide jurisdiction that was his, there were no depositions, no proof, no arguments, no due process. He held all unto himself; his "justice" was infallible; there was no appeal of the sentences that he pronounced, he did as he chose, and no one called him to account. In sum, he directed a kind of police inquisition. Nevertheless, to do him justice, if due allowance be made for the ideas of the time, he in fact did not much abuse his power, and in certain cases he exercised it exceedingly well.

Vidigal was a tall man, not very heavy, with an offhand air about him; his gaze was fixed in a downward slant, his movements were slow, and his voice low and soft. Despite this look of nonchalance, however, there surely was no man more fitted than he to his job—practiced, as it was, in the manner here described.

A detachment, usually of grenadiers, sometimes of other soldiers that he would choose from the corps in the city, all armed with heavy batons, would, under Major Vidigal's command, make the rounds of the city by night, while the rest of the police worked by day. There was not an alley or back road, street or plaza where the major had not performed a noteworthy deed enabling him to catch a miscreant or give chase to a vagrant. His sagacity was proverbial, and for that reason his name inspired great terror in anyone whose conscience might be less than pure with respect to fraudulent practices of any sort.

If, in the midst of the din of a good healthy party in which neither common decency nor neighbors' eardrums were being accorded much consideration, the words "Vidigal's coming around" should chance to be uttered, the scene would abruptly change character. Things would quiet down in but a moment, and the festivities would take on a sober tone. When—at night, with his cloak over his shoulders and guitar slung across his back, headed for the action—one of the "roisterers" of the time (who might not enjoy great fame as a diligent worker) was surprised by a soft voice saying simply "Come here, where are you bound?", the only response that might avail him was to flee, if he could. For that was his only chance to escape some days' residence in jail, or at least in the Sé Guardhouse—if, that is, the flogging of his backside wasn't involved as an inevitable consequence as well.

It was for such reasons that our sorcerers and their unfortunate victim scattered in confusion as soon as they recognized by the voice who it was they had in their midst. They tried to escape out the back of the house, but it was completely surrounded by grenadiers with the aforementioned weapons in their hands. The door was opened with little resistance, and Major Vidigal (for it was in fact he) and his grenadiers discovered the inhabitants in *fragrante delicto* of necromancy: The fire was still burning, and the objects that had played a part in the sacrifice were still there.

"Oh," he said. "You do wizardry here—"

"Major, sir, for the love of God . . ."

"I've always wanted to see how all this works; continue on—no need for formality; go on."

The unfortunate participants hesitated a moment, but seeing that resistance was useless, they started in anew with the ceremony—at which the soldiers laughed, perhaps foreseeing the impending outcome. Leonardo was absolutely abashed, all the more because he was a public figure; and he tried as best he could to cover himself with the dirty cloak. He again bent down, almost to the floor, in the same place as before, and the dance began again, with the major in close observation, his arms crossed and a lackadaisical look on his face. When the sacrificers, deciding that they had danced enough, attempted to stop, the major ordered, in a soft voice: "Continue."

After a great deal more time, they again tried to stop.

"Continue," said the major again.

They continued on for another half hour; at the end of that period, now very tired, they again sought to call a halt.

"Not yet. Continue."

They continued on until time became impossible even to calculate, to the point where they could go on no longer. Our Leonardo, kneeling by the fire, was almost melting away in sweat. At last the major indicated that he was satisfied, ordered them to stop, and without altering his attitude said to the soldiers in that sweet, deliberate voice of his, "Grenadiers, lay on."

At the command the batons were raised, then to fall square upon the backsides of that "honest" folk, making them, despite their wishes to the contrary, dance for some time more.

"Stop," said the major, after a good quarter of an hour.

He then proceeded to give each lawbreaker a lecture in which he expressed his deep regret at having to exercise such measures, and which he invariably ended with the question: "And what is your occupation?"

None of them had an answer. The major would then smile and add with a sardonic chuckle, "Hmm. I see!"

Leonardo's turn came.

"You, man, an officer of the justice system, who ought to be setting an example—"

"Major, sir," he responded, cowering, "it's that cursed girl that makes me do all this; I haven't been able to find any other way—"

"You we are going to cure! Let's move on to the guardhouse."

At that decision Leonardo despaired outright. He would happily overlook the baton blows he had received as long as they remained se-

cret; but to be taken to the guardhouse, and thence perhaps to jail . . .
that he could not bear. He implored the major to spare him; the major
was unbending. His shame then poured out in a stream of curses directed at that damned gypsy girl who was the cause of all his suffering.

The guardhouse was in the Sé Square; it was a kind of holding pen
where those taken into custody at night were held before being sent to
their sundry fates. And of course those interested in what was up in
town would go there in the morning and quickly find out all that had
taken place the night before.

There Leonardo spent the rest of the night and much of the morning, exposed to the scrutiny of the curious. It was his misfortune that a
colleague chanced to pass by and, seeing Leonardo, stopped to speak to
him—which meant that in short order the city's entire corps of bailiffs
had been informed about what had befallen their colleague. A severe
foot-stomp of disapproval was being prepared for him when the whole
business took another turn and Leonardo was sent off to the jail.

His colleagues made a superficial show of their regret, but secretly
they did not fail to calculate on the shortfall, for Leonardo commanded
a large clientele and while he was imprisoned the parties involved would
bring their business to them instead.

V I

First Night Away from Home

As soon as he realized that his godson was missing, the *compadre* became terribly upset; he sounded the alarm throughout the neighborhood, hunted, inquired, but no one had any news or information to
offer about the boy. Then he remembered the Via-Sacra, and it occurred
to him that the youngster might have gone off with it. He hurried along
all the streets the procession had traversed, anxiously asking everyone he
met for information about that precious treasure of his hopes. He got all
the way to the Church of the Bom-Jesus without finding a trace. There
they told him that they had seen three boys behaving in so reprehensible

a manner as the Via-Sacra entered the church that the sacristan had thrown them out. That was the only clue he was able to find.

He then wandered in the street for a long time, repairing to his house only after it was very late. When he arrived at his door, the wicket of a neighboring shutter opened, and a woman's voice called out: "No news, neighbor?"

"None," the *compadre* answered in a disheartened voice.

"From now on you'll believe me when I tell you that that child was born with a bad disposition."

"That's not a neighborly thing to say . . ."

"I'm telling you, and I say it again, the child was born with a bad disposition. God forbid, but I think he's bound for no good."

"Oh, *senhora*," the *compadre* shot back in an irritated tone, "what gives you the right to talk about my life and the things in it? Mind your own, stick to your bobbins and your tatting, and leave other people alone." And then he went into his house muttering, "Someday I'm going to raise some cain with that woman. It's always the same thing. It seems like a bad omen."

The poor man lay awake all night trying to come up with ways to find the child. And after he had hatched a thousand plans, he said to himself, "As a last resort, I'll go see Major Vidigal." And he awaited the daylight so that he could get back to searching.

In the meantime, let us satisfy the reader, who is probably curious to know where the youngster has got to.

Amidst the immigrants from Portugal there also came to Brazil the gypsy plague. A slothful, unscrupulous people, they earned here a well-deserved reputation as the worst of scoundrels; no one in their right mind would do business with them because they knew they would come out on the short end. The poetry of their customs and their beliefs, of which so much has been said, they left on the other side of the ocean; here they brought only bad habits, shady practices, and rascality. If you don't believe that, our own Leonardo can offer a few words on the subject. They lived in almost complete sloth, but no night passed that did not have its party. As a rule, they lived away from the main streets and enjoyed total liberty. The women dressed with a considerable ostentation relative to their resources: They wore a lot of lace and ribbons, they favored items that were red, and none of them would consider herself dressed without at least one gold chain around her neck. The men had nothing to distinguish them other than some characteristic features that made them recognizable.

The two boys with whom the fugitive youngster had struck up a friendship belonged to a family of these people that lived on Rossio

Square, a place that during a period of time back then had for that very reason acquired the name of "Gypsy Camp." Those boys were, as we have said, about the same age as he; nevertheless, accustomed to a vagabond life, they were familiar with the whole city and ran about it alone to no great concern on their parents' part. They never missed the Via-Sacra procession or anything else of the kind. Meeting our future clergyman that night, as the readers already know, they took up with him and ended up bringing him to their parents' house, where, as usual, there was a gypsy party (a custom that remains to this day). They held, as we have said, a celebration every day—always, however, with a specific reason. Today it would be a baptism, tomorrow a wedding, now this person's birthday, then that one's, feast day of this or that saint. On the evening of which we speak, there was an oratory set up, and a saint of their devotion—of whose name we are ignorant—was being celebrated.

On the way, the boy was overtaken by misgivings and wanted to go back, but his companions painted such a picture for him of what he would see if he went on with them that he decided to follow where they led. They arrived at last at the house, where the party had already begun.

On the left side of the living room, on top of a table covered with a white towel, a print cotton comforter serving as its canopy, was the oratory, illuminated by some small wax candles. Along the walls were seats of every sort, benches and chairs on which the guests were seated. It was no small number, both gypsies and native-born people; they wore dress of all kinds, ranging from the barely acceptable on down. They were jolly and ready to make the full most of the night.

The boys entered without anyone seeing them and went over and located themselves beside the oratory.

Shortly thereafter the fado commenced. Everyone knows what the fado is, that dance so voluptuous, so varied, that it seems the offspring of the most comprehensive study of the art. A simple guitar serves better as its accompaniment than any other instrument. The fado has different forms, each more original than the last. In one, just a single person, man or woman, dances for some time in the middle of the floor, performing the most difficult steps, assuming the haughtiest positions, accompanying all of this with a snapping of the fingers. Then he or she slowly begins approaching someone else of his or her choice. A few turns and movements in front of that person and finally handclaps say that the other has been chosen to go next. In that way the entire circle is called in until everyone has danced.

In other forms, a man and a woman dance together. Following the beat of the music with the greatest precision, they first dance together very slowly, then change to fast steps, one moment pushing each other away, the next joining back together again. Sometimes the man follows after the woman with quick steps as she, making slight movements with her body and arms, moves slowly away; at other times it is the woman who follows after the man, who retreats in his turn, until at the end they come back together again.

There is also the circle, in which many people dance, breaking off on certain beats to clap their hands and tap their feet, sometimes long and loud, other times in a brief and more subdued manner, though always at one and the same time.

And beyond these there are still other fado forms of which we have not spoken. The music is different for each one, though it is always played on the guitar. In some cases, the guitar player sings a song, which often is highly poetic in concept.

Once the fado begins, it is hard to stop it; it often stops only at dawn—when, that is, it does not take up entire days and nights on end.

The boy, having forgotten all else in the face of this pleasure, watched the party as long as he could. He was finally overtaken by slumber, and he and his companions curled up in a corner and slept lulled by the sound of the guitar and the tapping of feet.

At dawn he awoke startled, aroused one of his companions, and asked to be taken home.

The godfather was just coming out of the house to begin his hunt when he ran across him. "You little devil—where have you been?"

"I went to see an oratory. Aren't you always saying I'm going to be a priest?"

The godfather stared at him for some time and finally, unable to resist the air of ingenuousness that he displayed, burst out laughing and took him inside, completely appeased.

The Comadre

It is now our duty to say something about a figure who will play an important role in the course of this story and whom the reader scarcely knows, since we touched on her, in passing, only in the first chapter. She is the midwife who, as we said, served as godmother to the subject of these memoirs.

The *comadre* was a short, excessively fat, good-natured woman, simple, or simpleminded, to a certain extent, though in another sense quite discerning. She lived by her practice of midwifery, which she had adopted out of curiosity, and by pronouncing blessings to ward off the evil eye. She was widely known to be highly devout, the most assiduous churchgoer in the city. She was an unerring calendar of every religious feast day observed here, knew by heart the days on which Mass was said in this church and that, as well as the time and the priest's name; she was on time to every Mass, litany, novena, and septenary; she never missed a Via-Sacra, procession or sermon. In short, she kept her time so deployed and the schedules so organized that she never arrived at church to find Mass already at the altar. She began at dawn with the Mass at Our Lady of the Lapa; no sooner had it concluded than she was on her way to 8:00 Mass at the Sé; and leaving it she caught the 9:00 at the Church of Santo Antônio. Her habitual dress, like that of all the women of her civil and social standing, consisted of a black lisle skirt worn over any sort of dress, a thick, starched white kerchief at her neck, another on her head, a rosary hanging from the skirt sash, a sprig of rue behind her ear, all this covered with the classic mantilla, in the lacework of which was pinned a small amulet made of gold or of bone. On the days of solemn observance, instead of the kerchief on her head she would wear her hair combed up and held in place by an enormous chrysolite-set comb.

This use of the mantilla was a hollow imitation of Spanish custom. The Spanish mantilla, we have been told, is a poetic thing that invests women with a certain mystery and heightens their beauty. Not so its use by our women. It was the most prosaic thing imaginable, especially when the women who wore it were short and heavy like the godmother. The most brilliant of religious ceremonies (which were those most attended back then) took on a lugubrious apect when the church began to fill with those black shapes sitting side by side, now and again leaning over to whisper to each other.

But the mantilla was an article of clothing befitting the customs of the time: Because the actions of others were the principal concern of almost everybody, it was quite necessary to see without being seen. The mantilla played the same role for women's dress that shutters did for houses: Both provided an observation post that opened out upon the lives of others. The *comadre* led a busy and eventful life: midwife, devout practitioner, curer of the evil eye. She therefore had little time for visiting and keeping up with friends and acquaintances. She thus did not often go to see Leonardo. For some time she had had no news of him, or of Maria, or of her godson, when one day at the Sé she overheard the following conversation between two pious women in mantillas.

"That's what I'm saying; that Lisbon girl was the devil incarnate!"

"And she seemed like such an angelic little thing. What did Leonardo do to her?"

"Well, he let her have it with his fists, which is what made her run off with the captain all the sooner. But it was all her fault; Leonardo is a strong, healthy young man, he made good money and always treated her like a lady!"

"And what about the son? Even when he was little, that boy was a real handful."

"His godfather took him. He is extraordinarily fond of him . . . head over heels, poor man. He says the boy is slated for the priesthood. What a priest! He's full of the devil."

Just at that moment the Host was raised, and the two pious women broke off their conversation to strike their breasts.

One of them was the *compadre*'s neighbor lady, the one who was always predicting no good for the boy and with whom the barber had promised to raise some cain. The other was one of those who had come to the baptism.

As soon as she heard this, the *comadre* set out to find the *compadre*. It must not be thought, however, that her motive went beyond one of curiosity. She wanted to know about the affair in every minute detail; that would give her a great deal of material about which to talk at church and with which to entertain the soon-to-be-mothers who entrusted themselves to her care. She walked into the barbershop and, when she lay eyes on the *compadre*, started in, "Well, so the girl stuck us with the little monkey, huh? That's crazy, doing that to Leonardo, a man so well set up . . . a son of the old country."

"She just got homesick for her own country," said the *compadre* with an arch smile.

"I hope she just gets caught by the evil one in the end. What a beauty she was! . . . And you, *compadre*, you've ended up with the burden on your back."

"He's not a burden . . . I love him; he's a good boy . . ."

There then began a detailed question and answer session about what had taken place in Leonardo's house, and the two of them, *compadre* and *comadre*, unburdened themselves unreservedly. Afterward the *compadre*—without being asked, to be sure—narrated all their godson's excellent qualities and spoke of his intentions with respect to him. The *comadre* did not agree with them (which pleased the *compadre* not at all); she didn't see the boy as priest material. She thought it would be better to place him in the Conceição factory where he could learn a trade. Nevertheless, the *compadre* held firm in his plans, which he said he had great hopes would come to fruition. The *comadre* finally gave in.

Along the street she repeated everything that she had learned to whatever acquaintance she happened to meet, not refraining from the addition of one or another circumstance that might lend more color to the picture.

Meanwhile, the *compadre* was applying himself to work toward the realization of his plans: he started teaching the boy the ABC's. In an initial setback, however, the youngster got stuck on "F," and nothing could get him past it.

From that time on, the *comadre* continued to come by the house—for a reason that will become clear later.

For the present, let us pass on to an account of what happened to Leonardo.

The Rare Animal Garden

There still exists today in the vestibule of the Imperial Palace—which at the time when our story takes place was called the Royal Palace—a small chamber or room that the town wags, and the common people as well, called the "Rare Animal Garden." That name had been bestowed upon it because of the purpose that it then served: Every day of the year it was occupied by three or four high-ranking officers, old, no longer fit for war and useless in peace, who remained in the king's service, no one knew whether for some sort of extraordinary pay or just for the honor of being in the royal service. Seldom did the royal will call upon them actually to do anything, so they passed their time in resplendent idleness, sometimes in silence, other times conversing about the events of their own day and condemning those that they correctly judged not of that day, for none of them was less than sixty years of age. Sometimes it happened that they all fell asleep at the same time; then, with the resonance of their breathing passing through tobacco-constricted nasal passages, they would play a quartet, a piece of inestimable quality that the officers and soldiers of the guard, the servants, and other passersby would stop by the door to appreciate. The poor men were often the victims of practical jokes, which in those unharried times were many people's objects of study.

Now and again someone who found them sleeping would shout at the door, "Lieutenant Colonel sir, the King is looking for Your Excellency."

One or another of them would wake up with a start, grab up his cocked hat, buckle on his swordbelt—oftentimes with such haste that the hat went on crooked or the sword ended up on the right side—and run up to see the king.

"At your service, your Royal Majesty," he would say, a yawn still on his face.

The king, understanding the trick that had been played, would burst out laughing and send him away.

When the poor man got back downstairs, every one of those who hung around there would inquire, as seriously as possible, what the object of the king's summons had been.

Tricks of this and other sorts were played on them, and before long they would fall for another one.

Let us introduce the reader to one in particular of these "active" military men, for he also figures in our story. He was old, like his companions, but it surely was not he who was the reason whereby the room had received its peculiar nickname. His features, worn down a bit by the passage of time, still retained a certain regularity of line that indicated that in his youth he had not been ill-favored as regards masculine beauty; of his hair, what had survived the ravages of time were some crisp silver curls ringing his temples and the nape of his neck; his bald head was noble and imposing. He had been valiant and by dint of his exploits had won the epaulettes of a lieutenant colonel; he was the son of Portugal and had accompanied the king on his coming to Brazil. These qualities, however, did little to safeguard him, and, just like the others, he bore the brunt of the practical jokes played by the local wits.

Thus when one day a woman dressed in a mantilla came to see him and spent some time talking to him in private, one person or another would come by and clear his throat outside the door, or would utter some appropriate witticism.

"Old loves never die," said one.

"Bravo! I so like good taste," said another.

The woman in the mantilla is an old acquaintance of ours, for she is none other than the *comadre*. And the piece of business that has brought her is one that interests us as well, since it has to do with securing the release of poor Leonardo. The reader must therefore hear the conversation between the two.

"Lieutenant Colonel, sir," said the *comadre* when she arrived, "I come to ask a favor of Your Excellency. Mr. Leonardo, of whose child I am godmother, lies in prison."

"Leonardo? But why?"

"It's nothing. Just some craziness." And whispering in his ear the *comadre* told him in a low voice the cause of Leonardo's imprisonment.

The old man dissolved in laughter. "They've really got him," he said.

"I had hoped that Your Excellency would do me the favor of speaking on his behalf to Major Vidigal, for it was he who arrested him . . . poor man! It is a shame, but he just can't help himself!"

And proceeding on, the *comadre* told him in closest confidence—just as she had to all her acquaintants—the whole story of Leonardo's unfortunate love affair with Maria, all of the misadventures of the boy Maria had abandoned and the godfather was caring for. And she then went on to relate what had happened with the gypsy girl and got back to the story of the arrest, which she told and retold twenty times without omitting the smallest detail. At the end she made her request once more, which the old man promised to see satisfied. Then she left, receiving in the vestibule several sweeping bows and some malicious smiles. One cadet leaning near the exit door remarked to her, "I hope it all went well and that you won't forget me on baptism day."

"A curse upon you" was the only answer she gave as she walked by.

About how the old lieutenant colonel had come to know the *comadre* and Leonardo and why he took an interest in the latter's case the reader will hear more later.

The acquaintanceship was years old, and Leonardo no sooner found himself in jail than he thought of the protection that the old man could provide him in such a spot. Through the agency of a colleague, he had the godmother summoned and charged her with the mission of going to see the old soldier, a mission that she willingly accepted and—as we have seen—discharged most satisfactorily.

As soon as the *comadre* had left, the old man picked up his cocked hat, buckled his sword to his belt, and went out, after telling his companions what happens to people who get involved with their fortunes. One of them, who was himself enthusiastically inclined to witchcraft, grew very indignant about the case and promised to do everything he could for Leonardo as well.

Thus the reader can see that the business was not going all that badly. We shall shortly know its results.

I X

The Compadre's "I've Done Pretty Well"

The readers will probably recall what the *compadre* said while he was building castles in the air about his godson and considering having him take up his own trade—that "I've done pretty well" that we promised to explain further. We shall now make good on that promise.

If anyone were to ask the *compadre* about his parents, about his relatives, about his birth, he would have nothing to say—because he knew nothing at all about those matters. All that was recalled of his history amounted to extremely little. By the time he was old enough to be aware of life, he was in the house of a barber who was looking after him, but he never told him whether he was his father or not, or a relative, or even how he had come to be taking care of him. That, however, had never bothered him, nor did he ever have the curiosity to inquire.

That man had taught him his trade and, by some strange miracle, also to read and write. During the period of his apprenticeship he lived in the house of his . . . his master (for the lack of another name) a life that on the one hand resembled that of a family member, on another that of a son, on yet another that of a dependant and that in the final analysis was simply the life of a foundling, which the reader has doubtless already concluded he was. In exchange, his master gave him food and lodging, and repaid himself for what he had done for him.

When he ceased being a boy and became a young man and learned to barber and to draw blood reasonably well, he was obliged to support himself and pay for his lodging with the odd jobs that he did, since the income from his main work still belonged to the master. He submitted to this. But they wanted still more: They still required him to participate in the household chores. A surge of dignity stirred inside him as a result: He was now a journeyman barber and he didn't want to have his standing demeaned. The tide turned, and he steeled himself and left home with neither scruple nor remorse, for he knew well that the accounts had been evened between them. They had raised him, and he had done service in return. It must be admitted too that he found little resistance to his decision.

As soon as the initial bravado wore off and he had time to reflect, he almost began to regret his actions because he did not know how to get along on his own. He found himself on the street without knowing which way to go and having as his only possessions a barber's basin under his arm and a pair of razors and another of lancets in his pocket. It is true that he who possessed those instruments had the arms and uniform of the trade. That, however, was not enough; the poor youngster was in a difficult spot.

He spent his first night in a colleague's house, and at dawn the following day, taking his implements with him, he went out in search of work for the day and of fortune for all the days to come.

He found them both, one bringing the other along with it.

In the Palace Square a sailor sitting on a rock beside the sea called him over for a shave. To work, then! For now he wouldn't die of hunger today.

Now every barber is a gabber, and especially when he isn't fully occupied. He therefore struck up a conversation with his customer. It was his salvation and his fortune.

The ship to which the sailor belonged traveled to the African Coast, working in the slave trade. It was one of the convoys that brought merchandise to the Valongo slave market, and it was about to set sail.

"Master," said the sailor in the middle of their conversation, "aren't you a blood-letter as well?"

"Yes, I also let blood."

"Look, you would do right well for yourself if you went along with us . . . to work on the people on board; people die there at a terrible rate."

"Man, I don't know much about surgery."

"But didn't you just say you know how to let blood?"

"Yes . . ."

"Then you know all you'll need to know."

On the following day our man crossed the bar. Fortune had provided him with the means; now he had to know how to make the most of it. From the office of barber he was making the mortal leap to slave ship doctor; all that remained was for him to know how to make his new position pay. That was up to him.

By happy chance, in the first days of the voyage two sailors fell ill. The doctor was called. He did everything he knew: He bled them. And in a short time they were fine, perfect. As a result he gained a huge reputation and began being held in high regard.

After a good voyage they arrived at their destination. They took on their human cargo and headed back for Rio. Thanks to our man's lancet, not one Negro died, which greatly contributed to the growth of his reputation as one who knows his business through and through.

A few days outside of Rio the ship's captain fell ill. At first neither he nor anyone else had the slightest doubt that he would be well after the first blood-letting, but the case suddenly developed complications and neither the third bleeding nor the fourth seemed to accomplish anything. At the end of the fourth day the sick captain himself, and everyone else as well, realized that the end was near. But even so they did not blame our man.

"There's no blood-letting that will save him," they said. His running-aground time has come . . . and he's on his way in."

The captain had arrived at the point of making his last dispositions, and, as we have said, given the position of friendship and confidence that the "doctor" had won for himself, it was he who was chosen to carry them out.

The captain called him aside and secretly delivered to his care a leather belt and a wooden box, both stuffed full of gold and silver coins, and asked him as soon as he got to port to take them without fail to a daughter of his whose address he gave. Beyond that money he charged him as well to collect his pay for the current voyage and deliver it to the same destination. These were the only last wishes that he charged the "doctor" with carrying out, and he declared that he would be watching from the other world to see how he took care of them.

A few hours later, he expired.

From that day on not a single patient more escaped death, because the "doctor" no longer bled so much. He went about preoccupied, distracted, and he continued that way until they reached land.

As soon as he set foot on land he swore that he hadn't made out very well on the voyage and that he would never go to sea again.

As for the captain's instructions . . . stuff and nonsense. How could he possibly be held to anything? No one had witnessed what had taken place; nothing was known. The only ones who might suspect and try to do something about it were the sailors, but they shortly headed back to the Coast. The *compadre* simply decided to make himself the captain's heir and did so.

Such is the explanation for the "I've done pretty well"—and for many other like statements bandied about in the world.

X

Explanations

The old lieutenant colonel, albeit virtuous and good, nonetheless bore on his conscience a tolerable pair of sins, of the sort referred to as "of the flesh," which must not be called into account—sins not of today when age had made him inoffensive but rather of his youth. The result of one of them was a child that he had left behind in Lisbon, fruit of a late love that he had had at the age of thirty-six. As punishment the child had come out nothing like the father, and neither the advice nor the care nor the example of the latter directed him to the good path. At the age of twenty, having enlisted, he was an unruly cadet, a gambler, and the most insubordinate member of his regiment. He had visited a great deal of shame upon his poor father, who always endeavored by whatever means available to gloss over his defects and remedy those "honorable" things that he did, first paying his gambling debts for him, then hushing up his misdeeds, then curing with gold the breaches that he left in his adversaries' heads. There was one case, however, the circumstances and nature of which did not admit of such remedy. A short while before the poor father was to embark for Brazil in the king's retinue, as he was making preparations for the voyage, there came to his door a short, fat, ruddy-complected old woman dressed—according to the custom in that country for lower-class women—in a blue gingham skirt over a cotton print dress, a white kerchief worn in a triangle on her head and tied under her chin, and a pair of big, heavy shoes on her feet. She seemed beset by great agitation and anger: Her small blue eyes flashed deep in orbits sunken with age, her cheeks glowed red, her thin, shriveled lips pressed against each other violently as though holding back a torrent of insults, which made her pointed, somewhat upturned chin all the more prominent.

As soon as she found herself in the presence of the captain (such was the rank that the old man held at that time), she went up to him with a resolute and infuriated air. The captain instinctively retreated a step.

"Ah! Captain sir," she said at last, putting her hands on her hips and her mouth up close to his face and shaking her head angrily, "look; this isn't going right. It's got my head spinning . . . my blood boiling . . . I'm about to explode, you understand!"

"But what is it, woman? I don't even know who you are."

"I don't want any knowing. Like I say, it's not going right and I'm about to explode."

"But why? What is the matter? You have to tell me . . ."

"I've got nothing to tell. Like I said, I'm about to explode, Captain!"

"Well then explode away and to the devil with it! But at least say what you're exploding about."

"I've got nothing to tell, I said. Something like this makes a person's head go soft like a rotten onion; there's no place for it. Coming around buying fruit with that saintly look . . ."

"Who, woman, for the love of God? Won't you please explain?"

"What do you mean explain, or even half explain! Just because someone's an old woman that no longer has connections in the world, and she a poor, unsophisticated girl that just wants to experience everything, coming around putting one over on me right to my face, and her being even more susceptible . . ."

"But who put something over on the two of you? And who is 'she'?"

"Pretending not to know!" the woman went on, growing exasperated. "And didn't you actually consent to the marriage?"

"What marriage? Between whom?"

"Ay, ay, ay, now my head's spinning around like a loose mill wheel. You do know you have a son, don't you?"

"Of course I do," the other answered, beginning to see a bit of light within the mystery.

"And you know that he's one bad egg, don't you?"

To this the captain could surely have answered in the affirmative, though he was unable to bring himself to do so; he merely asked: "And what else?"

"And you also know that I have a daughter, my little Maria, that I brought with me from Lumiar, don't you?"

"How could I when I don't even know you?"

"Well, she's a very capable girl . . . and that damned cadet son of yours has spent a lot of time hanging around sidling up to her, a little courting here, some more there, gifts here, promises there. And in the end, bam, what do you think happened?"

The captain hit the ceiling.

"He even promised to marry her, saying that you had consented. Now I understand that it was just as much her fault, but I don't blame her, for I was a young girl once and I know that when the devil starts working in the body, it's good-night. But this'll drive a person crazy because . . . after all, the girl might have turned out real well."

The captain had now got a sense of it all and with several further explanations that followed saw himself reduced to the tightest of straits. This time the boy's behavior was irremediable. The woman was completely right; but to marry his son off to the daughter of a vegetable vendor, that wouldn't do. What was worse, he had nothing to leave to his son, and on just a cadet's pay the boy wouldn't be able to support a wife and household—not to mention the question of whether he would even agree to the match. He said good-bye to the old woman, not without promising to deal with the matter.

"See here now," she said as she left, "if this doesn't get worked out, I'll explode."

The poor man was in an awful situation. He went to talk to the wronged girl and, offering her a little something for her dowry, tried to get her to keep silent and not pursue her claims. She at first tried to refuse, but her mother advised her to accept—doubtless from the fear that she would explode. In this way the case was more or less remedied—given that the captain's conscience, which was that of a man of honor, was not at all satisfied. The times, however, did not allow for more, for the moment had come to set out with the king. He departed leaving his son recommended to all of his friends. The years passed, and when he least expected he found out that the girl was in Rio in the company of Leonardo—the same little Maria, who by then was the Maria the readers know so well. He tried to do everything he could for her, to appease all his scruples as an honorable father, though he chose to do it secretly. He went to see the *comadre*, whom he already knew, and charged her to advise him should she be aware of any need Maria might be experiencing. Never, however, did he have the opportunity to exercise his goodwill toward her directly. He was only able to do a small favor for Leonardo on an occasion in which the latter ran into trouble concerning an irregularity attributed to him with some documents and the *comadre* advised him to consult the lieutenant colonel, even without knowing him, because he was a very good man and everyone's friend.

This, then, is why Leonardo had recourse to the old lieutenant colonel, through the *comadre*'s mediation, in this his second predicament, and why the latter promised to see what he could do on his behalf—which indeed he tried to do.

As we have said, hardly had the godmother gone than he too set out and went to try to effect Leonardo's release. First he went to the jail, to get complete information from Leonardo himself, and he saw that what the *comadre* had told him was extremely accurate and that she had not omitted the slightest circumstance. Leonardo repeated and confessed everything that he already knew, in an affliction of embarassment and shame.

"Lieutenant Colonal sir," Leonardo said to him as the old man was preparing to leave, "Your Excellency once freed me from something that was not my fault. Free me from this as well . . . you can see that my honor has been compromised."

Leonardo was forgetting Maria's theory.

"It's not your honor," the old man replied. "What is compromised is your good sense; it will be said (and I am the first to say it) that you are crazy."

"I got away from a Lisbon rustic and fell for a gypsy . . . you're right!"

The old man left, smiling. From there he went to the house of a friend of his, a nobleman of influence, to obtain from him Leonardo's release. He lived in one of the narrowest streets in the city, in a big house with protruding wood shutters that had little peepholes that could be secretly slid open without anyone outside being able to see who was looking out through them.

The dust caked on the shutter pulls and the weather-beaten walls gave the outside of the house a somber look; as for the inside, it followed a similar fashion. The living room was small and had a low ceiling; the furniture that decorated it was all made of jacaranda wood in an old-fasioned style. All the pieces were enormous and heavy; the chairs and the couch, with curved legs and very high backs, had leather cushions, which was the fashion during the transition between cloth upholstery and caning. Anyone who wishes to get an exact idea of what this furniture was like might look into the consistory of some ancient convent, where we have seen some examples of it.

The walls were ornamented with a dozen paintings, or rather with glass cases that contained landscapes and flowers made of tiny seashells of many colors and were not altogether ugly, though they surely did not have the high value imputed to them at that time. To the right of the living room there stood upon a table an enormous oratory made in the same style as the furniture.

Finally, in one corner there was a blessed palm, the kind handed out on Palm Sunday. And if the reader will now imagine all this covered with a thick layer of dust, he will have a perfect idea of the place into which the old lieutenant colonal was received. It was with few differences the same as all the rich houses of that time, which is why we have given so much time over to its description.

Without making his guest wait long, the master of the house appeared. He was a man now along in years, with an unpleasant face. He came in in sandals without stockings, and shirt sleeves, with a checkered wool shawl over his shoulders and a snuff box and red handkerchief in his hand.

In few words the old man explained the case to him and entreated him to speak to the king on Leonardo's behalf.

At first, the latter put up some doubts, saying, "Man, you mean I'm supposed to go the the palace for the sake of some bailiff? The king will laugh at my protégé."

In the end, however, he was forced to yield to the bonds of friendship and he promised everything. The old man left, satisfied, and went to take the news to Leonardo, who jumped for joy. The release order arrived a few days later, and he was set free. He thought that he had just gone through the worst trial imaginable, but unbearable tortures began for him the day he left jail: the mockery, the ridicule, the laughter of his companions followed him for many days, incessant and excruciating.

Progress and Setback

Bearing in mind the explanations of the preceding chapter, let us now return to the subject of our memoirs, whom we have neglected for some little while. And let us hasten to give the reader some good news: The boy had finally extricated himself from "F" and was to be found all the way in "P," where unfortunately he had again become stuck. The godfather was extremely happy with this progress, seeing some brightening on the horizon of his expectations. He proclaimed positively that he had never seen a child with a better memory than his godson, and every lesson that the latter learned—on a four-day by four-day pace at minimum—was to him a triumph. There was, nonetheless, one thing that saddened him in the midst of this all: The boy had a decided aversion for prayer and in general for everything having to do with religion. He was incapable of making the sign of the cross from left to right; he always made it from right to left. And the godfather, despite all his patience and good will, could not get him to say even half of the "Pater Noster" from memory without making mistakes; instead of saying "Thy kingdom come," he would always say "Our bread be come." Going to Mass or to sermon was for him the greatest of all trials. This made the godfather despair at times, even to the point of agreeing with the *comadre* that the boy had no inclination for the clerical life. Those, however, were but passing clouds; there was always one thing or another that made all his hopes rekindle, and the man moved on reassured in his labor.

What he hoped for, however, was not expected by all; none saw in the boy anything other than a future vagrant of the highest order. The person who most expected that was the barber's neighbor lady, the one whom he had called the boy's "ill omen." That neighbor was one of those women they refer to as a shrew: Presumptuous and overbearing, she bragged that she had no fetters on her tongue. She was a widow, and she beleaguered everyone with the virtues of her late husband. Annoying and contrary, she never missed an opportunity to puncture her neighbor's expectations for his godson, saying that she couldn't see an aptitude for anything in him, that she wouldn't want his future for anyone she was responsible for, and that the best thing to do when he grew up would be to toss his carcass aboard some ship or clap a uniform across his back. The barber would get furious at that; he was able to contain himself for a long time, but one day he couldn't take any more and burst out at the woman. When he happened to come to the shop door, she asked from her window, in a mocking tone: "Well neighbor, how's the reverend getting along?"

An old man who lived across the street and was at his window at the time burst out laughing at the question.

The godfather hit the ceiling, his bald head turned red, he furrowed his brow, but he pretended not to have heard. The neighbor lady started laughing as well, perceiving the appreciation, and added: "A fado-loving priest . . . what do you know. When is he going back to the gypsies' house?"

The old man across the street redoubled his laughter. The neighbor lady went on, "Well, can he do the Pater Noster yet?"

The *compadre* grew exasperated and, trying to think of the biggest insult possible, finally came back with, "Yeah, yeah, Mrs. nose in everybody else's life . . . he's got the Pater Noster. And ⊺ make him say it every night for that dear departed husband of yours who at this very moment is kicking in hell!"

"What? What did you say, you old skin-scraper? Now you're attacking people who aren't even here to defend themselves?" said the neighbor lady, really getting her back up. "Remember that the person you're talking about was no blood-letter, and he didn't live off hair clippings either. Don't you start in with me or I'll really get nasty and spread it all over about your problems. . . . Kicking in hell! Can you believe that? . . . Kicking in hell! . . . Now listen to this, for I'm not one to have my tongue fettered: That wild-eyed so-called godson of yours is so total and complete a scoundrel that he's going to dishonor the very beard of the person who raised him. . . . And there's no surprise to it, because he's sprung from bad stock, do you hear me? Don't you start in with me—"

"And you," shot back the *compadre* as the woman took a breath, "why are you sticking your nose into something that's none of your business?"

She proceeded, "I'll stick my nose in where I want. That's none of your business, so don't come around here laying down the law; I don't need you."

"But what do you have against an innocent child who has never done anything to you?"

"A lot, because he keeps banging rocks off my roof, he makes faces at me when he sees me at the window, and he treats me like I was some Lisbon rustic woman or some barber's wife. I've said it before and I'll say it again: That boy was born with a bad disposition and he's headed for no good—"

"Okay, *senhora*," answered the *compadre*, who was generally even-tempered and was led to these excesses by his love for his godson. "Enough of this bickering; think of the neighborhood."

"Oh! Well! What the neighborhood needs is to be quit of that little devil!"

With that the boy came to the door and, standing up on his tiptoes, stretching out his neck and making it quiver like the neighbor lady's, he repeated, imitating her voice: "Be quit of that little devil . . ."

The *compadre* found that so funny that he considered it the ultimate comeback and, in his turn, burst out laughing.

"Oh," said the neighbor lady, "thank your stars, my little devil in the shape of a boy, it's not your fault. It's the fault of whoever eggs you on."

"It's the fault of whoever eggs you on," echoed the boy, mimicking her.

The *compadre* lost control of himself with laughter.

The neighbor woman, exasperated, banged her shutters closed and withdrew, though she went on for a long while talking out loud so all the neighborhood could hear, saying whatever offensive thing came into her head against the barber and the boy.

"The youngster's done me proud," said the barber to himself. "He got the better of that woman for me. But there's still that old man across the way who also chimed in laughing. The time will come."

We have forgotten to say that the barber, although he knew about Leonardo's imprisonment, had paid little attention to it, having merely said, in reference to the cause of the latter's troubles, "Just deserts, so he won't let himself be hauled around panting after every skirt he happens to set eyes on."

Nor did he go to the jail to visit him, or take his son to receive his father's blessing, for which the godmother heartily reproved him when she found out.

After Leonardo's release was secured, the old lieutenant colonel, being kept informed in detail by the *comadre*—as the reader knows—made up his mind to take the boy under his own protection. He believed that if he could put him on the right track he would cleanse his son of the sin of dishonoring Maria. He sent the *comadre* to offer his support in favor of the youngster and even offered to take him to live with him. The *compadre*, however, was by no means in favor of that, and it was only at the *comadre*'s insistence that he promised to accept the lieutenant colonel's protection on any matter whatsoever.

"I do not," he said, "want to be robbed of the pleasure of having made him into somebody. I started the job and I'm going to finish it."

"Man," the *comadre* retorted, "you're making a mistake. Look, the old man is a person of substance; see how he got Leonardo back out on the streets with just a couple of well-placed words."

"Absolutely not; I'm not going to give this wretched neighbor lady of mine the pleasure. I'm going to do this with my own hands. Now if the lieutenant colonel wants to do something for him, I'll accept it, but when it comes to taking him away from me, never. I've got up a head of steam; I'm going to keep right on going."

X I I

Starting School

It is now necessary to pass in silence over a number of years in the life of the subject of these memoirs, in order not to bore the reader with the repetition of a thousand boyish misdeeds of the kind already familiar. They were deviltries of all sizes and shapes that exasperated the neighbor lady, disgusted the *comadre*, but did not alter in any degree whatsoever the barber's affection for his godson: The more that affection grew, the blinder it became, if that were possible. With it grew the hopes for the glorious future that the *compadre* dreamed of for the child—all the more since during this period he had made at least some small progress: He could read passably, sounding out the words, and through an incredible triumph of patience on the *compadre*'s part had learned to assist at Mass. The first time he got through the ceremony correctly and respectably, his godfather exulted. It was a day of pride and pleasure: The first step on the path for which he had destined his charge.

"And they say that he has no aptitude for the priesthood," he thought to himself. "Now I'm on the mark, I've found his true inclination. He really was born for this, he's going to be a great clergyman. I'm going to try putting him in school, and then . . . it'll take."

Indeed, he went to see about this and to talk to the schoolmaster about taking the child. The latter lived in a small, dark house on Vala Street.

The barber was received in the parlor, which was furnished with four or five long pine benches long since dirtied through use, a small table that belonged to the master, and another larger one, where the pupils wrote, which had many little holes in it for inkwells. From the walls and ceiling there hung an enormous lot of cages of all sizes and shapes, in which little birds of many diverse sorts hopped around and sang; this was the pedagogue's greatest passion.

He himself was a man done all in infinitesimal proportions: short, slight, with a thin, gaunt little face, excessively bald; he wore glasses, had pretensions of being a Latinist, and whacked pupils' hands for the slightest thing. He was therefore one of the most highly regarded teachers in the city. The barber entered accompanied by his godson, who was a bit cowed on noticing the look of the school, which he had not imagined this way. It was a Saturday; the benches were crowded with boys, almost all of them dressed in jackets or lisle frock coats, dark sailcloth breeches, with an enormous case made of leather or cardboard held across their backs by a cord. The two arrived at the very moment of the chanting of the multiplication table. This was a kind of litany in numbers that was the rule in the schools back then, sung every Saturday in a kind of monotonous and intolerable Gregorian chant but one that the boys liked very much.

Their voices, mingled with the birds' singing, created a din that brought pain to one's ears. The master, accustomed to it, listened impassively with a huge ferule in his hand, and the slightest error committed by one of the pupils did not escape him amidst all that racket. He would stop the chant, summon the unfortunate young man up to him, correct in a chant of his own the error that had been committed, and then bring at least six lusty whacks down upon him. He was the conductor showing the orchestra how to keep time. It was in the midst of this uproar that the *compadre* set forth the purpose of his visit and introduced the youngster to the schoolmaster.

"He has a very good memory; he can read a little; he shouldn't give you any trouble," he said with pride.

"And if he does, I have the remedy right here: *Sancta Ferula!*" said the teacher, brandishing the ferule.

The *compadre* smiled, trying to suggest that he had understood the Latin. "That's true: It makes saints of the ferocious," he said, translating.

The schoolmaster smiled at the translation.

"But I trust that it won't prove necessary," the *compadre* added.

The boy understood what all of this meant and showed that he was far from pleased.

"He'll be here on Monday, and I beg you not to spare him," concluded the *compadre* as he took his leave. He looked for the boy and saw him already at the street door ready to leave, for he did not feel at all comfortable there.

"Why, boy, are you thinking of leaving without getting the master's blessing?"

The boy returned, constrained, received the blessing from a distance, and then they left.

On Monday the child returned armed with his own case across his back, his own writing slate, and his own horn inkwell; his godfather accompanied him to the door. On that very first day he comported himself in such a way that the master had no choice but to administer four whacks—which caused him to lose all the self-possession with which he had entered. From that moment he declared unrelenting war on the school. The godfather came to pick him up at noon, and the first thing he said was that he would not go back the next day, or even that afternoon.

"But don't you understand that it's necessary to learn?"

"But it's not necessary to be hit."

"You mean you've already been hit?"

"It wasn't anything, no sir; it was just because I tipped over the inkwell onto the breeches of a boy next to me; the master scolded me, and I started to laugh hard—"

"But if you're going to laugh when the master gets angry with you . . ."

This upset the barber very much. What the devil would that cursed neighbor lady say when she found out that the boy had been disciplined on his very first day at school? But he had nothing to complain about; what the master had done was right. It was a hard job to get the boy to go back to the school that afternoon; he was able to do so only with the promise that he would speak to the master and ask him not to engage in any more discipline. That, however, was not something that could really be done; it was merely a sop to get the boy back to the school. The latter went back inside in a state of despair and on no account wished to be calm and quiet on his bench. The master summoned the boy and had him kneel a few steps away from him. Shortly, he turned around distractedly and caught him in the act of raising his hand to throw a spitwad at him. He called him over again and gave him a dozen whacks.

"And on the first day," he said. "You certainly show a lot of promise."

The boy, grumbling, sent his way every dirty word he had memorized.

When the godfather came back to get him, he found him resolute and firm in his intention not to be lured back again—and never to return even if they tore him to little bits. The poor man lost his patience over the matter.

"On the very first day!" he said to himself. "This is the curse of that evil woman . . . but I intend to persevere, and we'll see who finally prevails.

XIII

Change in Life

By dint of huge effort, great travail, and above all much patience, the *compadre* got the boy to stay through two years of school and to learn to read very poorly and write even worse. During all that time, not a single day passed when he did not receive a greater or lesser count of whacks. And despite the reputation that the master enjoyed for cruelty and injustice, it must be confessed that he seldom acted thus with the boy: The latter had a nose for mischief, and that, along with the spoiling carried out by his godfather, resulted in the most highly refined ill-breeding that one could imagine. He derived the most delectable enjoyment from disobeying any instruction given him: If one wished him to be serious, he would burst out laughing like a crazy man, with the greatest pleasure in the world; if one wished him to be quiet, it seemed as if some hidden spring were driving him on and making him give a more or less faithful imitation of perpetual motion. A folder, an inkwell, a slate never lasted more than two weeks in his hands; he was regarded around the school as its most complete scoundrel. He would sell his schoolmates anything that might have value, be it his or someone else's, so long as it happened to fall into his hands: A pencil, a pen, a notebook, anything was fair game to him. And the money he gained he always employed for the worst ends he could come up with. At the end of the first five days of school he proclaimed to his godfather that he now knew the streets and didn't need him to go with him any longer. On the first day the godfather agreed to his going by himself, he played hooky. He took a liking to that practice and soon acquired among his schoolmates the name of chief truant of the school, which also meant principal punishment-catcher. One of the primary places where he happily whiled away the mornings and afternoons in flight from school was the Sé. The reader will understand that this in no way betokened any religious inclination: during Mass at the Sé, and even at other times, a lot of people came together—especially women in mantillas, against whom he had formed a particular antagonism because of their similarity to his godmother—and that was what he wanted, because by mingling in the crowd of those entering and leaving he could pass unnoticed and be assured that he would not be easily found if anyone was looking for him.

Because of his habit of frequenting the church he had come to meet the little sacristan—who, let us remark in passing, was every bit as good a piece of work as he—and to strike up a friendship with him. When they met they would first confine themselves to exchanging meaningful looks as the sacristan discharged his duties to the church; as soon as Mass ended, however, and as the truly devout were exiting, the two would come together and begin to recount their most recent misdeeds while hatching plans for a thousand new ones. For purposes of camaraderie or as a sign of fast friendship, his companion entrusted to our truant a candle snuffer, and they carried out the service—and their pranks—together. The least of the latter involved their going from altar to altar and sucking the last remains out of all the wine cruets—which only further inflamed their appetite for misadventure.

This life went on for some time. Finally, however, the truancies became so regular that his godfather saw himself again forced to accompany him school every day—which ruined all the plans that the two boys had cooked up. Our future clergyman had often thought about how pleasant it would be to go around dressed up like his companion in a cassock and surplice and be a sacristan too—having all the candle snuffers he wanted whenever he wanted them, having, with his friend, the run of the church, being able on feast days to take up the censer at Mass and suffocate the face of the nearest old lady with incense smoke. Oh, what a dream of adventure that was! Seeing himself deprived of the enjoyment of the pleasures of those days of flight because of the resumption of godfatherly accompaniment, he had his desires kindled and he began to confess them to the godfather, letting on that there was nothing more to his liking these days than the church, for which, he opined, he seemed to have been born. This was an absolute joy for the godfather, because in this newfound taste on the youngster's part he saw the route to furtherance of his plans.

"I was right," he thought to himself. "There's no doubt about it, I'm making progress. The boy is growing into it."

One day the boy made a final decision and proposed to his godfather that he become a sacristan. "It would be good," he said, "for me to become accustomed, for when I'm a priest."

At first the idea enchanted the godfather. But soon reflection set in, and he declared that this would demean the boy and compromise his future dignity. So great, however, were the youngster's arguments and appeals that he was finally obliged to give in. In this the child gained two enormous advantages: He would be satisfying his desires and he would be getting away from school, thus saving himself the daily ration of hand whacks.

"Okay," the godfather told himself, "he now knows how to read a little and how to write. I'll let him have his head for a while and put him at the Sé, so he can learn a greater love for that life. Later, when I see he has calmed down a little bit, I'll go ahead with the plan." As a result, he went to see that sacristan of the Sé who had danced the minuet at the baptismal celebration—and who was none other than the father of the little sacristan with whom our youngster had become friends—to try to place his godson, who wanted no other church but the Sé. Fortunately, he was able to get him in. With the practice acquired on his days of hooky-playing, the boy had learned just about the whole ritual necessary for a sacristan: He already knew how to assist at Mass, and he perfected the rest in short order.

He got ready in a few days, and one beautiful morning he left the house dressed in the requisite cassock and surplice, and set out to take up his job. When she saw him pass by, the neighbor lady of the ill omens first loosed an exclamation of surprise, supposing that this was another of the *compadre*'s idiocies. Looking more closely, however, she perceived what it was all about and burst into laughter. "And how about this?! . . . God protect you, sir Curate," she said, bowing in courtesy.

The boy shot her back a glare and responded through clenched teeth, "I am a curate, and what I'm going to cure is you." That was a promise of vengeance.

"Now what about this?" the neighbor lady went on grumbling to herself. "Something like that in the church is a sin!"

The boy arrived at the Sé panting with contentment; the cassock seemed to him a royal mantle. Fortunately, on that day there were two baptisms and a wedding, and he therefore had occasion to enter into the full exercise of his duties, which he initially undertook by investing himself with the greatest gravity in this world. The next day, however, things began to change form, and the rascalities started.

The first took place at a sung Mass. It was the youngster's function to stand holding a large candle while his companion held the censer at the foot of the altar.

By ill luck, the *compadre*'s neighbor lady, whom the boy had promised to "cure," unmindful of what she was doing, took a seat close to the altar and near the two. As soon as he caught sight of her, the new sacristan said some words to his companion, pointing out the woman with his eyes. Shortly thereafter the two moved stealthily to within a suitable distance and did so in such a way that she ended up with one of them more or less ahead of her, the other behind. Then the two initiated a most meritorious design: While one, having filled the censer with incense, swung it in just such a way that the billows of smoke it gave off came out right in the poor woman's face, the other at every step spilled gobs of melted wax all over the back of her mantilla, all the while pretending to gaze at the altar. The poor woman got angry and said something to them, we know not what.

"We are curing you," the boy responded in a serene voice.

Seeing that she wasn't getting anywhere, the devout woman tried to move to another place and get out, but the people were so densely crowded that she could not, and she had to endure the torture through to the end. When the ceremony was over, she went to the liturgy master and raised an enormous row, which cost the two boys a hefty reprimand. They, however, paid little heed to it, since they had successfully carried out their plan.

X I V

Further Vengeance and Its Result

The reprimand that the liturgy master gave the two youngsters as a result of what they had done to the poor woman did not, as we have said, produce any effect in them in the sense of correction. They did not, however, forgive the humiliation they had suffered in front of their victim or the revenge she had enjoyed. At the first opportunity they had, they evened the score with the liturgy master as well.

The incident was as follows.

The liturgy master was a middle-aged priest, moderately good-looking, a native of Ilha Terceira in the Azores, though he gave it out that he was pure Lisbonian; he had graduated from Coimbra. On the outside he was a complete Saint Francis of Catholic austerity, on the inside a thorough Sardanapalus who all in and of himself could have furnished Bocage with material enough for an entire poem. He was a preacher who always took honesty and corporal purity in every sense as his subject; on the inside, however, he was as sensual as a follower of Mohammed. The public might have been unaware of these matters, but such was hardly the case with the two boys, who knew everything about it. The liturgy master, confident that given their youth they would pay little attention to certain things, had sometimes used them in his service, to deliver messages to a certain person who—let the reader secretly understand—was none other than the gypsy girl object of Leonardo's late affections, with whom at one moment His Reverence had been living in the closest of relations, maintaining, of course, the appearance of total respectability.

The day arrived of one of the principal church celebrations, in which the liturgy master was always the preacher. The sermon for this day was one on which, some time ago, he had worked very hard, turning the library upside down and expending an enormous effort of intellect (which, in his case, was not exactly a character strength). Thus it is clear that he loved his sermon—so much so that one year when he was ill and could not deliver it he nearly burst with frustration. It was his belief that everyone listened to him in rapt delight, that the audience was transported by the sound of his voice. In short, that annual sermon was the means through which he had hoped to achieve all his goals and to which he expected to owe his future elevation. It was his talisman. Let us nonetheless observe that that particular sermon was an exceedingly bad route to that end, for if it demonstrated anything it was the priest's inadequacy as regards anything in this life except being liturgy master, in which office he knew no equal. Now it was on this delicate point that the two boys sought to attack him, and chance favored them beyond their wildest hopes and desires, making their vengeance totally complete.

The day of the celebration arrived, as we have said. For the past three or four days the master had not set foot outside his house, so involved was he in memorizing this important presentation. Our novice sacristan was charged with going to inform him of the time for the sermon. He went to the gypsy girl's house, where the priest was habitually to be found; he knocked on the door and, despite all the monitions he had received, asked in a loud voice: "Is the reverend liturgy master in?"

"Speak quietly, boy," said the gypsy through the shutters. "What do you want with His Reverence?"

"I need very much to talk to him about tomorrow's sermon."

"Come in, come in," said the priest, who had overheard.

"I've come to tell Your Reverence," said the boy as he entered, "that you have to be at the church by ten o'clock tomorrow."

"Ten? That's an hour later than usual . . ."

"Just so," answered the boy, laughing with delight inside as he took his leave. He then went to let his companion know that his plan had worked out perfectly, for he wanted the priest to miss the sermon and, being the person in charge of telling him the time, had himself changed it, saying ten o'clock instead of nine.

Everything was set up; the barbers' music was ensconced at the church door; everything was boiling right along; at nine o'clock the celebration began.

The celebrations of those times were carried out with as much richness as those of today and, in certain respects, with greater propriety. Nevertheless, they had their comic sides, and one of those was the barbers' music at the door. No celebration could be carried out without it; it was generally considered to be almost as essential as the sermon itself. Its great value was, however, that nothing could be easier to arrange: a half-dozen apprentice or master barbers, usually black, one armed with an out-of-tune cornet, another with a diabolically hoarse trumpet, formed a tuneless but extremely loud orchestra that delighted those for whom there was no room inside the church or who did not wish to go in.

The celebration followed along its normal course. As the hour drew near, however, the preacher's lateness in arriving began to cause consternation. One ceremony was performed a second time, another one repeated, but still the man did not appear. One of the boys who had not figured in the ritual was dispached to look for him. He gave a quick look about the neighborhood and returned to say that he had not been able to find him. Concerns grew further; there was no way around it, a sermon was necessary, no matter what kind it might be.

An Italian Capuchin friar was in attendance and, observing the general plight, in the name of goodwill offered to improvise the sermon.

"But Your Reverence does not speak our language," it was objected.

"*Capisco!*" he responded, "*ed la necessità.*"

After no small dose of perplexity, the good offices of the Capuchin were finally accepted, and he was led to the pulpit. The boys smiled at one another in triumph. No sooner had the preacher appeared before the people than a general murmur arose; the wags smiled, counting on all the material they could get out of this for a goodly number of laughs; at the sight of the preacher's immense beard, some old women prepared themselves for a great contrition; other less pious women, seeing that it was not the accustomed orator, exclaimed in irritation: "Curses!" "God forgive me." "Is *that* our preacher for today?"

In spite of all this, however, attention was profound and general, a great curiosity enlivening everyone. The orator began and spoke for a quarter of an hour without anyone's understanding him. Some old women were beginning to protest that a sermon all in Latin was of no interest when suddenly the pulpit door was seen to open and the figure of the liturgy master entered, bathed in sweat and red with fury. There was a general whisper. He stepped forward, with his hand pushed aside the Italian preacher—who stopped for an instant in surprise—and then intoned in a husky and powerful voice his "per signum crucis." At the sound of that familiar voice the audience awoke from its boredom, made the sign of the cross, and prepared itself to listen. But not everyone was of such a mind: Some thought that the Capuchin should be allowed to finish, and they began to mutter. The Capuchin would not yield his right and went on with his harangue. It was a truly comic scene, at which the great part of those present laughed until they could laugh no more. The two boys, principal authors of the work, were in complete ecstasy.

"*O mei cari fratelli*!" proclaimed the Capuchin on one side in a mild, reedy voice, "*la voce de la Providenza . . .*"

"Just like the trumpets of Jericho," croaked the liturgy master on the other side.

"*Piage al cor . . .*" added the Capuchin.

"Announcing the fall of Satan," continued the liturgy master.

And so on went the two of them for some time, accompanied by a chorus of laughter and confusion, until the Capuchin chose to abandon his post, muttering angrily, "*Che bestia, per Dio!*"

With the sermon over, the liturgy master descended from the pulpit now somewhat calmed by having succeeded in making himself heard but still sufficiently furious to come proclaiming that he would pull off one by one the four ears of the two youngsters who he suspected of being the source of what he had just undergone. He got to the sacristy, which was full of people. Seeing the two boys, he descended upon them and, grabbing each in one hand by the surplice collar, "And so—and so—" he said with his teeth clenched, "what time did you say the sermon was?"

"I said nine o'clock, yessir. You can ask that young lady, for she heard me . . ."

"What young lady, boy, what young lady?" asked the priest, displeased that there were so many people around to hear.

"That young gypsy lady where I found Your Reverence; she heard me say nine o'clock."

"Ooh!" said the company present.

"That's not true," responded the liturgy master forcefully, releasing the boys to avoid further explanations and trying to mollify the others with protestations of the falsity of what the boys had just said.

After a while the uproar calmed down, the celebration ended, the people left. The liturgy master, seated in a corner, was thinking to himself, "Now how about this? Did I or did I not miss my sermon this year on account of that little devil? Ever since that cursed boy came into this church everything here has been going wrong! And he topped it off by saying right in front of all those people that I was at the gypsy's house! Enough . . . I'm going to get rid of him."

And in fact he set out to get the two boys, or at least the newer one, dismissed. He was successful with no great effort, for the boy certainly did not enjoy any great sympathy.

This was the worst thing they could have done to him: It was as though he had been in a paradise and they were expelling him from it. And then that cursed neighbor woman, what satisfaction she would find in his dismissal! And his godmother, who had formally opposed his entering the Sé. . . . All this made him anxious.

He had not been wrong in his expectations: No sooner had he arrived back home and had the outcome become known in the neighborhood than the neighbor lady, finding a way to catch up the barber, said, "Well, didn't I say he was born with a bad disposition?"

"*Senhora*, for the love of God, mind your own business . . ."

"I am avenged. He thought my new mantilla was going to end up the same way . . ."

The *compadre* retired to avoid any further outbursts.

The *comadre* too, as soon as she heard of the incident, came to see the *compadre* and say to him, "I'm telling you, he's not going to be good for that. It would be better to put him in the Conceição; there's more discipline there. You know, I can arrange it with the lieutenant colonel . . ."

The *compadre*, however, did not seem disposed to accept that advice.

X V

Scandal

Despite everything he had suffered for the sake of love, Leonardo did not really endeavor to change. While he remembered the jail, the grenadiers, and Vidigal, he forgot the gypsy girl—or, rather, he thought about her only to swear to forget her. As his companions' jibes gradually ended, however, his passion began to rekindle, and a great battle took place between his tender impulses and his dignity, in which the latter had almost carried the day when an unfortunate discovery came to upset everything. Leonardo one day discovered, we know not through what means, that the lucky rival who had driven him off the field was the liturgy master of the Sé!

At that, the blood rushed to his head, "But a priest!?" he said. "I must save that poor creature from hell, for that is where her life is taking her." And he set out anew with entreaties, with promises, with pledges to the gypsy girl, who would give in to none of them.

One day when he caught her at the window he approached her and began *ex-abrupto* to speak to her in this manner: "You are already in hell in this life! . . . A priest?!"

The gypsy interrupted him, "There were lots of bailiffs to choose from, but I didn't like any of them—"

"But you're committing a mortal sin . . . you're condemning your soul . . ."

"Man, do you know what? You're a rotten preacher, you just don't have the knack. I'm fine exactly as I am. I've never gotten along well with bailiffs anyway; I was born for better things—"

"Well, then, what do you have to say about me? I'm going to have my revenge . . . and a sweet one it'll be."

"Ha!" responded the gypsy, laughing. And she began humming the refrain of a *modinha*.

Leonardo understood that this talk about hell and punishment in the next life was going nowhere, so he decided to mete the punishment out to her in this life itself. He withdrew, murmuring, "I'm going to blow the whole thing sky high, let the chips fall where they may."

It so happened that a few days later the gypsy girl was celebrating her birthday. According to custom, upon that kind of pretext a party was planned. We will not take the trouble to describe it; in one of the preceding chapters the reader has already seen what it would have been like: guitar, *modinhas*, fado, din, and the celebration was complete. Leonardo soon found out what was going to happen, and he swore that this would be his day of vengeance.

Being a ruffian was at one time an actual calling in Rio de Janeiro. There were men who made a living from it: They would beat people up for money and go anywhere to purposely start a riot no matter what the outcome, as long as they were paid.

Among the honest citizens thus occupied there was, at the time of this story, one Chico-Juca, duly infamous and feared. His real name was Francisco, and he was therefore at first called "Chico." But, since he was successful with his own hands in bringing down from the throne of ruffiandom a companion who had the greatest reputation of the time in this line of work, and who was called "Juca," people added that name to his in honor of the victory, and he was from then on known as "Chico-Juca."

This man was Vidigal's greatest challenge; he made no few tries, but he hadn't yet found a way to catch him. The grenadiers knew him at a league's distance, but they had never been able to lay hands on him.

Having lain in watch all day, Leonardo saw the liturgy master enter stealthily around the time of the Ave Maria, when the party had not yet begun.

"Ah! He's not going to miss even tonight?! Well he's going to pay dearly for his little spree."

He left and went to look up Chico-Juca, who was an old acquaintance of his. He found him in a tavern across from the Church of the Bom-Jesus. Chico-Juca was a dark-skinned man, tall, heavy, with red eyes, a long beard, and close-cropped hair; he always wore a white jacket, full-legged pants, black slippers, and a small white hat ever tipped at a rakish angle. He was usually affable, clever, full of jokes and sayings. When what he called the "rumpus" started, however, he bordered on outright brutality. Just as some have the vice of drunkenness, others the vice of gambling, and still others that of debauchery, he had the vice of ruffianism. Even when he was not being paid, all he had to do to start a brawl was to take it into his head to do so. And only after he had thrown punches until he could throw no more was he satisfied. He profited greatly from this: There was not a tavern-keeper who did not extend him credit and did not treat him exceedingly well.

He was at the tavern door sitting on a sack when Leonardo came up to him. "Hello, Master Pataca!" he said when he saw him. "I thought you were still in the pokey working on your fortune on account of that gypsy girl."

"It's precisely on account of that devil that I've come looking for you."

"Man, I can dish out head butts and good old-fashioned beatings, but sorcery? I've never had the calling."

"I'm not talking about sorcery," said Leonardo in a low voice. "I'm talking about those good old-fashioned beatings."

"Oh boy! You mean we have a dance? Go on . . . you're not capable of starting a rumpus yourself; you've always been a noodle."

"I know, I couldn't . . . but you . . . you're the past master of it."

"Me? Well what do you know—and where do you want me to start this rumpus?"

"You won't regret it," said Leonardo, tapping his vest pocket suggestively.

Chico-Juca read the line; he tipped his hat a bit further to the side and got ready to listen with curiosity to what Leonardo was going to propose.

Then Leonardo told him what he wanted: It was nothing less than for Chico-Juca that very night to get into the gypsy girl's party whatever way he could and to start a big fight there late in the evening. He cautioned him that Vidigal would likely be in the area, so as soon as the fight was well under way he should take it on the lam. Leonardo did not explain to him the reason for this, and he showed no great curiosity to know: It was a fight, and he was always ready for one whatever the reason. Thus, after dickering over the price, the two reached an agreement and all was arranged.

Leaving Chico-Juca, Leonardo went and found Vidigal, informed him about what was going to take place that night at the gypsy's house, and assured him that the business would necessarily end up in a fight. Therefore it was incumbent upon the major to go there and be prepared for what might come about.

"Very good," said Vidigal to him. "You want to get back at her, that's fine with me. I'll be there, and I didn't need your information, for I already knew that there would be a birthday party there today and I had every intention of stopping around."

Leonardo left, happy to see his plan working out so famously, and, from a convenient place where he could watch, settled back to enjoy the outcome. The high jinks started. A half dozen *modinhas* had already been sung and the *tirana* had been danced for some time when Chico-Juca appeared and, through the intermediary of someone he knew—for he knew people all over town—secured entrance to the room and began to observe the goings-on. The room had a door that led to a side room, and that door was closed. The gypsy girl would now and again go in through that door, stay a while, and then come back out. After a while she would go in again, now taking with her one or another of her closest girlfriends, and then come back out; then she would do so again, taking another girlfriend. Some of the guests remarked on this, while others did not notice anything strange in it. The party went on, and around midnight, when it really began to heat up, it was suddenly interrupted. One of the young men playing the guitar was seen suddenly to stop in the middle of the *modinha* refrain he had been singing and call out in fury: "That's enough of that . . . I won't stand for it . . . Mr. Chico-Juca, stop your gross jokes with that young lady; she belongs to me . . ."

Chico-Juca had in fact for more than half an hour been directing some of his own brand of humor at a young woman who he knew "belonged" to the guitar player. He had carried on so long that the other, having noticed what was happening, had uttered the words we have just heard.

"You're talking back to me?" said Chico-Juca back to him.

The young man, who was not one to shrink away, stood up and replied, "I said what I meant. Stop teasing her!"

No sooner had he uttered those words than Chico-Juca grabbed the guitar out of his hands and hit him full over the head with it. The other retaliated, and a melee ensued.

Chico-Juca was overwhelmed for a moment, but, quick and fearless, he began dishing out doses of head butts and kicks in all directions. Some women got into the fray, and they dished out punishment and caught their share just like anyone else; the other women, however, started screaming. Chico-Juca suddenly wheeled around, burst out through the door, and disappeared.

It was indeed time, for only a few moments had passed when there appeared in the still-open doorway the tranquil figure of Vidigal, surrounded by a number of grenadiers. Chico-Juca had escaped them, even though they had seen him leave, because the major, having with him on this occasion but a small number of soldiers, chose not to go in pursuit for fear that he would end up short on personnel, for he saw that matters had grown pretty ugly inside the house. Letting him go, then, he entered the house.

As soon as they saw him, everyone stopped in fright.

"Now what squabble is this?" he asked, in his slow voice.

They each began to give their excuse as best they could, and justice was meted out according to the credit that the reputation of each merited: If the person was well known and this was not the first time he had been in this situation, he was kept to one side with a grenadier guard; the others were sent away. During this period the gypsy girl kept eyeing the door into the other room and giving signs of nervous agitation. This did not escape Vidigal's notice, and after the process was over he said to one of the grenadiers, "Go search that room . . ."

The gypsy screamed; the grenadier did his duty and opened the door to the room; a little noise was then heard. Vidigal said from his side of the door, "Bring on out whoever is in there."

At that same instant he saw the grenadier reappear bringing along by the arm the reverend liturgy master dressed in short, baggy drawers, black stockings, shoes with buckles, with a skull cap on his head. In spite of the predicament in which they found themselves, everyone burst out laughing. Only the priest and the girl wept, with shame.

The latter threw herself at Vidigal's feet, but he was unbending and the reverend was hauled off to the Sé Guardhouse with the others, being permitted only to put on some more respectable clothes first.

X V I

The Plan's Success

So that our readers may remain calm—for you are doubtless gravely concerned about the liturgy master—let us hasten to say that he did not actually go to jail: Vidigal wanted merely to give him a taste of the medicine, and after exposing him to public scrutiny for some hours in the guardhouse, as had happened to Leonardo, he let him go, ashamed, cowed, cursing that idea he had had of attending his mistress's birthday party from inside that little room. As for Leonardo, he was brimming over with joy. His revenge was virtually complete: He had seen his rival arrested by the grenadiers, just as had happened to him, and taken to the guardhouse, to suffer there the scrutiny of the curious. True, the whipping and the days in jail were missing, but it was also the case that he was a mere bailiff while the liturgy master was a respected priest, and therefore anything at all would have the effect of wounding him gravely.

Beyond this, the liturgy master, knowing that he had not come off well in the eyes of his colleagues because of the scandal he had caused—even though he was well aware that in this regard none of them was in a position to cast the first stone—and hearing a low murmur rise to threaten him with the loss of his position at the Sé, decided after serious meditation to abandon the gypsy girl. And abandon her he did. With this, Leonardo considered himself completely satisfied, and there rekindled within him the desire to reconquer his former position, now that his principal enemy had abandoned it. The gypsy girl, seeing herself rejected, undoubtedly would not wish to remain unattached for long. And as he found himself with petition already filed and could point to unremunerated services, it was likely that he would obtain favorable dispensation—especially too because she would not be able even to dream that everything that had happened was his doing.

The sentimental Leonardo therefore began passing by the door of his old paramour: If he saw her at the window, he would stop at the corner and direct looks of supplication her way; passing nearby he would let out a plaintive sigh or a bitter remonstration.

All these scenes put on by a figure such as Leonardo cut—tall, corpulent, red-faced, wearing a dress coat, breeches, and cocked hat—were so comic that the entire neighborhood was entertained by them for some days. Some of the more imprudent individuals began casting arch remarks the gypsy girl's way as they talked from their windows; she was goaded on by this, and that turned out to be Leonardo's "fortune." One day as he passed by she gave him the eye to come on in.

Leonardo experienced an inexplicable sensation: His face turned every shade of red, from crimson, which was his habitual color, to dark purple; then it gradually lightened to a marble pallor. As he walked from where he was to the gypsy's door, he could not feel the ground under his feet; when he came back to himself he was, with his eyes full of tears, back in the arms of his old lover, who was asking a thousand pardons and promising from that time on to be faithful to her last dying breath—although she did not fail to declare in the midst of it all that if she received him anew in her house it was because she wanted to halt the wagging of those evil neighborhood tongues that kept prying into her life. The poor man was beside himself; he looked like a traveler who has returned to his old haunts, or an army officer who has just liberated a besieged fortress from an enemy's control. In short, all the bonds that had been so stretched were pulled taut again.

Leonardo made the mistake of telling his colleagues that he had finally been victorious in this intricate suit of his. This let him in for a tremendous tongue-lashing from everyone and serious reprovals from some. But on that occasion he paid no heed: Joy blinded him to the point that he could not see what was coming in through his eyes.

No sooner did the *comadre* hear what had taken place than she went to see Leonardo and undertook a long sermon seeking to persuade him that he was off on the wrong track. "Why, man," she said to him, "you haven't changed at all!"

"Oh, nonsense! I'm just crazy on this subject, that's all."

"But, man, you haven't fared very well with either Lisbon rustics or gypsy girls. Why don't you at least try a daughter of this country?"

The *comadre* had a daughter who lived with her and who represented a considerable burden for her. For a long while now she had therefore nourished an idea with which the reader will become acquainted later on—when it comes to pass—or before, should it be perceived in the *comadre*'s words.

"No, I'm not very fond of these people."

"But you have no reason for that. There are many very capable young ladies around here. It is true that what they want is the old 'first you take and then you give' down here under the Southern Cross . . ."

"That's exactly the reason why I'm not fond of them."

After several more attempts, the *comadre* left a bit miffed but not wholly discouraged. She counted on the gypsy girl to aid her in her plan, and, as we go on, the reader will see that she was right in doing so.

As for our ex-sacristan, he continued on in a futureless state, which greatly concerned the *compadre*, without, for that, disheartening him. Coimbra was his *idée fixe*, and nothing could get it out of his head. At the behest of the *comadre* the old lieutenant colonel had even come personally to speak to him but had got nowhere. Exasperated with this obstinacy, he had dropped the business and decided to have nothing further to do with it.

X V I I

Dona Maria

In this city a procession day has always been a time of great celebration, of frenetic comings and goings, of movement and of agitation. And if still today it is as the readers know it to be, at the time when the personages of this story lived it was at a somewhat higher pitch: The streets filled with people, especially women in mantillas; houses were decorated; magnificent quilts of silk or damask in all colors were hung out of windows; and choruses gathered on nearly every street corner. It was almost everything practiced today but at a larger scale and greater scope, because it was done "for the faith," as the old women of those good times used to say. We, however, would say it was done for fashion: Decorating windows and doors on procession days or contributing in some other way to the splendor of the religious festivals was as much a matter of style as donning a dress with puff sleeves or wearing a formidable high comb two palms tall in your hair.

In those times there were many more processions, and each sought to be richer and to display greater pomp than all the others. The Lenten processions were ones of extraordinary magnificence, especially when the king deigned to participate in them, thus obliging all the court to do the same. Outshining all the others, however, was the one called the Goldsmiths' Procession. Nobody stayed at home on the day it was put on: Either on the street or in the houses of those friends and acquaintances that were lucky enough to live in a place that it passed, everyone found a way to see it. There were some people so devoted to it that they were not content with seeing it only once; they would go from one person's house to another's, from this street to that, until they had seen it pass by from beginning to end two, four, even six times before considering themselves satisfied. The principal reason for this, we suppose, aside perhaps from others, was that this procession contained something that none other did. The reader will doubtless find it extravagant and ridiculous, as do we, but it is our obligation to tell about it. We refer to a large company called the "Baianas" that walked at the head of the procession, attracting the attention of the devout as much or more than did the saints, the biers, and the sacred emblems. That company was formed by a great number of black women dressed in the style of the province of Bahia—whence the name—who, in the intervals between the "deogratias," would dance impromptu dances. To tell the truth, the thing was curious, and if it had not appeared as the first part of a religious procession it certainly would have been more excusable. Everyone knows how black women from Bahia dress: It is one of the prettiest modes of dress we have observed. Nevertheless, we do not advise its adoption by anyone else. A country in which all the women wore that dress, especially if it were one of those fortunate countries in which the women are white and beautiful, would be a land of sin and perdition. Let us try to describe it.

The so-called Baianas did not wear dresses; they wore only some few skirts, held at the waist, that hung down barely below midleg and were adorned with magnificent lace. From the waist up they wore blouses of very fine cloth, the collar and sleeves of which were also adorned with lace. At their throats they would put a string of gold or a necklace of coral; the poorest of such wear was a string of glass pearls. Their heads were bedecked with a kind of turban called a *trunfa* formed of a huge white kerchief, very starched and stiff. They wore high-heeled slippers so small they held only the toes, leaving the heel outside. And on top of all this they covered themselves elegantly in a black cloth cape, leaving outside their arms, which were laden with metal rings like bracelets.

A few days after the last events narrated in the preceding chapters came the day of the Goldsmiths' Procession. Our customs at that time as regards openness and hospitality were not what one would term highly praiseworthy; that day, however, represented an exception, and, as we have said, those who lived on streets that saw the procession pass opened their doors to all their friends and acquaintances. By virtue of this it happened that in the house of a certain Dona Maria there were to be found gathered together the *compadre* accompanied by his godson (richly dressed for the day in his black serge frock coat and otter cap), the *comadre*, and the neighbor lady of the ill omens.

Dona Maria was an elderly woman, very fat; she must have been quite beautiful in her day, but all that now remained of that beauty was the pink of her cheeks and the whiteness of her teeth. On this day she wore her white dress with the high waist and puff sleeves, a kerchief, also white and highly starched, at her throat. Her hair was done up *bugres* style, which consisted of two thick swirls falling over the temples; a bun was done up on the crown of her head in such a way as to simulate a plume. Dona Maria had a good heart, was generous, devout, a friend to the poor, but in compensation for those virtues she had one of the greatest vices of that time and those customs: a mania for lawsuits. As she was rich, Dona Maria nourished that vice lavishly; her suits were the very food of her life. Awake she thought about them, asleep she dreamed about them; rarely did she speak of anything else; and as soon as she found a tangent line she would fall right back into that favorite of topics. Through the long practice she had in those matters, she knew them like the palm of her own hand. There was no lawyer who could best her; she knew all the legal terms and the whole structure of a law case so well as to take a back seat to no one in that regard. In her, this mania attained the status of obsession, and it bored to the point of desperation anyone who had to listen to her talk of the latest charges that her lawyer had advanced on her behalf in the documents in her property suit, of the final arguments that had been advanced in her action against one of her father's executors, of the deposition of witnesses in her suit regarding the sale of her houses, or of the summons that she had had served upon a tenant of hers who had borrowed twenty *doblas* from her and now refused to acknowledge the debt, and a thousand other cases of the same kind.

As soon as the *compadre* entered—he being an old friend of hers whom she had not seen in a long time—Dona Maria started in by telling him that that old suit against her father's executor was still unresolved. She started to go on according to her custom when the *compadre* introduced his godson and for his part began to recount the latter's story.

He started with the boy's origins, going all the way back to the foottromp and the pinch with which Maria and Leonardo had launched their relations during the voyage between Lisbon and Rio de Janeiro—which elicited peals of hearty laughter from Dona Maria. He then went on to the baptismal celebration, which he described in detail. Up to that point it was a bright and happy drama. Then came the tragedy: He told all the stories of Maria's treachery, Leonardo's jealousy, and the final quarrel that had resulted in bringing the youngster into his hands.

Dona Maria listened to it all with the closest attention and interrupted the *compadre* only occasionally to cast a curse at Maria, evince compassion for Leonardo, or laugh at the boy's misdeeds. When the conversation reached that point, the neighbor lady of the ill omens, who was also present but up until then had paid little attention, intervened in the conversation—needless to say, against the youngster. She then mentioned some of his stunts, always adding at the end of each statement, in words addressed to the godfather, "Our neighbor, no matter how much he may love the child, can't deny that . . ."

The *compadre*, who in the midst of all this had always painted the boy's history in highly favorable colors, never ceasing to boast of his gentleness and good disposition and always gilding his deviltries under the title of innocent acts, ingenuous games, or childish pranks, was increasingly exasperated by the resistance the neighbor lady was putting up, which, by contrast to his practice, painted everything in shades of black. The *comadre* chimed in on this occasion as well, though maintaining a duplicitous position: First she would agree with the *compadre*'s view, then with the neighbor lady's.

Dona Maria, who was crazy about chitchat, especially gossip, took the greatest interest in the story; no one could recall her ever forgetting her lawsuits for so long at one time.

The boy, seated in a corner, listened to it all in an observant silence. The *compadre* was barely able to contain himself—out of respect for Dona Maria—at the neighbor lady's invectives; she, judging herself safe given the circle she was in, unburdened herself at great length against the boy. In the end, she addressed herself to Dona Maria, saying in her usual phrase, "So, my lady, is he what I say or isn't he? He was born with a bad disposition."

"Bad disposition?" cut in the *compadre*, the bald spot on his head now very red. "Bad disposition? C'mon . . ."

From his place the boy cast a thunderous stare at the neighbor lady, which more or less signified, "I'll get you for this; you just wait."

Dona Maria, seeing that the godfather was beginning to become exasperated, took up the role of mediator, and, addressing herself to the neighbor lady, said, "You are too angry with him. Now the wax on the mantilla is enough to get anybody's goat, but, as the master here so rightly says, 'show me a child that doesn't act up.' It'll pass with age." Then, addressing the boy, "Come here, little sir mischief-maker," she said in a kind voice, "come defend yourself against what's being said about you."

The boy came over with an air of hurt and at the same time of cunning, and stood between his godmother and the neighbor lady.

Dona Maria then asked him some questions, to which he responded readily but in a sullen manner. The neighbor lady did not judge herself very secure with this fine neighbor so close beside her, and she decided to get up. The boy, perceiving her intention, did not want to miss this opportunity to do her whatever ill he could; he reached out the toe of his shoe and stepped as hard as he could on the hem of the black skirt that she was wearing, having taken off her mantilla. The woman, observing his move without fully comprehending its import, understood only that he was up to something, and she tried to get up quickly. There went a good four palms from the bottom of her skirt!

"Oh!" said the boy, pretending to be surprised.

"Lord help you, boy," said the *comadre*.

The neighbor lady looked at her ripped skirt and said to all present, "There! Didn't I say he was bad?"

The *compadre* smiled a hidden smile seeing the vengeance the boy was taking for what the neighbor lady had said.

"Now, now," Dona Maria summed up, with an air of uncertainty about what she was saying, "he was just careless; it wasn't intentional . . ."

The boy went back to his seat, and the conversation proceeded. They got to the matter of the future that the godfather wanted for his godson, and, as was usually the case, a great difference of opinion then arose between the *compadre* and the *comadre*; she could speak only of the Conceição, while he could speak only of Coimbra.

Dona Maria, asked to give her opinion, said, "Look, if it were up to me, I'd put him in a law office and make a good civil law solicitor out of him."

"Oh no," answered the *compadre*. "Pardon me, *Senhora* Dona Maria, pardon me if I offend you with this, but I distrust those lawsuits like the devil."

"But see here, there's no reason for that; they give me some concern, but I'm used to it. For example, that property case, it has gone on forever; the heirs of my *compadre* João Bernardo, who didn't know much about the court system, had me served . . ." And, from that point, on she went, no one knowing where she would end, when fortunately she had to stop because the procession was approaching. Everyone ran to the windows.

That put an end to the discussion. The procession began to pass by, and it made a very pretty scene, especially viewed from Dona Maria's house, which was—and we had forgotten this detail—right on the very Street of the Goldsmiths. The candlelight reflected in the metalwork of the doors and in the signboards from which hung the gold and silver objects in the process of manufacture that the goldsmiths put out to show on this off-day for their businesses—which presented a general aspect of wealth and luxuriance, albeit of bad taste as well. Of everything that the procession included, the greatest reception from the devout was earned by the Baianas, with whom the reader is already familiar, and the Sacrifice of Abraham, which was put on with live figures.

In front walked a boy playing the role of Isaac, with a bundle of firewood over his shoulder. Right after him came a huge fellow dressed in a gaudy costume holding a huge wooden sword over the boy's head; he was Abraham. A bit farther back, an angel suspending the fierce sword on a ribbon three or four yards long.

When the procession was over, the guests took their leave.

As the barber went to leave with the youngster, Dona Maria came up to him and said, significantly, "Drop by and we'll talk about the child . . ."

Thus we can see that the boy was hardly an unfortunate, for if he had his enemies he also found protectors in many quarters. The readers will observe henceforth the role that Dona Maria will play in this story.

X V I I I

Love

The readers must by now be weary of stories about boyish misdeeds; you are sufficiently aware of what the subject of these memoirs was like as a child, the hopes that he held out and the future that he promised. We shall now skip over a number of years and see some of the hopes realized. The stories now beginning are, if not more important, at least a bit more sensible.

As always happens to those who have much from which to choose, the boy whom his godfather wished to send to the University of Coimbra to become a cleric, whom his godmother wanted to send to the Conceição to become an artisan, and whom Dona Maria wanted to send to a law office to become a shyster, whom, in sum, every friend or acquaintance wanted to provide with the future that they judged most fitting to the inclinations they perceived in him, the boy, we repeat, having so many good possibilities, chose the worst possible of them. He did not go to Coimbra, nor did he go to the Conceição, nor to any law office; he did none of those things, nor, for that matter, anything else. He in fact became a complete idler, a master idler, the very prototype of the idler.

The godfather despaired of this twenty times each and every day, seeing his pretty dream dashed, though he could no longer summon up the courage to confront his godson and just let him go his own way.

The *comadre* had achieved her goal as regards her daughter: So forcefully had she insisted that Leonardo, after catching the gypsy girl in a new infidelity, made a decision . . . and the thing was done. This was when he began to live a more settled life; the winds of age were beginning to extinguish the flames of his affectionate nature.

Dona Maria had aged a bit, but she had by no means lost her mania for lawsuits: The last one she had had was perhaps the most excusable, the most reasonable, of them all. The issue in question was the guardianship of a niece of hers, who had been orphaned by the death of her brother. This brother had a *compadre* who did not enjoy a good reputation. Now, as the orphan had been left mistress of some thousands of cruzados left her by her father—even though, as she was his only and legitimate child, he had not made a will—the *compadre* presented himself to be named her guardian.

Dona Maria, comprehending the situation, presented herself as well, and in the end she emerged victorious: She was named guardian, and the niece came to live with her. The latter was grateful for this, all the more because her age made her need not so much support as companionship.

The rest of our personages continued on the same as before.

We shall henceforth refer to the subject of our memoirs by his baptismal name. We do not recall if we have said before that he bore the same name as his father, but if we have not said so before, let it be stated now. And that it be understood when we speak of the father and of the son, we shall give the latter the name of "Leonardo" alone and add the surname of "Pataca," by this time in common use, when we wish to refer to the former.

Leonardo had, then, reached the age when young men begin to notice that their hearts beat harder and faster when, on certain occasions, they meet certain individuals, about whom, without the slightest idea why, they dream for some nights in a row and whose name continuously appears tickling their lips.

We have said that Dona Maria now had her niece living with her. The *compadre*, as Dona Maria had requested of him, continued to visit her, and on those visits they would spend long periods in private conversation. Leonardo always accompanied his godfather and, when he was younger, would act up in the house; when he lost the taste for that, he would sit in a corner and drowse in boredom. The result of this was that he hated the visits profoundly and tolerated them only when forced by his godfather.

On one of the last times they had gone to Dona Maria's house, she called to the *compadre* as soon as she saw them come in and told him very happily, "Now, I've finally won my campaign—yesterday the girl was given to me. My brother's scoundrel of a *compadre* didn't get what he wanted."

"Congratulations! Many congratulations!" answered the *compadre*. Leonardo paid little attention to all of this; he had been hearing about some niece for a long time now. He sat down in a corner and, as usual, began yawning.

After the exchange of a few more words between the two, Dona Maria called for her niece, and she came in. Leonardo's eyes fell upon her, and he could scarcely repress a laugh. Dona Maria's niece was already well developed, save that, having lost the graces of a girl, she had not yet acquired the beauty of a young woman. She was tall, skinny, and pale; she walked with her chin buried in her chest, kept her eyes aimed downward, and looked by furtive glances. Her hair, cut short, barely came down to neck level, and since it was badly done up and she always held her head down, a great portion fell over her forehead and eyes, like a visor. On this day, she wore a very long cotton print dress, almost formless, with a very high waist; she had around her neck a red Alcobaça kerchief.

Question as he might, the *compadre* was able to get her to murmur only a few unintelligible phrases in an indistinct, hoarse voice. As soon as she was left free, she exited the room without looking at anyone. As he watched her go, Leonardo again laughed to himself.

After they took their leave, he laughed out loud on the road. His godfather inquired about the cause of his hilarity; he answered that he could not think of the girl without laughing.

"Then you seem to be thinking of her very often, because you're laughing a lot."

Leonardo saw that this observation was true.

Over several days he spoke of Dona Maria's niece some few times. And as soon as his godfather told him that they would have to pay their customary visit, he thrilled with satisfaction without knowing why, and, contrary to the other days, he was the first to get dressed and say he was ready.

They went out and set off for their destination.

XIX

Pentecost Sunday

That day was Pentecost Sunday. As everyone knows, the feast of the
Holy Ghost is one of the favorite celebrations of the people of Rio
de Janeiro. Even today when certain habits are being lost, some of them
good, others bad, that feast day is still the occasion of great activity.
What happens today is, however, far from what used to take place in the
time back to which we have taken our readers. The celebration did not
begin on the Sunday marked on the calendar; it started much earlier, so
that the novenas could take place. The first announcement of the celebration was to be found in the *Folias*. In his childhood, the writer of
these memoirs had the opportunity to witness the *Folias*, although they
were then in their last stages of decadence, so much so in fact that only
children such as he paid attention and found enjoyment in them. For
everyone else, if they paid heed at all, it was merely to lament how different the celebrations were from those of yesteryear. What went on
back then, if closely examined, was not very far from deserving of cen-
sure. Nevertheless, it was a custom, and let no one say to an old woman
from those times that it really must have been scandalous back then, because he will get a laugh right in his face and hear a tremendous philip-
pic against the celebrations we have today.

In the meanwhile, let us just say what the *Folias* of that time were
like, even though the readers will probably know a little something
about them. On the nine days that preceded Pentecost Sunday, or
maybe even earlier, a company of boys would go out into the streets of
the city, all of them from nine to eleven years old, costumed "shep-
herd" fashion: pink shoes, white stockings, breeches the color of the
shoes, sash around the waist, white shirt with long, loose collar,
broad-brimmed or silk-lined straw hat, all topped off by garlands of
flowers and prodigious quantities of loops of scarlet ribbon. Each of
these boys brought a "pastoral" instrument, on which he played: a
tambourine, a *machete*, a small drum. They marched in a square formation, in the center of which walked the so-called Emperor of the
Divine. All of this was accompanied by barber musicians and preceded and surrounded by a throng of "brothers" in tunics carrying
scarlet banners and other emblems, who begged alms as the singing
and playing went on.

The emperor, as we have said, walked in the center. Ordinarily, he was a boy smaller than the rest clad in a dress coat of green velvet, breeches of the same material and color, silk stockings, buckle shoes, cardboard hat, with an enormous, glittering emblem of the Holy Ghost on his chest. He walked with a pausing gait and a solemn air.

Let the readers allow if it was not a truly extraordinary thing to see an emperor dressed in velvet and silk marching through the streets surrounded by a company of shepherds to the sound of tambourine and *machete*. And no sooner was the whining music of the barbers heard in the distance than everyone ran to the window to see the *Folia* pass by; the "brothers" used the moment to collect alms door to door.

As the company marched, the barbers' music would be playing. When it stopped, the shepherds, accompanying themselves on their instruments, would sing. The songs were more or less of the same genre and style as this:

> He's nothing but a fraud,
> That Holy Ghost divine;
> He really eats a great deal of meat,
> And a whole lot of bread and wine.

That is what the *Folia* was like, and that is what the godfather and his godson encountered on their walk through the streets.

This episode of the *Folia* was followed by others that we shall soon recount to the readers. For now, however, let us return to our visitors.

They arrived at Dona Maria's house and found everyone at the window because the *Folia* had just passed. Dona Maria received them with her customary amiability. As he entered Leonardo had glanced at Dona Maria's niece. Without knowing why, however, this time he experienced no desire to laugh, even though the girl was still ugly and odd—that day, even more so than on the others. Dona Maria had taken it into her head to make her presentable: She had dressed her in a very short white dress, put a kerchief of red silk around her neck, and had her hair done *bugres* style. Therefore, with her customary visor of hair gone, we can see her face; let us say for honesty's sake that if on that day she was in general odder, it might be noted that her face was not as ugly as first might have seemed to be the case.

The fact is that Leonardo began to glance at her with no desire at all to laugh; he looked one, two, three, four—in short, many—times without ever satisfying what he inwardly called his "curiosity" to appraise that figure.

For her part, the girl continued on in her inalterable silence and con-
centration, chin on her chest, eyes upon the floor. But a keen observer
might have seen a certain quick lifting of the eyelids and a fugitive
glance directed Leonardo's way.

Dona Maria and the *compadre* conversed as was their wont.

As they were taking their leave, Dona Maria, addressing the *compadre*, said, "Listen here; we're going to the campo today to see the fireworks. We could all go together. What do you say?"

"Yes, we could," replied the *compadre*. "I was going to go alone with
my boy, but as you've made the offer, we'll all go together. And you're
taking your girl, aren't you?"

"Oh, certainly! Poor girl, she's never seen fireworks; when her father
was alive, she never went out . . ."

Unconsciously, Leonardo quivered with pleasure; it seemed to him
that this way he might have a greater opportunity to satisfy his curiosity.
The girl did not react; the whole matter seemed one of complete indifference to her.

"Well then, we're agreed," added the *compadre*, "and tonight we'll
come by for you."

And they left.

X X

Fireworks on the Campo

At the appointed time the two, godfather and godson, came for
Dona Maria and her family according to arrangement. It was not
much after the Ave Maria, and already there were to be found upon the
roads great crowds of families, groups of people, some bound for the
campo and others for the lapa, where, as is well known, the Holy Ghost
was also celebrated. Leonardo walked along seemingly oblivious to what
was taking place around him: He would trip and bump into those whom
he came across. One idea and one only was gnawing at his brain; if he
were to be asked what idea that was, perhaps even he would not have

known. They had arrived more quickly than the barber had estimated, because tonight Leonardo seemed to have wings on his feet, so swiftly had he walked—and obliged the godfather to keep pace with him.

Dona Maria was ready and waiting for them, along with some other people with whom she had also arranged to go in group, and they immediately set out. They formed a large party, accompanied by no small number of black women and girls, Dona Maria's slaves and their children, who carried woven mats and baskets of food. Dona Maria gave the *compadre* her arm, and the other ladies did the same with the other gentlemen. As a jest Dona Maria had Leonardo give her niece his arm; he accepted the assignment with pleasure but not without feeling somewhat embarassed. And he gave the poor girl some bumps, befuddled as to whether to offer his left arm or his right. Finally, he decided to give her his left, which would leave him on the city side. He offered his arm, but Luisinha (let us henceforth refer to her by name) seemed not to comprehend the offer, or not to trust it. Leonardo therefore contented himself with walking at her side.

They arrived thus at the campo, which was full of people. Back then there were not yet the stalls with dolls, lottery drawings, freaks, and shows that we have today; the few that there were served food. After they passed by in front of them, Dona Maria and her company walked toward the império. Luisinha was dazzled in the midst of all that movement and spectacle that she was seeing for the first time. For what Dona Maria had said was true: When her father was alive she rarely if ever went out of the house. Thus, without being aware of it, she sometimes stopped open-mouthed to stare at something, and Leonardo often saw himself obliged to pull her by the arm to get her to move on.

They reached the império, which at that time was nearly across from the Church of Santa Ana, on the site now occupied by one end of the Fusiliers barracks. Everybody knows what the império is, so we shall not describe it. There in his seat was the emperor, whom the reader has already seen marching through the streets in the middle of his phalanx of revelers. Upon seeing him, Luisinha stood up on tiptoe, craned her neck, and stared at him for a long time, absorbed in wonderment. Seeing this, Leonardo had a funny feeling inside—of animosity for the boy who had attracted Luisinha's attention. And it ran through his mind to turn the clock back six or seven years in his own life and be an Emperor of the Divine too.

There was an auction being held on the steps of the império, just as is done today, the tightly packed crowd of people being entertained by the auctioneer's heavy-handed jokes. Our acquaintances spent some time there in amusement and then they went into the middle of the campo to find a place where they could settle down, have dinner, and watch the fireworks. They found one, not without some difficulty, for many other families had got there ahead of them and had taken the best places. A great part of the campo was already covered with those groups seated on mats, eating, talking, singing *modinhas* to the accompaniment of *guitarras** and guitars. It was a delight to walk through this scene and to hear here a story being told by someone who was well-spoken, there a *modinha* being sung in that passionately poetic tone that is one of our rare originalities, and to witness the movement and animation that reigned overall. This was—permit us the expression—the truly entertaining part of the entertainment.

Our acquaintances, like the others, seated themselves upon their ring of mats and began to eat their dinner. Leonardo, despite the new emotions that he had been experiencing for a certain period of time and principally that night, had nonetheless not lost his appetite and for a while forgot his female companion to attend exclusively to his plate. At the height of the supper they were interrupted by a skyrocket streaming up; it was the start of the fireworks display. Luisinha shuddered, raised her head, and for the first time spoke so that her voice could be heard, exclaiming in ecstasy as she watched the fiery tears fall from the rocket and light up the whole campo: "Look, look, look!"

Some of the bystanders burst out laughing. Leonardo was upset by the laughs, finding them thoroughly out of place. Fortunately, Luisinha was so ecstatic that she paid no attention to other things and as long as the fireworks lasted she did not move her eyes from the sky.

After the rockets, as the readers know, come the pinwheels. The girl's ecstasy then turned into a frenzy; she applauded with enthusiasm, craned her neck to see over the heads in the crowd, and only wished she were two or three yards tall to be able to see everything exactly as she wished. Without knowing how, she came up close to Leonardo, braced herself with her hands on his shoulders so she could stay on tiptoe longer, talked to him and expressed her enthusiasm to him. Her happiness ended up making her completely familiar with him. When the "moon" was set off, her appreciation was so great that, trying to steady herself on Leonardo's shoulders, she all but hugged him from behind; Leonardo thrilled inside and begged heaven to make the "moon" last forever. Turning his head he saw over his shoulders that girlish head illuminated by the pale light of the burning remains of the last charge,

---

* A "Portuguese guitar," which is something like a bass mandolin.

and he went into ecstasy in his turn. At that moment it seemed to him the prettiest face he had ever seen, and he wondered at himself that he could ever have laughed at it and thought it ugly.

When the fireworks were over, everything sprang into motion: The mats were picked up and the people dispersed. Dona Maria and her party too set out for home, using the same disposition as when they had come. This time, however, Luisinha and Leonardo went not arm in arm as the latter had wished when they came to the campo but, going beyond that, they walked hand in hand very familiarly and ingenuously. This "ingenuously" may not, in the strictest of senses, be applicable to Leonardo. They talked all the way as though they were two very old friends, brother and sister from little up, and they were so absorbed that they even walked past the door and were quite a bit farther down the street when Dona Maria's beckoning "ssst" got them to turn around. The leave-taking was happy for all and extremely sad for the two. Nevertheless, as was always the case when they said good-bye, the *compadre* promised to return, and this served as some alleviation, especially for Leonardo, who had taken much more seriously everything that had happened.

X X I

Complications

We believe, from what we have related, that it will come as no surprise to any reader that the time had come for Leonardo to pay the tribute that no one escapes in this world, although it may be light and easy for some people and heavy and burdensome for others: The boy was in love. We do not even need to mention with whom.

How it could be that Dona Maria's niece, who at first incited his laughter for being odd and ugly, had subsequently come to inspire his love is a secret of the boy's heart that it is not given to us to plumb. It is a fact that he was in love with her, and we must be satisfied with that. It should be recalled that, if a father's destiny forecasts that of a son, in matters of love Leonardo held out no great promise. Indeed, soon after the night of the fireworks on the campo, during which matters began to take shape, the wheel of fortune began turning awry for him in just about every way. Luisinha's enthusiasm, activated by the emotions she had experienced on the night of the fireworks, had awakened her from her apathy, but when that enthusiasm subsided she returned again to her former state. And as though she had forgotten everything, on the first visit that the barber and Leonardo paid to Dona Maria after those events, she did not even look up for the latter of the visitors but rather kept her head down and her eyes upon the floor.

Now, for someone like Leonardo who after that happy night had been led to build those castles of elaborate design that we dream of during the blissful days of our first love, this was an indescribable setback. When he saw himself so treated, he almost broke into tears; he restrained himself only with the fear that he would be unable then to justify his weeping on some other grounds. This first reaction was followed by a moment of calm, and then a flame of rage welled up within him and he all but rushed over to the girl, pulled her chin up off her chest, and called her four or five kinds of fickle and ugly. He ended up sulking a little and muttering a "What does it matter to me!" that endeavored to be scorn but came out nothing but spite instead.

That first visit after the night of the fireworks was followed by many others in which things took more or less the same course.

Nevertheless, one day a new incident took place that gave events another color and another direction: It was the meeting of the two, godfather and godson, at Dona Maria's house, with someone who was a stranger to them both. He was an acquaintance of Dona Maria's who had returned shortly before from a trip to Bahia. The reader must imagine a little man, born in the days of May, about thirty-five years of age, thin, long-nosed, with a sharp, penetrating look in his eyes, dressed in black breeches and stockings, buckle shoes, cloak and cocked hat, and he will have a good idea of the appearance of this recent arrival, Mr. José Manuel. With respect to morality, if physical signs tell true, anyone looking into the face of Mr. José Manuel would there and then assign him a distinguished place in the family of scoundrels of the highest order. And one who would do so would by no means err: The man was exactly what he appeared to be. If he had any virtue, it was that his appearance did not mislead. Among his many qualities, he possessed one that in those days—and perhaps still today—positively and clearly characterized the native of Rio, and that was his venomous tongue. José Manuel was a living chronicle, albeit a scandalous one, not only of all his friends and acquaintances, not to mention their families, but even of the friends and acquaintances of his acquaintances and friends, and their families. On the flimsiest pretext he would take the floor and spin out a two-hour disquisition on the life of so-and-so or what's-his-name.

For example, in the discussion of some other topic, the conversation happened to touch on Dona Francisca Brites. "I used to know Dona Francisca Brites very well," the indefatigable talker immediately broke in. "She was the wife of João Brites, who was the bastard son of Captain Sanches. When she was married they used to talk about her, and the cause of that was Pedro d'Aguiar, a person who had a bad reputation, especially after he got into that mess about the false will that was attributed to Lourenço da Cunha, who, if truth be told, was indeed capable of such a deed, for he was a real saint that fellow. He was the one who kidnapped the daughter of Dona Ursula, who was the "girl" of Francisco Borges, whom she abandoned to go off with Pedro Antunes, who, needless to say, gave her a pretty rough time. And she shouldn't have expected any better from him, since a man who would dare to do what he did to three daughters that he had is capable of anything. He went so far as to drive the poor girls out of the house with a stick, after beating them horribly. But one of them came out of it all right: She found a sea captain somewhere who treated her well. Not so the other two, poor things . . ."

"Not so . . . why? one of the participants might perchance ask. "They married . . ."

"Yes, they did marry," he retorted, taking another deep breath. "But what sort of husbands? One went on drinking binges of various lengths, the other lost everything he owned gambling. I knew them both very well . . ."

And he would go on from there to probe deep into the entire family background of the two husbands. He was quite capable of spending whole hours in the task.

From the first day the godfather and godson met José Manuel at Dona Maria's house, neither of them liked him much, to say the least, and that dislike grew day by day, especially on Leonardo's part. And the fact is that he was right: It was instinct that told him that he had an enemy there. So overblown were the compliments that José Manuel bestowed on Dona Maria, and so fully did he extend them to Luisinha as well, that it was very easy to see some hidden purpose lurking there. After a while, the business became clear. Dona Maria, old and rich as we have stated, had no heir other than her niece. If she were to die, Luisinha would be left very well off, and since she was very young and seemed to be quite simple, she would be a presumptive wife for any slicker who, like José Manuel, might find himself at the right place at the right time. He was, then, paying court to the old lady with designs upon the niece. When Leonardo, enlightened by his godfather's sagacity, came to understand what was up, he was beside himself, and the most peaceable of the ideas that he came up with was that, when he went to visit Dona Maria, he could easily arm himself with one of his godfather's sharpest razors and sever José Manuel's throat with a single swipe when the first good opportunity presented itself. He nonetheless had to calm down and heed the advice of his godfather, who knew of all his sentiments and approved of them.

XXII

Alliance

If Leonardo had despaired, in the way we have just seen, at the setback that he had suffered with the arrival and designs of José Manuel, his godfather was no less upset by the situation: Seeing that his godson was becoming a man and having definitively abandoned his monumental plan of sending him off to Coimbra, he had seen in Dona Maria's niece an excellent means of livelihood for his charge. He knew, it is true, that, should things continue on, at the moment of decision Dona Maria could, with very good reason, deny her niece to a youth who worked at no job and who had no future. For this reason he had often urged his godson to break into the trade on the face of some stupid customer or other; the latter, however, obstinately refused. The *comadre*, on the occasions when she came to the barber's house, never ceased insisting on her old project of having the boy go into the Conceição. On one occasion when she spoke of that in his presence, the story cost her a sharp reprimand: The boy had taken a liking to the life of an idler and on no account wished to leave it. And if on other occasions he was of that disposition, now after the latest events, when love and jealousy filled his heart, he certainly did not want to hear of such things. He believed that his best job should consist of putting an end to the rival who had gotten in ahead of him.

In the midst of all this, what was worse was that José Manuel seemed to be making progress in his designs; astute as he was, he skillfully insinuated himself into Dona Maria's mind and captivated her with all sorts of attentions. The *compadre* began to meditate on the situation, and one day an idea came to him: The *comadre* should be informed of what was going on and involved in the entire matter. She was very capable, if she chose, of dealing with José Manuel and spiking his weaponry; she enjoyed a great reputation as one who had a knack for "those things." So he in fact sent for the *comadre* and told her all.

"Yes!" she answered, upon hearing the narrative. "So that is the situation? Well the guy looks capable of it. But I'll show him what I'm made of. I'll visit Dona Maria this very day."

José Manuel had no idea how great the storm was that was being raised against him. He had long perceived that Leonardo and his godfather could scarcely stand him and also that they had other designs with regard to Luisinha. But it never entered his mind that he would have to do battle with them. He would soon see that he was mistaken. The *comadre*, as she had promised, went to Dona Maria's and, finding José Manuel there, ostensibly endeavored to make herself his close friend but now and again made some subtle remarks against him in Dona Maria's hearing.

For example, when José Manuel finished telling a story, in all the usual detail, about the life of this person or that, the *comadre* would mutter, "What a mouth! It does run on . . ." And with such and other words she proceeded to profile her adversary's character without ever seeming to have that intention.

In addition to his proficiency as a gossip, José Manuel lied with an aplomb such as is rarely seen. Dona Maria, herself a lover of gossip and very credulous to boot, was an easy target for whatever falsehood he wished to dish out for her consumption. A story that he frequently told was one he called "The Shipwreck of the Pots." It had happened to him on his last voyage to Bahia, and he told it in the following manner.

"We were about to come to the anchorage; next to my ship there sailed a huge one-masted cargo boat loaded down only with pottery. Suddenly a storm came up, so bad the world seemed to be turning upside down; the wind was so strong that, despite the darkness, we could see from the ocean the tiles blown up off roofs in the old city dancing the quadrille in space. Finally, when everything seemed to be calming down and the weather was beginning to clear, there came a wave so strong in such a direction that the two vessels ran together with tremendous force. Already badly beaten by the storm that they had just endured, they could take no more damage, and both of them split open.

The ship lost its cargo and passengers overboard, and the boat lost its entire cargo of pots. So many were there that the sea was absolutely clogged with them! The sailors and other passengers tried to save themselves by grabbing onto floating planks, crates, and other objects, but I was the only one who escaped alive. It was because of a fortunate idea I had. From the piece of the ship I was on I leaped to the pot that was floating nearest; because of my weight, the pot went under and, filling with water, disappeared from under my feet. That, however, did not take place until I, perceiving what was going to happen, leaped from that pot to another. The same thing happened to that one and all the others after it, but I made use of the same strategy and thus, since the force of the waves was taking us in to shore, I went from pot to pot all the way to land without the slightest mishap!"

José Manuel told thousands of stories like this one. At the same time, they provided a way that the *comadre* took advantage of to undercut his standing with Dona Maria—always, to be sure, very cleverly.

We shall see the results that the *compadre* and Leonardo achieved through their alliance with the *comadre* against the rival for Luisinha.

X X I I I

Declaration

While the *comadre* was deploying her plan of attack against José Manuel, Leonardo burned with jealousy, with rage, and there was nothing that could console him in his despair, not even the promises of good results that his godfather and godmother made to him. All the poor boy could see before him was the detestable figure of his rival, ruining all his plans, scattering all his hopes. In the times when he was calm he sometimes absorbed himself in the imaginary contruction of magnificent castles—castles in the air, to be sure. But there were times when they seemed to him the most solid castles in the world. Then suddenly the terrible José Manuel would rise up from somewhere, with his cheeks puffed out, and he would blow the construction down in the blink of an eye.

What was most notable all this time was that Luisinha, the cause of so many torments, was ignorant of it all and went on indifferent to everything. Leonardo came to understand, after much meditation, that this was one of the principal weaknesses of his position. If his godmother and godfather were to be successful in defeating José Manuel and rendering him unable to enter into combat any further, what was there to say that the triumph was complete? Was there not as well a second campaign to be waged, against Luisinha's indifference? Hence he concluded that it was essential to start opening up a front in that area. And, since it seemed to him the key area, he did not choose to confide his attack to either of his allies but determined to launch it in person. As the majority of the readers know very well indeed—for they are doubtless very experienced in the matter—he had to begin with a formal declaration.

But in love, as in everything else, the first sally is the hardest. Every time this notion came into the poor young man's head, a dark cloud passed in front of his eyes and his body broke out in a sweat. It took him many weeks to plan and compose what he would say to Luisinha when the crucial moment arrived. He easily came up with a thousand brilliant ideas, but no sooner had he decided that he would say this or that than this and that no longer seemed good to him. He had had several favorable opportunities to carry out his task, since he had been alone with Luisinha. On those occasions, however, he could summon up nothing to overcome a tremor that took hold of his legs and would not permit him to rise from the place in which he found himself, and a choking that came over him and prevented him from articulating a single word. In short, after many battles with himself to conquer his timidity, one day he resolved to put an end to the fear and say to her the first thing that came into his mouth.

Luisinha was in a window recess peeping through the shutters out onto the street. Leonardo approached, trembling, step after step, stopped, and stood still as a statue behind her, while she, engrossed in what she was watching, noticed nothing. He stood thus for a long time, trying to decide if he should speak standing or if he should kneel. Then he moved as though to touch Luisinha on the shoulder, but he quickly withdrew his hand. He thought that that was not a good way to do it, that it would be better to give a tug on her dress. And he was already lifting his hand when he thought better of that as well. During all these false starts the poor youth was sweating profusely. Finally, an incident took place to extract him from the difficulty. Hearing footfalls in the corridor, he realized that someone was coming. Seized with terror that he would be caught in this position, he suddenly took two steps back and uttered a very choked "Ah!" Luisinha, turning around, realized that he was close to her and, retreating, pushed back against the shutters. She then made another "Ah!" but it never got out of her throat and she ended up merely making a face.

The sound of the footfalls ended without anyone's entering the room. The two remained for some time in their positions until Leonardo, with a supreme effort, broke the silence and, in a tremulous voice and the most graceless tone imaginable, asked dismally, "You . . . know what?" And he laughed with a forced, pale, idiotic laugh.

Luisinha did not respond.

He repeated, in the same tone, "Well . . . do you know . . . or not?" And he laughed again in the same way.

Luisinha remained silent.

"You do know . . . that's why you won't say.'

No answer.

"If you wouldn't get mad . . . I'd say."

Silence.

"It's okay . . . I'll go ahead and say. But are you going to get mad or not?"

Luisinha made a gesture of impatience.

"Well, then I'll say . . . you don't know it . . . I . . . I love you . . . a lot."

Luisinha turned cherry red and, making a half turn to her right, put her back toward Leonardo and walked away down the corridor. The timing was good, for someone was coming.

Leonardo watched her go, a bit stupefied by her response but not entirely discontent: His lover's eye had perceived that what had just taken place had not wholly displeased her.

When she disappeared from sight, the youth heaved a sigh of relief and sat down, for he was as exhausted as if he had just engaged in hand-to-hand combat with a giant.

VOLUME II

I

The Comadre in Action

The readers will recall that our old acquaintance Leonardo-Pataca, whom we have forgotten for some time now, had united in amorous bonds with the *comadre*'s daughter and was living with her in holy and honorable peace. Now in due time that holy and honorable living produced its result. Chiquinha (that was the name of the *comadre*'s daughter) found herself "expecting" and soon to give birth. As the readers can see, the line of the Leonardos is one that is not going to be easily extinguished. Leonardo-Pataca had not by any stretch of the imagination lost those old affectionate ways we have seen in him, and in the current circumstances, when he could see at the gates of life the fruit of his latest love, that customary violent flame swelled within him: The poor man fairly glowed inside and out and outdid himself in demonstrations of affection for his mate.

The day finally arrived for the long-awaited result to appear; the first symptoms manifested themselves at dawn. As a consequence, Leonardo created a huge stir around the house: He wandered in and out, chaotic and confused, trying to do a thousand things without accomplishing anything at all. He had the *comadre* called; she hurried right over and got the preparations under way. Some readers will perhaps have an idea of the infinite world of arrangements that back then were set in motion on such occasions. The first thing that Leonardo-Pataca saw to was to have the great bell at the Sé toll nine times. This custom was practiced only when a woman in labor was in danger, but he wanted to get everything done ahead of time. He then sent a request to the woman next door, for there was no blessed palm leaf to be found in the house—an unpardonable oversight. The *comadre* brought a pair of scapulars of Our Lady of Mount Carmel, which had a powerful reputation for being miraculous, and she put them at Chiquinha's neck. She put the palm leaf at the head of the bed, and in the living room she set up an improvised oratory using a tablecloth, a glass of rue, and a porcelain figure of Our Lady of the Immaculate Conception decorated with gold string. So that none of the prescribed procedures would be overlooked, Chiquinha tied a white kerchief around her head, crawled under the sheets, and started in praying to the saint of her devotion. The *comadre* sat on a small bench at the foot of the bed and fingered a large rosary, all the while keeping her eye on Chiquinha and pausing frequently to give orders to Leonardo-Pataca and respond to what was being said outside the bedroom.

After everything was set, Leonardo-Pataca, when he saw that nothing more remained but to "wait for nature to take its course" (as the *comadre* put it), dressed down—that is, he took off his breeches and vest, which left him in his drawers and slippers. In obedience to time-honored custom, he tied a red kerchief around his head and set in to pacing the living-room floor from wall to wall with an anguished expression on his face. It looked as though he, and not Chiquinha, were suffering the labor pains. Every so often he would stop at the bedroom door, which was closed, peek inside with a look of curiosity and fear, and, shaking his head, murmur, "I'm not any good at this . . . my temperament isn't suited for this sort of thing . . . I'm shaking as though it were me . . ."

And in fact, at every moan that emerged from the bedroom, the man shuddered and turned a thousand colors.

Inside the room, the *comadre* was urging the patient on, in terms more or less like these: "Don't be a baby, my lady . . . this as no big thing . . . no more than a cinder in your eye. Just a 'Benedictus' and you'll be free of it. Under my care these things go quickly. It's just that it's your first and that's making you afraid. But there's no reason for you to worry. You just have to help nature along. 'Do thine own part and I shall aid thee'—those are the words of Jesus Christ."

The patient was, however, petrified; despite the *comadre's* urging, she did not even move. In the meanwhile, time was passing and the poor girl was suffering. The *comadre* rearranged the scapulars, putting them on her breast, and tilted the blessed palm further down over the bed. Still no change. Leonardo-Pataca started to grow impatient; from time to time he would come to the bedroom door and ask, in a weary voice, "Well?"

"Man," replied the *comadre*, "I've told you that it's not good for a woman in her state to hear a man's voice! Shut up and wait!"

Time kept passing. The *comadre* emerged to light a new consecrated candle to Our Lady and after a brief prayer she returned to her station. She then took a long blue ribbon out of her skirt pocket and tied it around Chiquinha's waist. It was a measure-ribbon of Our Lady of Childbirth. Then she said, with a triumphant air, "Well now we'll see, because this isn't going at all to my liking. But the fault is yours, girl; I told you nature has to be helped along."

Some more time passed. Suddenly, the *comadre* shouted out the door: "Oh, *compadre*, bring me a bottle."

Leonardo-Pataca rushed to obey. Afterward, from inside the bedroom, came a sound such as might be produced by a human mouth blowing as hard as it can into something. It was Chiquinha, who, at the *comadre's* instruction, was blowing into the bottle that had been brought until she was dead with fatigue.

"Hard, girl, harder yet; Our Lady doesn't abandon the faithful. Be brave, be brave; this doesn't happen more than once a year. Ever since our mother Eve ate of that cursed fruit we have been subject to this. 'I shall multiply the labors of thy delivery.' Those are the words of Jesus Christ."

You can see that one of the *comadre's* strengths was sacred history.

In the outer room Leonardo-Pataca's knees were shaking so hard that he could not continue his pacing and ended up sitting in one corner with his fingers in his ears.

"Blow hard, girl," the godmother said over and over again. "Blow with Our Lady; blow with Saint John the Baptist; blow with the apostles Peter and Paul; blow with the Angels and Seraphim of the Heavenly Court; blow with all the Saints of Paradise; blow with the Father, with the Son, and with the Holy Ghost."

There was at last an instant of silence, which was broken by the squall of a baby.

"There now, the bad time's gone," the *comadre* exclaimed. I was right when I said it was no more than a cinder in your eye. Oh, *senhor compadre*, come in. It's your turn now; come see your little girl . . ."

"It's a girl," exclaimed Leonardo-Pataca, beside himself. "Now this is a good omen, for I wasn't very lucky with the other one, and he was a boy."

The house was then infused with the pleasant smell of lavender. The *comadre* came into the living room and put out the candles that had been lit to Our Lady. She then untied the ribbon from around Chiquinha's middle and took the scapulars from around her neck.

The newborn, diapered, swaddled, banded, ribboned, and with an array of *figa*-signs, half-moons, Solomon's seals, and other protections against the evil eye attached to her band, passed from Chiquinha's hands to those of Leonardo-Pataca, who could not contain himself in his delight. She was a beautiful little baby, gentle and happy—completely the opposite of her brother on the father's side, our friend Leonardo.

Leonardo-Pataca went immediately to the calendar of saints to see whose name the girl should receive. As that option did not please him, however, he initiated a discussion with Chiquinha about what name to give her.

The *comadre* availed herself of this moment to finish up her arrangements; she then put on her mantilla and went out to attend to other duties.

I I

Intrigue

The *comadre* went through many other scenes every day just like the one we have depicted, for she was one of the most sought-after midwives in the city. She enjoyed a great reputation for skill in these matters, and in the most serious cases it was always she who was chosen, with her miraculous scapulars, blessed palm, measure-ribbon of Our Lady of Childbirth, and bottle to blow in. With the invocation of all the legion of saints, seraphim, and angels she could get herself out of the most difficult situations. And let no one try to dictate to her, for she would not listen to them! Not even the royal surgeon, should he try to butt in. She had only to look at an "expecting" woman to tell with no problem at all which sex and what size the baby that she bore within her would be and with miraculous accuracy the day and hour in which she would see herself unburdened of the child. At times, by certain signs known only to herself, she could even tell what temperament and inclinations that entity about to be born might have. Obviously, this life was an arduous one that required great devotion, but the *comadre* was able to carry on a high level of activity. And despite spending a lot of time on the duties of her trade and on the church, she always had some left over to dedicate to other things. As we have said, she had taken to heart the matter of Leonardo's love for Luisinha and had sworn to put José Manuel, the new rival, out of the picture.

She set out, then, to use her spare time in that grave business and began a very subtle and constant intrigue against her godson's competitor. Enjoying Dona Maria's intimate friendship and esteem, she never missed a chance to undercut José Manuel's standing with her, which was all the simpler for her to accomplish the easier a target he made himself, and Dona Maria—she of the litigious and chicaning frame of mind—was susceptible to such suggestion. Here is one of the traps that she set for her adversary.

Everyone in the city knows where the Stone Oratory is, but what everyone may not know is what uses it served in earlier times. Doubtless there was the image of some saint in that oratory, and the devout among the populace would go there to pray to it? Exactly. But why has that practice not continued on down to today? Why do we retain only that sort of stone sentry box atop the wall, without any image, without light at night, which everyone passes by irreverently without taking off their hat and genuflecting? First and foremost, it lapsed for the same reason that many other good things from those good times lapsed: People started becoming bored at finding them so good and stopped doing them. Then too there were many good police reasons for the Stone Oratory to cease being what it had been.

The reader, who surely knows very well what thorough believers our forebears were, devout and God-fearing, will perhaps be surprised to read that there were police reasons for the discontinuance of an oratory. It is, however, true. And if our friend Vidigal, of whom we have had occasion to speak in some of the chapters of this little history, were still alive, he could tell how many boys he caught *in flagrante delicto* right there in front of the oratory, kneeling contrite and pious.

When the Via-Sacra passed and the oratory lamp was lit, a paterfamilias who lived in the neighborhood would take up his cloak, call all of the people of his household, sons, daughters, slaves, and slave-children, and they would go to pray, kneeling before the oratory amongst the people. But should that pious man, through lack of caution, forget about his eldest daughter, who was kneeling a bit behind him, should he, absorbed in his prayers, not remain alert, he might at times return home with his family reduced in number: the daughter would avail herself of the opportunity and slip furtively away in the company of some devout young man who had been kneeling nearby wrapped in his cloak and whom, two minutes earlier, everyone had seen fervently engrossed in his supplications of God.

It was the execution of a plan worked out during the Ave Maria of the evening before, through the wicket of the shutters. At other times, when all those in attendance were absorbed in their devotions and the litany melodically intoned was filling them with contrition, a sharp scream of pain might come to interrupt the hymn. All would race to the place from whence it had come, to find there a man stretched out on the ground with a stab wound or two in him.

And we shall not even take into account the innocent tricks that the wags played at every opportunity. This, then, aside from other motives, is why we have said that there were police reasons for putting an end to the pious practices of the Stone Oratory.

In the time in which the scenes we have narrated took place, the Stone Oratory was still in its heyday. A day or two after the birth of Leonardo-Pataca's second child, the news made the rounds of the city about a great scandal that had taken place in that classic location of scandals: a young lady who lived with her elderly, wealthy, and devout mother, as she was going with her to pray at the Oratory, had, on the occasion of the Via-Sacra's passing, run off, taking along with her the foot of a black stocking containing a goodly portion of gold pieces. The business was much talked about, not because at that time it was itself anything to be remarked on but rather because there was a mystery about it: No one knew with whom the girl had fled.

Dona Maria, like everyone else, was anxious to see the matter cleared up when the *comadre* dropped by her house to pay a visit.

Dona Maria was seated on her little bench, in front of her an enormous lace cushion with six- or seven-dozen bobbins on it; she was involved in making a long join. Beside her seated on a mat and surrounded by a number of little black girls, slave-children in Dona Maria's house, was Luisinha, who was also busy making lace.

When the *comadre* entered, Dona Maria immediately removed the cushion from her lap, pulled off of her nose the pair of silver-rimmed glasses that she had been using in her work and pushed them up on her forehead, and then began to refer to the case that was occupying her thoughts. The *comadre* made a gesture indicating that she should send Luisinha and the other children away, and the conversation proceeded on freely.

"Now what do you say, *senhora*, about the poor old woman's misfortune? When people raise a girl with every affection and then get that kind of treatment in return! . . . In my time you didn't see that kind of thing . . ."

"What do you expect, *senhora*?" the *comadre* replied. "After all, it happened right there, under the very noses of all of us. Almost no time had passed since she arrived with the old woman and the two of them knelt down right beside me . . ."

"Right beside you? You mean you were there?"

"I was. I only wish I hadn't been."

"Well the devil of it, my lady," Dona Maria added, "is that nobody knows who the reprobate was that ran off with her."

The *comadre* broke in with a sardonic little chuckle.

"I've asked everyone, and no one can tell me."

"That's because they were all blind."

"What do you mean?"

"But I was not, for all my sins; would only that I had been . . ."

"Why, you saw and know who it was . . .," said Dona Maria, quivering with delight atop her little bench. The idea of knowing some information that no one else did filled her with joy.

"Well, then, who was it? Come on, I want to know who that thief was who stole the girl and the money . . ."

"I'll tell you," responded the *comadre* after some hesitation, "only if you promise me to keep it all secret, for it is a matter of the utmost seriousness."

"Now, you know well that I . . . it's just like throwing it down to the bottom of a well."

Even though they were alone, the *comadre* leaned over and said in Dona Maria's ear, in as quiet a voice as she could, "It was our great friend—that piece of work of a José Manuel."

"What are you saying, *comadre*?"

"I saw him," she replied, pushing her eyes open with two fingers, "with these eyes that the earth will one day reclaim . . . . Why, they were right beside me . . ."

For some time, Dona Maria sat in silent stupefaction.

Defeat

Those last words from the *comadre* had the effect of a thunderbolt on Dona Maria: The old woman squirmed on her bench, overcome by the greatest chagrin.

"Well, *comadre*," she exclaimed after the initial shock had subsided, "if this doesn't beat the devil . . . that's why I follow the time-honored rule: Don't trust anything that wears breeches. Hmm! This really makes me see red."

The *comadre*, seeing these good results, took full advantage of them to play her role better and replied, "Well, after all what could you expect from a person like that? . . . a man who doesn't open his mouth except to lie . . . who's got a tongue like Lucifer's own? Anybody who trusts in him is just asking for a fall."

"That is true, my lady; I have never seen a greater liar, or a greater scandalmonger . . ."

Dona Maria had previously never seen in José Manuel the qualities she was now discovering to be so pronounced. "If I were a relative of the girl, I'd slap such a lawsuit on that monster as would teach him. . . . That's why he hasn't been by to visit me for so long . . . he's been hatching his plans."

Hardly had Dona Maria finished pronouncing these last words when they heard a knock at the door and the voice of José Manuel requesting admittance.

"It's him . . . shhh . . . I don't want him to know it was me," said the *comadre* quickly.

"Don't worry," Dona Maria replied, "you can count on me."

José Manuel entered. Dona Maria, unaccustomed to restraining her feelings, greeted him coldly. The *comadre*, by contrast, received him with an effusive greeting, "A good welcome to you," she said, "You're a sight for sore eyes."

"I have been busy making some plans . . ."

"Plans," said Dona Maria, exchanging a meaningful glance with the *comadre*.

José Manuel, innocent on all scores, was puzzled, not understanding what that was supposed to mean. But, as was his custom, he did not miss the chance to tell a tale. "Yes, some plans," he said. "There was a very serious business I was involved in, and it sure has been running me ragged. I'm sorry I can't tell you the details; they're secret."

The *comadre* made a gesture as if to say "Here comes a lie." Dona Maria, however, who was still concentrating on the prior conversation, thought that José Manuel was referring to the abduction of the young woman, and, shaking her head, she said through clenched teeth, "Hmm . . . I understand."

The *comadre* trembled with the fear that Dona Maria would let the cat out of the bag and the question of the abduction would have to be adjudicated in her presence—in which case she would be caught in a flagrant lie and all would be lost. She therefore started to goad José Manuel into telling what this serious business was that he was involved in. She was counting on his putting out some of his lies, thereby turning the conversation away from the point that she did not wish to see dealt with in her presence.

Let us leave her in that attempt to deal with the tricks and fictitious mysteries of José Manuel.

Ever since the day Leonardo had made his declaration of love, Luisinha had begun to undergo a remarkable change; the difference in her, both physical and mental, became more evident hour upon hour. Her contours had begun to fill out; her arms, until then thin and gangly, became fuller and more robust; her thin, pale cheeks rounded out and took on that color peculiar to a woman's face at a certain time of life; her head, which she had habitually carried downturned, was now becoming gracefully erect; her eyes, previously lifeless, began to sparkle brilliantly. She spoke, she moved about, she was lively.

The order of her thought processes was altered as well; her internal world, until then withdrawn, narrow, dark, and vacant, began to find broader horizons, to brighten, to fill itself with millions of images, now pleasant, now melancholy, but always beautiful. Previously indifferent to what was going on around her, she now seemed to take part in life, in everything around her; she spent entire hours contemplating the sky, as though she had noticed only now that it was blue and beautiful, that the sun illuminated it by day, that it was layered with stars at night.

All this, with respect to our friend Leonardo, resulted in a considerable surge in love. And he was the first person to pay attention to those changes in Luisinha. But in spite of the growth of his love, no increased hopes sprang up within him. After his declaration he had not pushed even an inch further forward. The only thing that perhaps gave him encouragement was a certain flush that quickly rose on Luisinha's cheeks on the rare occasions when her eyes happened to cross his. The sum total of these new phenomena was a fury that grew daily in his heart, ever increasing in strength, directed at José Manuel, to whom, according to his calculations, his inertia was to be attributed.

These explanations having been given, let us now return to give an account of the remainder of the scene that we have left in suspense.

By the sheer force of insistence, the *comadre* got José Manuel to say what the highly secret business was in which he had found himself involved.

"Very well," he said finally, "if you promise total discretion, I'll tell you."

"Of course; that goes without saying."

With the tricks and mysteries that he had employed up to that point José Manuel had merely gained time to dream up the lie that he was going to tell. The *comadre* was counting on that.

He began, "You ladies should know that a few days ago I was called to the palace."

"Un-hunh!" the *comadre* exclaimed.

"That is the final result," said Dona Maria, "but paid for not in the next life but right here in this one."

"Final result of what?" asked José Manuel in befuddlement.

"Nothing. Go on."

José Manuel then, taking as his theme those first words that had come into his mouth, spun out a very insipid lie—from which we shall spare the readers. The *comadre*'s goal of diverting the conversation away from the girl's abduction was, however, not achieved. When the story ended, José Manuel began insisting that Dona Maria explain the dubious words that she had said with regard to him. The minute she saw the game turning in that direction, the *comadre* started trying to withdraw—after exchanging with Dona Maria a glance saying "don't give me away."

At first Dona Maria tried to keep the secret, but after a while she could not contain herself and loosed a great diatribe upon José Manuel, saying that the whole city was full of the horrible scandal that he had perpetrated by abducting a respectable young woman.

The man hit the ceiling; he swore again and again that he was innocent in the entire matter. Nothing availed him, however; Dona Maria was inflexible.

She proclaimed again that if she were a relative of that girl, Mr. José Manuel would really find himself in a tight spot over the matter. And she ended by informing him that he was too unsavory a man to be admitted into respectable people's homes.

José Manuel left completely befuddled and wondering who could have authored an intrigue such as this.

As for Dona Maria, she was highly satisfied, for, having a great fund of honesty in her character, she felt that she had done a good deed in breaking with José Manuel, who ended up, as the *comadre* had calculated, losing greatly in her esteem.

I V

The Prayer Master

Everything that had just taken place in Dona Maria's house had put José Manuel's head in a whirl. He realized that he had an enemy there, whoever it might be, since obviously all this was nothing more than a plot directed specifically at him. It remained, however, for him to discover who that enemy was and, cogitate on it as he might, he could not come up with an answer. Because of the kind of plot it was, he realized that the motivation must have to do with his intentions with regard to Luisinha, which had doubtless been perceived; he began to suspect that there must be a rival. In the circle that frequented Dona Maria's house, he saw no one who seemed to be in that category. He did often think of the young Leonardo, but he did not find him capable of such things.

That is how scoundrels are! How often they touch the enemy with their hands and neither see him nor sense him!

No matter the source of the blow that had wounded him, however, what was sure was that it was delivered with accuracy—and with both hands.

Dona Maria, as extreme in her hatreds as in her affections, would only with great difficulty consent to José Manuel's rehabilitation.

He, however, did not shrink from the task as a result, and set to work. Through a peculiar chance, just as Leonardo had found in the *comadre* a protectress of his cause, so too did José Manuel find an advocate of his own. Let us tell the readers who José Manuel's advocate was.

In the time in which these events were taking place, there were some very unusual "institutions" in Rio de Janeiro; some of them were noteworthy for their ends, others for their means. Amongst them was one whose vestiges we had occasion to see even in our childhood: it was the institution of the prayer master.

In that period, the prayer master was as highly regarded and as revered as the schoolmaster. To the esteem ordinarily accorded preceptors in general, one very noteworthy circumstance was added: The prayer masters were invariably old and blind. They did not exist in great numbers, and for that reason they were very active and earned a considerable amount of money. They went from house to house teaching the children, slaves, and slave children of both sexes how to pray.

The prayer master did not wear any distinctive dress; he was clad like anyone else. The only thing that distinguished him was a huge ferule, with which he was always armed, it sticking up out of one pocket; it was the sole compendium through which he gave lessons to his pupils. When they came in for their lesson, he would gather them all in a semicircle in front of him, pull the ferule out of his pocket, and set it on the floor propped against the chair in which he sat. Then the work began.

The master would say the "By the sign . . ." aloud, in a slow, measured voice, and all the pupils would accompany him in chorus. As to the making of the signs, he was almost always deceived, as is easily imagined. As regards the repetition of the words, however, so practiced was he that, no matter the number of the pupils, he could discern if this or that voice was missing in the midst of the chorus whenever anyone dared to keep silent. Then the work was immediately suspended, and the culprit was rewarded with a levy of whacks that in no way failed to bespeak the fame that "the blind man's buffet" enjoys. Once that was done, the work recommenced, starting over at the beginning every time there was an error or an omission. When the "By the sign . . ." was over—which, with the diverse interruptions it usually underwent, could take a good half-hour—the master would repeat, always alone and in a loud, rhythmic voice, the prayer that he had selected. It was then repeated from beginning to end by the pupils, in a manner that was neither speaking nor singing—interrupted at each error, of course, by the corresponding number of whacks. A new prayer followed the last, and so on, until the lesson ended with the chanted litany. As he left, the master would receive a small gratuity from the head of the household.

Dona Maria, having in her house no small number of slave-children, did not fail, like all those in her circumstances, to have her own prayer master. He was a blind man very famous for his great rigor with the pupils and therefore one of the most highly sought-after of the prayer masters. At that time that quality was required above all else. He had another merit as well: He enjoyed a high repute as a good maker of marriages.

This was José Manuel's advocate.

José Manuel had previously made an alliance with him and, now that he saw himself imperiled, took recourse there. He explained the situation to him, communicated his intentions, and asked for his collaboration. He let him know most especially that there was a rival to contend with, and one all the more fearsome as his identity was unknown. The old man then began to gather the most minute pieces of information, and, after calculating for some time, said, "Now I know who it is I'll be contending with."

"Then who is it?" José Manuel instantly inquired.

"Relax, don't worry about anything else."

"But, man, just be aware that you'll have to be very careful, because whoever it is is as clever as the devil."

"Ha! Nonsense. I can handle matters of this kind in my sleep, and, blind though I am, I can see through this better than most people with perfect sight."

"It addles my brain not to be able to figure out who's meddling in my affairs—be aware that that story about the abduction of the girl was a master stroke."

"I too am a master, and we shall see who ends up teaching better."

The two of them left matters at that, and the blind man set to work.

We must advise the reader that in such hands the cause, while not decidedly won, was at very least hanging in the balance. The auspicious factor was that the *comadre* was on the opposing side.

The old man began his work in a calculated way: On the very first night he went to give a lesson at Dona Maria's house, he steered the conversation toward the girl's abduction and gave it to be known that he knew all about the case and was aware of the identity of its author. Dona Maria said that she too knew who it was and in fact was personally acquainted with him. The old man smiled, merely letting drop, in a dubious tone of voice, a meaningful "Hmm."

Dona Maria frowned, raised her glasses, and exclaimed: "So you think I'm not up on these things? Well, don't you worry . . . I know who it was, and I know it through and through. He's a bad actor with the face of a liar who'll get back into my house only if I decide one day to become a jailer."

"He is every bit of that. But I'm telling you, *senhora* Dona Maria, you don't know who it is; I know all the ins and outs of the business."

"I do know, I do know . . . and I know about it from a very reliable party, so it's easy to see which one of us is mistaken. Go ahead and say who it was."

"Oh, me, no never," exclaimed the old man quickly, as he rose to his feet. Never; I don't reveal anyone's confidence."

Dona Maria writhed in vexation; persist though she did, she was unable to drag anything out of the old man, who, the better to play his role, insisted on withdrawing, thus giving her to understand that he wanted to end the conversation at that juncture.

If he had succeeded in nothing else, the old man had at least sown doubt in Dona Maria's mind about the issue that was for her the cornerstone of the scandal involving José Manuel.

V

Upset

While all these events were taking place, a sad occurrence, and one of the greatest importance, came to alter Leonardo's life—or actually to turn it upside down. His godfather fell gravely ill. At first the upset seemed to be a matter of little importance, and the *comadre*, who was the first person called in, felt that the discomfort would completely disappear within a couple of days if the patient would take some rosemary baths. That prescription, however, had no effect; the illness continued. They then had recourse to an apothecary known to the *comadre*, who extended his trade—whether with the sanction of the law or without it we know not—to the profession of physician.

He was an old man, a son of Oporto, who had come and established himself here many years ago and who had pulled together a pretty good pile of money in his trade. As soon as he arrived and saw the patient he declared that he would have him back on his feet in a very few days; all he had to do was to take some pills that he would send from his shop. They constituted a perfect remedy, according to him, except that they were a bit on the expensive side; but a man's life was worth it. When she heard the word "pills," the *comadre* frowned.

"Piulls," she said to herself. "Then it's serious business. And I, I've got no faith in piulls; I've never seen a person yet who's taken 'em and escaped." And her eyes immediately started growing red.

The apothecary left, taking Leonardo with him to bring back the pills. The *comadre* looked at them and shook her head. "Well," she said, "I thought he'd have him take some baths; I would think that ones with rosemary would do the trick."

The *comadre* was right up to a point, for in three days' time, after receiving all the religious rites, the *compadre* gave his soul to God.

Dona Maria had been called on the last day, and she came with Luisinha and her entire batallion of slave-children. Some other people from the neighborhood had come as well. They were all seated on a huge settee on the veranda totally absorbed in discussion of the most diverse subjects; some even found in the conversation a cause for laughter. Suddenly the bedroom door opened, and the *comadre* came out with a handerchief to her eyes, sobbing uncontrolledly and shouting again and again, "I said I had no faith in piulls; there's yet to be anyone I've seen take 'em and escape. Poor *compadre* . . . such a good creature . . . I never saw him do ill to anyone."

These words from the *comadre* constituted the call to arms for the grief of those present. General sobbing broke out, each person crying as loud as they could. Leonardo was devastated, and in his shock he huddled on the settee with his head on his knees, sliding—"naturally" without intending to, so much did the pain disorient him—as close as possible to Luisinha. The rest continued on in the chorus of weeping led by the *comadre*. They did not, however, content themselves merely with weeping; they also now and again offered some pronouncements in honor of the deceased.

"He was always a very good neighbor; I never heard a bad word about him," said one. That was the neighbor woman who had predicted a bad end for Leonardo and with whom the *compadre* had fought no few times on that score.

"A good soul," said Dona Maria, "a good soul. If anyone wanted to have a good soul, they'd have to be like him."

"I who had my run-ins with him," said the *comadre*, "I know best what he was made of. His was a saint's soul in the body of a sinner."

"A good friend . . ."

"And very God-fearing . . ."

After this scene was carried out for a period of time, some people took their leave while others remained. The weeping was subsiding, and shortly before Dona Maria, still wiping her eyes, had begun explaining in detail to a lady who was sitting next to her the genealogical history of each one of the slave-children present.

Finally everyone had gone except Dona Maria, her people, and the *comadre*, who, since the *compadre* had fallen ill, had been running the household. Night was approaching. They lit candles beside the deceased and carried out all the other customary preparations.

Dona Maria and the *comadre* began to converse, in low voices.

"Well, *senhora*," Dona Maria began, "this man must not have just died without making a will; he wouldn't have wanted to leave his godson unprovided for in the world and let other people enjoy what it cost him so much hard work to accumulate."

"To me," replied the *comadre*, "he never spoke of any such thing; but after all, since those are secret affairs . . . maybe he did."

"It would be good to look for it. Perhaps it's in a drawer around here. He wouldn't just not make any disposition of his possessions at all. Many is the time I counseled him to do just that."

"You are right, Dona Maria; I too think that there must be something."

And the two women went to look through the drawers of a large bureau in the dead man's bedroom to try to find the will. While they were thus occupied, Luisinha and Leonardo were talking together, or rather, as the common phrase has it, were "whispering together." What they were saying I cannot tell the reader, for I do not know; doubtless the girl was consoling the boy on the loss that he had just experienced in the person of his beloved godfather.

At last the two women came across a will, and they were quite satisfied.

They returned to the veranda and surprised the two young people deep in their conversation. Upon seeing them thus the *comadre* smiled, and Dona Maria, doubtless drawing the same conclusion as have we regarding what they were talking about, said tenderly, "She has such a good heart!"

"And his is no less so," replied the *comadre*. And she added, significantly: "They'd make a beautiful couple."

"Oh, *senhora*," said Dona Maria ingenuously, "leave the girl be; it's still very soon."

"I don't mean now, but in its own proper time."

Dona Maria smiled a smile that by no means displeased the *comadre*, and they changed the subject.

The night went by. The next day the burial was carried out with all the customary formalities. After it was over, they tried to resolve an important question: with whom would Leonardo go to live? The reading of the will on that same day answered the question. The *compadre* had made Leonardo his sole heir. The *comadre* informed Leonardo-Pataca of the situation, and he presented himself to take charge of his son. The boy did not seem highly pleased with the gesture. There came to his mind, I know not how, the image of that terrible kick that had driven him to flee his home. Also, he had seen his father a scant few times since then and was now completely unaccustomed to him. There was, however, no other choice; he needed to obey and go home with him, where he would encounter his baby sister and the person who had brought her into the world.

Leonardo-Pataca set out to deal with the will like a man familiar with those matters and brought the process to a speedy conclusion.

It must be noted that if, during the *compadre*'s life, seemingly exaggerated rumors flourished about his worth, upon his death it turned out that those murmurings had in fact fallen far short of the truth, for he left a good couple of thousand cruzados in coin. After some small legacies and other such items were paid out, the remainder came into Leonardo-Pataca's hands as his son's inheritance.

In the first days, all was sweetness and light in the Leonardo-Pataca household, even though, if the truth be told, young Leonardo had, from first sight, not taken a liking to the face of the object of his father's new and recent affections.

The *comadre* proclaimed that it was her duty to take the *compadre*'s place in love for their godson, and she decided to go live with him in Leonardo-Pataca's home. She would thus also be reunited with her daughter and her granddaughter. Leonardo-Pataca, who was an accommodating person, was in favor, and so the entire family was brought together.

It all went very well at first, as we have said. Young Leonardo and the *comadre* kept up their visits to Dona Maria's house, and, let us say it straight away, the young man and the young woman were becoming as thick as thieves. It is true, however, that José Manuel kept working, aided by his blind prayer master, and certainly had not relinquished his hopes.

The tranquility in Leonardo-Pataca's home did not long endure. Chiquinha (such was the name of the *comadre*'s daughter) began to conceive an antipathy to her stepson, while he—who, as we have said, had not taken a liking to her—started a series of noisy rows. Day in and day out they went head to head over each little trifle, and then everything would be up in the air. Leonardo-Pataca and the *comadre* would play mediating roles, but the other two were both very headstrong, and the person doing the mediation often ended up badly used because the one who had been judged to be in the wrong would then turn on the mediator. If, for example, it were the *comadre* and she found Leonardo in the right, her daughter would come after her arguing that her mother was abandoning her to take the side of her godson. If, by contrast, she favored Chiquinha, Leonardo would complain that a motherless child was doubly bereft, for he could never find anyone to listen to his side. The same would happen to Leonardo-Pataca whenever he tried to bring peace to the pair.

Matters thus went badly, for if not one day then the next there would be a big blow-up in the house.

V I

A Greater Upset

One day Leonardo came home highly mortified because, having gone to visit Dona Maria, he had spent a long time with her without Luisinha's appearing, so that after some hours he was obliged to leave without seeing her. Anyone who has ever been in love, no matter how slightly, and has had to undergo such a disappointment; anyone who has been obliged to endure for long the conversation of an old woman, having to agree with her on every tiny point in order not to incur her displeasure, all only with the goal of exchanging with "someone" a quick glance, a fugitive smile, or some other such; and who, after all was said and done, had not succeeded even in that, will agree that Leonardo had every reason to be put out at what had just happened to him and will forgive him for whatever mood might come over him on that occasion. There are, however, spirits so perverse that they take pleasure in building on someone else's ill humor and who, the more irritable the unhappy person they see, the more they enjoy throwing brickbats at him.

Chiquinha, Leonardo-Pataca's beloved, was just such a spirit. And ever since they had all begun living together she, by virtue of the antipathy that she had for the boy, had not missed a single opportunity to give poor Leonardo a good working-over with her tongue. The latter, choleric of temperament and little accustomed to being opposed, would hit the ceiling when that happened. And if quarrels were constant in the house on the ordinary occasions when he was in a good humor, just imagine what he would do in moments like the one to which we refer, when he had such motivation—and, what is more, what a motivation!

Seeing Leonardo come in the door with a thundercloud face and without so much as a "God save you" for anyone, Chiquinha smiled malignly to herself and, clearing her throat, said between her teeth, "Here's hoping tomorrow will bring with it a better face."

Leonardo, who understood what that referred to, made an angry gesture as he sat down in a chair—with, however, such ill luck as to send onto the floor a lace cushion that was lying next to him. The fall caused threads to pop, and a bunch of bobbins rolled all over the house. With even greater ill luck, the cushion had been Chiquinha's, and Chiquinha was very protective of her lace cushion.

Boiling with fury, she arose from where she was sitting, put her hands on her hips, and, wagging her head as she spoke, exclaimed, "Now there, have you ever seen such shameless impudence? . . . He comes in off the street with his dander up, all overheated, and on purpose, totally on purpose, he does what you've just seen, just to spite me, as though he were the master of the house and can do anything he pleases to anybody without any cause at all!"

Leonardo listened to it all without interrupting, endeavoring to get control of his anger. And when Chiquinha stopped to take a breath he replied in a choked and trembling voice, "Stay out of my business, since I certainly don't give a fig about yours; talk about having dander up—"

"Oh for a good uniform on you!" Chiquinha cut in. "Oh for the deck of some ship! Oh for Major Vidigal!"

"I told you—"

"Phooey to 'I told you,' to even half of 'I told you'—you stupid, lovesick calf—"

These words produced the same effect as a match in a keg of gunpowder. Leonardo advanced on Chiquinha with fists clenched and foaming with rage. "If you say one half a word more to me—I'm going to lose my respect for you—I never did actually trust you. And even though you may be the lady, or whatever it is, of my father—I'm going to lose my respect for you—"

"You never cease to show me that you've got Lisbon rustic in your veins," Chiquinha retorted, stiffening and standing her ground.

Leonardo-Pataca, who was in the back part of the house, rushed out at the noise and arrived to find the two of them toe to toe. Seeing his son about to do damage to the beloved object of his latest affections, he did not hesitate in bursting out at him, "You thug—do you think this is like that house of your godfather's you used to live in? What I want here is respect for everybody—if not—then if once before I gave you a kick that sent you away for a good many years; this time I'll give you one that'll put you away forever—"

"I never dreamed," interrupted Chiquinha, addressing Leonardo-Pataca and wishing to make the situation appear as ugly as possible, "I never dreamed that I'd have to undergo such a thing living with you—"

"Don't let it bother you, my dear; he's just a wastrel I'm going to have to teach a lesson. I'd kick him out for your sake above anyone else's."

"For her sake!" the boy cut in. "Well think of that! I'm sure she'll pay you well for it—as well as the gypsy girl—"

"But I'll never treat him," Chiquinha hurried to add, infuriated at that insult, "I'll never treat him the way your mother did—"

At this point Leonardo-Pataca lost control completely, what with the flood of bitter memories that those few words had brought down upon his head! "You wait, you no-account. Just wait; I'll teach you," he exclaimed, crimson with fury. "Just wait; I'll teach you." And running into the front bedroom, he rushed back, armed with the smallsword from his uniform, and charged his son. It should be noted that the smallsword was still in its scabbard.

"Don't risk ruining your life for me," exclaimed Chiquinha, grabbing hold of him by the cotton nightshirt he was wearing.

Chiquinha's fear was unnecessary, however, because the youth, seeing that the whole affair was turning ugly and harboring an instinctive terror of his father as the result of that kick that had never left his memory, had headed for the open street, closing the shutter behind him.

"Ah, you ruffian!" said Leonardo-Pataca once more. "I'd cut you up in little pieces—"

Leonardo was fleeing on one side and the *comadre* was arriving on the other, for the latter had been absent during the whole scene. Hardly had she removed her mantilla and seen the two actors, who still remained on stage in positions corresponding to the last tableau, when she sought to inquire into the play that had just been staged.

"Oh, it was just one of your beloved godson's usual," answered Chiquinha, not yet calmed down.

"But it cost him dearly this time," added Leonardo-Pataca.

"Well really," cut in the *comadre* in indignation. "Were you really using the sword to attack the boy with?"

"You bet! He was going to catch it as hard as bone!"

"But why? How many people did he kill with a single blow? Where did he start the house afire? A motherless child is a sad thing! . . . I'll bet that if I had been here none of it would have happened!"

"Of course not," replied Chiquinha, "because you'd take his side just as you always do. It's the same old story: Many children do have mothers, and their mothers are only good for taking someone else's side and leaving them out."

"What? Nonsense! It's just that there are two sides to everything."

"Oh *senhora*," interrupted Leonardo-Pataca, "if we keep going this way, there'll never be a moment's peace in this house. As soon as one row ends another one starts. What will the neighborhood say? And remember that this is the home of an officer of the law."

"All right," said the *comadre*, "where's the boy? Where have you buried the body?"

"He lit out of here like his tail was afire, and I hope to God he never comes back."

"Now that's very nice! Tell me it isn't so, that you didn't run the boy out of his home! . . . He's no urchin, you know; he has what his godfather left him."

"That's part of what has him on the road to perdition."

"You bet! Give him the airs of a rich man and you'll see how he turns out!"

"Poor boy," the *comadre* lamented, "he was born under a bad sign." And putting her mantilla back on she went out with tears in her eyes in search of Leonardo.

As she left, three or four neighborhood women were waiting for her at their windows.

"What did they do to the youngster, then?"

"What happened, *senhora comadre*?"

"He passed by here going ten leagues an hour!"

"Leave me be, leave me be," responded the *comadre*. "This isn't working out the way it should."

V I I

A Cure for Ills

The poor boy had exited, as we have said, straight through the door and traveling fast. He kept looking back over and over again, for he could still see the menacing smallsword raised against him in the hand of his father, who seemed to want to finish the job on him that he had begun with that kick. He moved at a goodly pace for a long time and finally found himself in the area of the Cajueiros. Panting and weary, he sat down on some stones, and anyone who had seen him with his air of gloom and self-absorption might have judged that he was contemplating his situation and the road that he should take. But anyone who so judged would have been roundly mistaken: He was thinking about something much more pleasant; he was thinking about Luisinha. And it is true that he could not think of her without having appear before his eyes the terrible José Manuel, and that explained certain gestures of impatience that could from time to time be observed in him. He had spent a long time in this meditation when he was brought back to his senses by occasional bursts of laughter emitting from some nearby bushes. He trembled from head to toe; it seemed to him that the very thoughts going through his mind were being read and he was being laughed at. He turned around—but saw nothing. Guided by the noise he kept hearing he began to search, and with no great effort found, behind some especially tall bushes, a number of young men and women. Seated on a mat amidst the remains of a meal, they were bent forward with curiosity over two of their number who, with a deck of dirty, crumpled cards, were engrossed in an intricate game of *bisca*. The laughter that he had heard a moment ago had come in response to a slam that one of them had just suffered. At the sight of the leftovers from a meal that, while it did not seem particularly abundant, nonetheless made him recall that he had left the house just before mealtime, his stomach began to give out some formidable noises. Even so, he started to turn away, not wishing to interfere in other people's celebrations, when one of the players raised his head and he recognized an old comrade, the boy who had been sacristan at the Sé. Despite this revelation he started to withdraw, but it was too late, for with the movement that he made the player, catching sight of him, recognized him in turn.

"Hi Leonardo! What downpour dropped you on these parts? I thought that the devil had licked your bones by now, since I never laid eyes on you again after that cursed day when we caught it on account of the liturgy master."

Leonardo approached the group and, after the expectable greetings were exchanged with his old comrade, was invited to partake of whatever remained of the meal. He wanted to stand on cerimony and refuse, but he was in no condition for that; one of the girls handed him some food, and, as the game of *bisca* went on, he ate until he was full.

"Polish off that last bottle," his friend said to him, "and see if it's as good as the wine that we used to pinch from the cruets at the Sé, to the anguish of my father and the fury of the liturgy master."

When Leonardo had done with eating, the two players also finished their game. He then took his friend aside and asked him, "What kind of people are these you're hanging around with?"

"They're my kind of people."

"Your kind of people?"

"Yes, you see that dark-haired girl over there?"

"Yes, and so?"

"Well, what do you think?"

"You mean you've got married?"

"No, but what's that got to do with it?"

"Oh, I see; you're shacked up with her."

"And how about you?"

"I . . . there's so much to tell . . . my godfather died."

"Yes, I heard."

"I went to live with my father . . . and suddenly, just today, I get into a fight with that something-or-other of his; he comes at me with a sword, and I beat hell out of there. I finally stopped over there and then I heard the laughing coming from this direction . . ."

"I know the rest—And now you have no place to go?"

"Man, I was going to see . . ."

"See what?"

"See about something to do, somewhere here . . ."

"Somewhere? Where?"

"I really don't know."

And the two of them burst out laughing. When we bear only eighteen or twenty years on our backs, which is still a very light burden, we sneer at the past, laugh at the present, and give ourselves carelessly over to blind trust in the future, which is the best appanage of youth.

"You know what else?" Leonardo's friend went on. "Come along with us; you won't regret it."

"Along with you? Where?"

"Where? You mean you've got better offers to choose from? Are you trying to stand on cerimony?"

Night was beginning to fall.

"Let's call it quits for tonight, people," said one of the participants.

"Yes, let's."

"No, not yet. Vidinha's going to sing a *modinha*."

"Yes, yes, a *modinha* before we go. Let's have 'If only my sighs could'."

"No, not that one. Sing 'When the glories that I have enjoyed'."

"C'mon, make up your minds," said a girl in a high, languid voice.

Vidinha was a mulatto girl some eighteen or twenty years old, of average height, with broad shoulders, salient breasts, a slim waist, and tiny feet. She had very black, dancing eyes, thick, moist lips, and extremely white teeth. Her speech was a bit slow but sweet and melodic. Every sentence she uttered was punctuated with a long, sonorous giggle and a certain backward toss of her head that would perhaps have been characterful if it had not been so highly affected.

It was finally agreed that she would sing the *modinha* "If only my sighs could." Vidinha took up a guitar and, accompanying herself with a melody that today would be considered old fashioned but was very popular back then, sang as follows:

> If only my sighs could
> Find their way to your ears
> You would know that love
> Is a deadly power to fear.
>
> My lament comes not from zeal,
> Nor from jealousy strong,
> But from the torments of love's absence,
> Which impel me to long.

Leonardo, who perhaps suffered from a hereditary weakness for such things, listened to the *modinha* with his mouth hanging open, and such was the impression it made on him that he could scarcely thereafter take his eyes off the singer. The *modinha* was duly applauded, and everyone rose, put everything they had brought back into baskets, and took to the road, Leonardo accompanying the merrymakers.

New Love

A fter a long walk under a sky in which shone one of those magnificent moons that are to be seen only in Rio de Janeiro, they all
reached a house on Vala Street. In those times a moonlit night was made
the most of: No one stayed inside; those who did not go out on a stroll
would sit in their doorways on mats and pass long hours in music, at
their supper, and in conversation. Many slept the whole night in the
out-of-doors.

It being the case that our acquaintances had already strolled some
distance, they adopted the expedient of the mats in the doorway, thereby
extending well into the night the festivities in which they had spent the
day. For what Leonardo had witnessed in the Cajueiros, and indeed had
taken part in, was but the finale of an outing that had begun at daybreak, one of those pilgrimages of pleasure so common and so highly regarded back then.

It is now our duty to acquaint the reader with the new people in
whose midst our Leonardo finds himself. If we could here enlist the aid
of our friend José Manuel, he would doubtless pluck for us every leaf off
the genealogical tree of that family that Leonardo's friend called his
"kind of people." But let the readers be satisfied with the present without inquiring into the past. And let them therefore be apprised that the
family consisted of two sisters, both widows—or at least claiming to be
so—the one with three sons, the other with three daughters. Each of
the two was past her forties; they were both fat and very similar looking.
The three sons of the first sister were three husky young men in their
twenties, all employed in the Royal Arsenal; the three daughters of the
second were three unpretentious young women of about the same age as
their male cousins and good-looking, each in her own way. One of them
the readers already know: She is Vidinha, the *modinha* singer. She was
single, as was one of her sisters; the other was single too, but not like the
other two. Let Leonardo's friend explain what that means, and by that
explanation he will make clear what he himself was within the family.
The rest of those present were in the main neighbors that regularly got
together for such festivities, which were traditional in the family.

When they got to the house, Leonardo's friend took the two elder
women aside and began to talk to them, doubtless about Leonardo,

since all three of them looked over at him during the exchange and someone with keen hearing could even have heard these words from the women: "Poor boy!" "Imagine what a hard-hearted father!"

Anyone older—or, to be precise, anyone with more sense and better rearing—would have been ashamed, and perhaps greatly so, at finding himself in Leonardo's position, but he did not give that a thought. And in addition he gave no more thought to something that until then he had been unable to get out of his mind, namely Luisinha on the one hand and José Manuel on the other. Now he could see only the dancing black eyes and white teeth of Vidinha and could hear only the echo of the *modinha* she had sung. He was, then, absorbed in an ecstasy of contemplation. To everything else he would put his mind when he had time left over.

Hardly had they all sat down on a wide mat near the threshold of the door that opened out onto the sidewalk when Leonardo proposed that another *modinha* be sung.

"Aww," Vidinha replied, accompanying that "aww" with her customary giggle. "I'm so tired now . . . that I just can't."

"Now, now . . .," said no few voices. In addition to giggling, Vidinha had another habit, which was to begin everything with a very emphatic "aww."

Therefore, she answered, "Aww . . . I might've already sung everything I know. Aww, my God! I just can't do any more."

"You still haven't sung my favorite one," said one of the company.

"Mine either," said another.

"Same with me," added yet another. "I still haven't asked you for the one I keep in my heart."

"Aww, my God! Where is this ever going to stop?"

"C'mon sis, stop playing coy."

"Ah, my child," said one of the elder women, "what do you want? For people to get down on their knees for you to sing a *modinha*?"

Leonardo, seeing his cause being advocated by so many voices, remained silent.

After several other tactics were tried out and more avoidances put up, Vidinha agreed and, taking up the guitar, at the request of one of the elder women sang the following:

> Hard irons held me fettered
> At the moment I saw thee;
> Now I want to break them:
> Too late, it cannot be!

That last phrase absolutely completed Leonardo's bedazzlement: The song's last notes had not even died away and already, as a whirlwind of ideas rushed about in his mind, he marveled that he had even for an instant felt an inclination toward an insipid and odd girl like Luisinha when there were women like Vidinha in the world. He was decidedly smitten with the latter.

The reader should scarcely wonder at this, for we have not ceased to repeat that Leonardo had inherited from his father that overabundance of amorous humors that was his chief characteristic. Along with that heritage, however, he seemed to have received one other as well: that of always undergoing some contretemps in such affairs. José Manuel had been the first; let us now see what—or, rather, who—the second was.

If the reader has thought about what we said a moment ago, namely that in that family there were three male cousins and three female cousins, and if we now add that they all lived in the same household, he or she must have done some wondering about that fact. Three male and three female cousins, living in the same house, all young . . . nothing more natural: One male cousin to every female cousin, and it all works out. It must be observed in addition, however, that Leonardo's friend had accounted for one of the female cousins, so that there came to be three male cousins for two female cousins—that is, a one-male surplus. In this light, the business becomes even more complicated. For, to make a long story short, be it understood that there were two male cousin suitors for a single female cousin, and she was Vidinha, the prettiest of the three. Be it understood as well that one of them was encouraged, the other rebuffed. Our friend Leonardo, then, will now have to contend with two contretemps instead of one.

But for now he knew none of this and tranquilly gave himself over to his emotions without remembering what anyone else would remember: That among male and female cousins there is a certain mutual right in matters of love that greatly disadvantages any outside suitor.

They spent a great part of the night sitting there, retiring only when it was very late.

Leonardo's friend, to whom we shall henceforth refer by his proper name of Thomas and the added qualification "of the Sé"—both of them inherited from his father—declared that his buddy would be staying there for the night, as it was very late. He wished thus to spare him any embarassment and in so doing proved himself a good friend.

Now that our Leonardo is installed in safe quarters, let us go occupy ourselves with another important matter, which we have previously left in suspense.

José Manuel Triumphs

The *comadre* had run all over the city and nowhere had she found Leonardo. While she was wearing herself out in the search, he was calm and relaxed gazing into the eyes of Vidinha, contentedly listening to *modinhas*, as the readers well know, completely heedless of what was going on in the world.

The poor woman, after wearying herself to the bone, took refuge in Dona Maria's house. It was by then deep into the night.

As she was entering, the prayer master was leaving, having given his lesson to the household slave-children. For some time now the *comadre* had been suspicious of the prayer master; adding up the talk about the confidence in which he was held and certain things that she had had occasion to witness, she had all but concluded that he was José Manuel's emissary to the court of Dona Maria. The meeting, then, was not one to her liking, and it bothered her deeply to see him leaving at that time of day, since lessons ordinarily did not go so late. To try to get a rise out of him, she said, "The lesson ran late today, my pious one . . . the girls seem to like gossip more than they like prayer."

"No," the old man answered in his nasal voice, "they're not doing badly. They get stuck in some places but they keep making progress. And you know that I always bring the blessed cure-all with me." And he caressed the handle of the ferule with which he was always armed.

"Ah! Then you must've been deep in conversation. You do like to wag your tongue . . ."

"I'm not opposed to it, no. But at the same time I say only what I know—that is, what I hear. Other people spend their time both seeing and hearing; I, since I can only hear, take up in talking what others use in seeing. I talk; I talk a lot. But then I have time aplenty for it. And what's more, you know it's not tiring work. My parents were Algarvian, and I don't want to let my ancestry down."

"Then I'm sure that the dead have been disinterred and the living buried this day. Well, I can't match that, because you find me as irritated as can be with my life. If, my pious friend, being a man who gets about the city very widely, you should hear anything of my godson Leonardo, please come let me know. He left home today on account of some sort of nonsense, and I haven't been able to find hide nor hair of him."

"Now just you leave that to me; nothing easier than to find out where he is."

And with that the conversation, which had taken place at the street door, came to a close, the *comadre* feeling quite displeased with its upshot. Dona Maria, who had heard it all, came out to meet her and, before the latter had time to take off her mantilla, said to her, "Then the boy's not at home any more? *Senhora*, that's nature; he was born with it and he'll go to the grave with it. I've been told what he was like, and despite that smart air he has about him, I've never thought very well of him."

"As far as I'm concerned, you're casting the blame on someone who doesn't deserve it; this time the boy is completely in the right—"

"Now, now, stuff and nonsense. You just say that because you love him like a mother. But mark my words: Young men today go around with their heads too high in the air. Our dearly departed *compadre*— may God rest his soul—was the one to blame for all of this, what with those pretensions about Coimbra that he s..ffed the boy's head with—"

"But, my dear *senhora*, his brute of a father actually went after him sword in hand—"

"And what do you suppose the boy did first? And what of it anyhow? His father wasn't going to cut him up in pieces. Oh, I know about his temper all right; it was anger, and it'll pass. The child should have given in—he is his father, after all."

"By the Holy Virgin! But it was over nothing at all! A lace cushion! Does that sound reasonable? ... And now where's the poor child to go?"

"He's probably around here in some gypsy fado or other. Don't you remember what he did when his godfather was still alive?"

"Oh, stuff of childhood. Why bring that up?"

This dialogue was going on interminably in the same vein when Dona Maria, abruptly changing the subject, said to the *comadre*, "Oh, that's right! Sit down right here, for we have a score to settle."

"A score?"

"And very long ones, I'll begin by saying," added Dona Maria, who did not seem to be in a very good humor on this occasion. "I'll begin by telling you right to your face that when you go to confession this year you must try to atone for a great sin that you have committed."

"And I who have no small number of them! But what are you speaking of?"

"A bit of slander, *senhora*, of great slander that you raised against someone who did not merit it."

The *comadre* needed to hear no more to realize where all this was headed: She knew through and through what the most recent bit of slander was of which her conscience accused her. She started to see it all, clear as day: She saw José Manuel completely exonerated in Dona Maria's eyes with regard to the abduction at the Stone Oratory, and she saw as well the blind prayer master as the mediator of that exoneration. She was, then, visibly discomfited; she shifted back and forth as though the bench on which she was seated was covered with thorns, and she had a violent coughing spell when Dona Maria finished speaking those last words.

"Everything you told me about José Manuel in relation to the story of the girl," Dona Maria went on, turning red, which in her was a bad sign, "was untrue—and very untrue. I know this from a very reliable source—"

The *comadre* was overcome by a new coughing spell.

"Now, look here," Dona Maria continued. "I took your story on trust, so much so that I broke off relations with the poor man. I won't make that mistake again; that one time taught me a lesson."

The *comadre* saw that the wind was switching quarters; she realized that Dona Maria was very well informed and that it would be useless even to attempt to insist upon the truth of all that she had said. It would serve only to make her position worse. She thus, there and then, forged a new plan, saying, "you're not telling me anything I don't already know, *senhora*. I know it all too well: In this matter, that man is like Pilate in the Creed."

"But recall now, you told me you saw it with your own eyes."

"Ah, *senhora*, it must've been the very devil in his place. I never saw anything like it, so similar were they. I found out the truth the other day, and I am repentant."

"For that reason I sent for the poor man," Dona Maria went on, "who was so offended by the way I had treated him that it was hard for him to come back. I had a heart-to-heart talk with him. And I'll tell you one thing: You don't come out well in the whole business. He confided in me about some things . . . that I didn't want to believe."

"Then you told him that it was I who . . ."

"I wasn't the one who told him. He already knew, and I wasn't going to deny it. That's when he started to open my eyes on other points—"

The *comadre*, who could see all the soup spilled in those "other points," tried to change the topic of conversation, pretending that she had not heard the last words. "But then," she asked, "who told him about how the business got started? I want to see if that goes together with what I know."

"The person who got me to see the light left just a short time ago."

"Ah," said the *comadre*. And she bit her lips in a gesture that said "I had that one right!"

Dona Maria went on to tell the *comadre* that, when she talked to the prayer master about the affair, he had rejected everything she had said to her about José Manuel. She had argued with the old man a long time trying to get him to say what he knew about it and what he based his rejection on. Finally, after great resistance, he had just the day before brought the girl's father to her house, and he had confessed everything, even giving the name of the man his daughter had run off with, whom he already knew and with whom he had made his peace.

"That's exactly what what I found out," said the *comadre* at the close of the narrative. "It was just like that. Look, *senhora*, at what can happen to a person in this life: even bearing false witness against others."

Let us now inform the reader that everything that had just taken place had indeed been the work of the prayer master. By bits and pieces he had learned about what was going on in Dona Maria's household with regard to his client José Manuel. He had succeeded in discovering who had plotted the intrigue. He had also inquired into goings-on in Leonardo-Pataca's house, and, as there was a lot of talking out loud in that house about Leonardo's intentions, putting two and two together he came to the correct conclusion about what had in fact happened.

Dona Maria seemed to accept the *comadre*'s repentance and that began to placate the rather unfriendly humor she was in. They returned to the matter of Leonardo's leaving home, and this time Dona Maria did not show herself so inflexible toward the youth. Still the *comadre* could not get out of her head Dona Maria's words "he opened my eyes on other points," and, when she saw her more pacified, she endeavored to bring the conversation around to that juncture again and try to ferret out explanations. She could foresee the meaning of the words, which without any doubt whatsoever referred to her designs, or those of her godson, upon Luisinha. But she still wanted to know the colors in which the business had been painted for Dona Maria by José Manuel.

This, however, proved fatal to her, for she found out (which was not at all to her liking) that the business was at a complete stop as far as her godson was concerned and, by contrast, well advanced in favor of his adversary. Dona Maria—after declaring that José Manuel had registered a complaint against the *comadre* in which he attributed to her everything that had taken place, which amounted to nothing more than a plot cooked up to get him out of this house because suspicions had fallen upon him (which he confessed were well founded)—added finally that José Manuel, completely exonerated thanks to the prayer master's intervention, had ended up by giving her to understand something with regard to Luisinha that she, Dona Maria, confessed she had not received with total displeasure. For after all, she alleged, José Manuel was a man of good sense and of judgment, had seen a goodly part of the world, and was no wet-behind-the-ears boy (those words wounded the *comadre*) unable to treat a young woman properly. The *comadre* lost heart completely at these last statements. What, however, could she do under the circumstances? She herself had confessed just a short while ago about the risk one runs at every moment of being unjust with one's fellow man and she could not without risk venture something against José Manuel, at least not on this occasion — all the more given how badly her first plot had turned out. She thus contented herself with repeating an observation that Dona Maria herself had made to her a short time ago, and she said, referring to Luisinha, "Well, the child is near the age for it! . . ."

"Yes," Dona Maria replied, "she is still a bit green, but that's not a big problem."

The *comadre* let her breath back out, for she saw that there was still time to emerge victorious.

X

The Dependant

S ome weeks passed in the following fashion: Leonardo, after all the ceremonies were performed, was declared a "dependant" attached to the household of Thomas of the Sé and remained comfortably ensconced there. Let no one wonder at the ease with which such things were done; in the time in which the events we are narrating took place, nothing was more common than for every house to have one, two, or at times more such dependants.

In some households these figures were very useful because the family derived great benefit from their services — we had occasion to give an example of this when we told the story of Leonardo's late godfather. In other instances, however — and these were the more frequent — the dependent, a confirmed lay-about, became a veritable parasite latched onto the family tree, partaking of its sap without helping it to yield fruit. And, what is more, he sometimes ended up killing it. And it is the case that, in spite of everything, if, on the one hand he was crushed under the weight of a thousand demands, if favors done were thrown up to him on every occasion, if the oldest son of the house, for example, took him for his amusement, or at the slightest and most justifiable complaint the parents leaped all over him taking the side of their own child, on the other hand whatever disturbance might arise in the house was also tolerated with martyrs' patience. The dependant became almost a king in his castle, proposing and disposing, punishing the slaves, reproving the family children, intervening, in short, in the most private of affairs.

In which of the two categories was our friend Leonardo, or would he soon come to be? Let the reader decide on the basis of what is about to occur.

Let us begin by observing that from the very beginning the two elder sisters had taken a decided liking to him, and that was the only point on which we can judge him moderately happy: While at every step he met resistance and opposition, he also encountered counterbalancing sympathy and favor. This amounted to half the battle won for any project he might formulate, any intention he might have, or any desire that might awaken within him. But, to be faithful to the law of countervailing forces, which law constantly weighed upon him, it must be noted that the particular project, intention, or desire that he had just happened to relate to a "certain someone" that had already incited a similar project, intention, and desire on the part of two other people—which is equivalent to saying, as we already have, that he had to contend with two difficulties.

Vidinha was a young woman as pretty as she was flighty and shallow: A breeze, no matter how soft, would make her take flight, another of similar nature would send her off again, and she would flit and flutter about in the direction that every breeze that passed over her was headed. That means, in plain language stripped of rhetorical blandishment, that she was a shameless flirt, as we say today, not to say a coquette, as they said back then. Therefore, Leonardo's first gallantries were by no means ill received, especially as he had now become much bolder, whether because the business with Luisinha had loosened his tongue or because his passion had grown stronger—the latter hypothesis going against the opinion of the ultra-romantics, who loudly trumpet so-called first love. May they learn from Leonardo's example how enduring it really is.

If one of Vidinha's male cousins, who we have said was at that time the one favored, had reason to rise up against Leonardo as his rival, the other, who we have said was the one scorned, had double the reason for doing the same. For, in addition to his brother, Leonardo was now appearing as a second contender, and the fury of one defending himself against two is—or doubtless should be—much greater than that of one who defends himself merely against another. Therefore, as soon as the symptoms of whatever there might be between Vidinha and our house guest began to appear, a war of two against one, or of one against two, was declared. At first it was deaf and dumb: A war of looks, of gestures, of slights, of ugly faces, of rudeness on the part of some to others; then, in correlation with Leonardo's advance, it went on to nasty words, taunts, and insinuations. One day it finally broke out into full-fledged abuse, into threats the size of the Tower of Babel. And the cause of this was that one of the cousins had surprised the happy Leonardo in flagrant enjoyment of a first fruit of love: An embrace he was exchanging with Vidinha in the backyard of the house.

"There you have it, auntie," the young man had said in a fury to Vidinha's mother, "that's what you get for letting a pair of legs into the house that don't belong to the family."

"Where, oh where is the fire breaking out?" said the old woman in a mocking tone, presuming it was all some foolishness on the young man's part, for he tended to exaggerate everything.

"Fire!" he retorted. "If he actually starts a fire, there won't be water to put it out . . . and mark what I say, if he's not starting a fire . . . he's as least gathering the wood!"

Vidinha, who was coming up just at that moment, broke in and talked for a straight half hour, hurling upon her two cousins (for the other one had also come in) a blistering catalinarian in which the word "aww" was repeated an enormous number of times. Leonardo had to defend himself as well, and he acquitted himself admirably. The two old women chimed in with the four, accompanied by the remaining two girls, who tossed in their own spoonfuls now and again as well.

It would be useless for us to attempt to reproduce each interlocutor's exact words; it would be more or less like trying to count the raindrops that fall in a storm. Only someone who has had occasion to be present can really evaluate what one of these family quarrels was like—and perhaps still is. Everyone talks at the same time, each trying to speak louder than all the others combined; no one seems to pay any attention to the excuses that are offered or to the recriminations advanced, and, minute by minute, each, growing hotter and hotter all the while, deems him- or herself more and more offended. Oaths cross in the air, threats crash into each other; no choice term is left behind in the dictionary but instead is trotted out for use. Some issues lead to others, and the others to yet others. Past, present, and future offenses are summoned up to be heaped upon adversaries' heads. In sum, everything is said and nothing is accomplished. The quarrel lasts many hours, at the end of which the combatants, *fagitatis sed non satiatis*, abandon the field, bitterer against one another now than they were at the beginning. And if by chance, the retreat having been sounded, someone should still dare to loose a final slur, the thing catches fire again and lasts a goodly time longer. Most of the time, it all remains in the realm of words.

This time, however, it did not turn out that way: One of the male cousins, who possessed a short fuse, advanced toward Leonardo after, as a combatant, having hurled a considerable insult his way; and, catching hold of him by the shirt collar, he gave him two resounding punches. Leonardo, who in this world feared only his father, fought back. The two old women and Vidinha, in trying to part them, succeeded only in tearing their clothes and adding to their rage; everyone else occupied themselves in beating on the walls and calling to the neighbors. The two scuffled for some time without either suffering any serious damage as a result, and they finally separated. Leonardo, upon seeing himself free of his adversary, kept trying to get out to the street; ever since his childhood, a kind of destiny like the Wandering Jew had borne down upon the unfortunate youngster. But the old women, who throughout the fracas had taken his side, would not hear of it; they proclaimed that they were in their own house and could run it as they chose. Leonardo insisted, despite this and despite protestations from Vidinha. At the very moment he was trying to open the street door, however, the *comadre* walked in through it.

"Well, thank God I've found you, Mr. stone-crazy."

Leonardo recoiled two steps. At that moment, just as had been the case since he ran out of his father's house, the idea had never passed through his mind that he had a godmother, a father, or any other relative in the world. There was a general reaction of surprise and curiosity in the group, for no one in the house knew the *comadre*.

The good woman had done so much digging that at last she had learned of the burrow wherein her godson had holed up—and she immediately took herself there. Having entered and spoken those initial words, she then intended to continue on to her godson with a great exhortation when, laying eyes on the two elder women, she decided that it would be better to address herself to them first. Indeed, she did so, and the three went into conference.

Betrayal

T he three old women conversed for a long time, not because there was much to say about what had just been going on but because the *comadre* had taken it into her head that in order to explain how much she was interested in her godson's return home it was necessary for her, going back into the distant past, to tell the boy's entire life story from its beginning, that of his mother, that of his father, and her own — which had been the longest of all. And because the two sisters took it into their heads that in order to assert that Leonardo was doing quite well where he was and that they would not consent to his leaving it was necessary to do what the godmother had just done: Tell the story of their lives and that of their entire family from times long past. Now as all these stories recounted from one party to another were full of episodes that were sometimes sentimental, sometimes gripping, sometimes gay, it happened during the conversation that among many chuckles of laughter some tears also flowed. There is nothing that works better to create and confirm friendship, even intimacy, than laughter and tears: Those who have once laughed together, and even more so those who have once cried together, find it easy to become friends. Indeed, by the end of the conversation, the three old women had come to feel an incredible degree of mutual esteem.

If this facility of expansiveness had not been accompanied by the great failing of ruptures and intrigues, it might have been one of the great virtues of the age. But the close relationships that were created in an hour of talk could be transformed into hatred in a moment of discord.

While the old women talked, the combatants calmed down, the storm passed, and if everything was not completely over it was at least for some while forgotten. Leonardo now found himself disposed to heed the entreaties of Vidinha and the other girls, who did not want him to leave the house for any reason whatsoever. The two defeated rivals seemed to resign themselves.

When the three women's conference ended, the *comadre* felt that the time had come for her to start her preaching to Leonardo, and she did so in these terms: "Young man of the three hundred demons, may the seraphim stand by you . . . you've got rocks instead of brains in that head of yours! The sun doesn't shine on another creature as stubborn as you! You're an idler; you've become a ne'er-do-well with no direction and no gumption, a burden to everyone in this life—"

"If you're talking about us," interrupted one of the old women, "let him stay right where he is, and he'll be fine."

"Nonsense, *senhora*! Why now he's off raising a rumpus in somebody else's house! He's just a fighting cock!"

"Aw, that's just stuff that boys and girls do; leave 'em alone and they'll work it out," retorted the old woman.

The childish ingenuousness of the old women of that day!

The *comadre* was going to proceed, but as she was interrupted at every step she decided it was easier to call the matter done. She withdrew, it being agreed that Leonardo would remain where he was.

Vidinha was extremely happy; the male cousins, however, grimaced, because they were not expecting that outcome. Once they saw that everything was going to go on as before, their resentment was rekindled. They uttered a few insinuations, at which the business threatened to catch fire anew, but they restrained themselves. One of them called the other aside, and they went into their own conference, though in secret. Nothing more natural: Theirs was a common enemy and they joined forces to combat him; after he was defeated, the issue would be decided between the two of them.

After this final conference, everything was definitively calmed, each person withdrawing to his or her own position, and many days passed in blessed peace. During those days, the bonds between Leonardo and Vidinha grew tighter and tighter. This is always the way of it: If you want us to bind ourselves closely to something, then make us suffer for its sake. The two of them had suffered for each other, and that was a powerful reason for them to fall more and more in love.

The *comadre* came regularly to see her godson and visit her new women friends. Everything, in short, seemed to be turning on its natural axis. The two male cousins, however, were plotting, and plotting at length. But no one could have guessed what they were up to.

Leonardo was leading the life of a complete idler, staying at home the whole blessed day without showing the slightest care about what was going on out in the world. His world consisted solely of the eyes, the smiles, and the coyness of Vidinha.

One day they organized an outing like the one that had precipitated Leonardo's acquaintanceship with the family. They planned to leave the city early in the morning and spend the whole day out in the country.

Everything was ready: baskets of food, mats, and other preparations. Vidinha had her guitar re-strung; all the usual participants were notified. At the appointed hour, they set out.

Anyone not as caught up in the pleasure of the outing as were its various participants might have noticed that now and again the two male cousins lagged behind the rest and whispered to each other as though they were plotting a conspiracy. But no one was paying any attention.

Just at daybreak they arrived at the designated spot. They had scarcely begun to lay out the breakfast when they saw emerge, nobody knew from exactly where, the tall, thin, severe, and sarcastic figure of our celebrated Major Vidigal. A sense of unease ran through them all, save for the male cousins, who exchanged a look of recognition and of triumph. Vidinha's eyes fell instinctively upon Leonardo.

Major Vidigal allowed the initial moment of shock to subside and then, smiling, said in his usual slow voice: "Don't be afraid of me; I don't eat children and I don't go around ruining other people's pleasures. I just want to know which one of you is friend Leonardo."

At that Vidinha looked as if she were going to cry. Leonardo stood up without knowing how he managed to do so and said, trembling, "I am he . . ."

"Well look at that," Vidigal answered in a mocking tone, "I would never have guessed! . . . Now, my friends, don't be afraid; the case isn't all that serious. One partier less on a picnic is practically no change at all. This friend is coming with us. If he can, he'll be back in a while—but I don't think it'll be in time to finish up the party with you."

"Oh my God! But why? What harm has he done?"

"He hasn't done—and doesn't do—anything. It's precisely because he doesn't do anything that this is happening to him. Take him, grenadier." And one of the grenadiers who accompanied the major led Leonardo away.

Vidigal followed them tranquilly, at a measured pace, saying politely, "Good-bye, folks."

Vidinha burst into tears, crying, "He was betrayed!"

"He was betrayed!" everyone repeated, except for the two male cousins.

The party broke up.

XII

José Manuel's Complete Triumph

It was a Saturday afternoon. In Dona Maria's house there was intense activity: The slave-children and other slaves were hurrying in and out; the drawing room was being dusted; the chairs were being arranged; there was much running, talking, shouting.

Out of her usual practice, the lady of the house was wearing an elegant dress of fine muslin embroidered in silver, with a very low bodice and puff sleeves. Be it said in passing that the silver of the embroidery had grown tarnished and the rest of the dress somewhat soiled. Dona Maria was also wearing an outlandishly high hairdo, a heavy pair of chrysolite earrings in her ears, and ten or a dozen rings of various sizes and designs on her fingers.

Luisinha also was wearing a dress that anyone less experienced on the topic would have suspected was the legitimate offspring of her aunt's; she wore a headdress of white plumes and a rosary with very thick gold beads around her waist.

The two, thus attired, had just entered from the dressing room when a carriage was heard coming up and stopping at the door of the house. Luisinha trembled; Dona Maria raised her handkerchief to her eyes, and shortly took it away moist with tears. "The carriage is here," called one of the slave-children, who had been stationed as lookout at the window.

The carriage was formidable, a monstrous leather mechanism bobbing heavily atop four huge wheels. It did not seem a very new thing; indeed, given an additional ten years of life it might very well have figured in the number of the unfortunate earthquake remains of which the poet speaks. No sooner had this machine stopped at the door than the sound of another was heard, which came to a halt beside the first. What we have said with regard to the apparel of Dona Maria and her niece can perfectly well be applied to the two vehicles: the second seemed the legitimate offspring of the first.

Out of that second to arrive stepped José Manuel. He entered Dona Maria's house, she coming to receive him at the door.

It goes without saying that the entire neighborhood was at the windows and watched all that movement with eyes bulging with the most unbridled curiosity.

José Manuel was dressed in a black silk dress coat and breeches of the same cloth and color; he wore black stockings as well and low-cut shoes adorned with enormous silver buckles, a smallsword, and a top hat. Two friends similarly attired accompanied him.

José Manuel wore an air that mixed compunction with triumph, and he outdid himself in the ceremony he used with Dona Maria.

After all this, does the reader still need us to state that Dona Maria's niece was marrying José Manuel that afternoon?

The moment arrived for their departure. Luisinha, led by Dona Maria, who was serving as her godmother, embarked in one of those refugees from Noah's Ark that we have called a carriage. José Manuel, accompanied by the man who was to serve as his godfather, did the same, and they hurriedly departed for the church. They did well to depart quickly, because if they had delayed some minutes longer they ran the risk of being completely devoured by the neighbors' eyes.

Hardly had the noise of the carriages ceased when these latter began a contentious chatter, a small sample of which we here present.

"*Senhora*," said one individual who lived near Dona Maria's house to another woman who lived across the street, "that bridegroom may well be all right, but I wouldn't give a jot for that face of his."

"And what about the bride?" responded the other. "I'm not fond of such a skinny look."

"And what happened to Leonardo's boy? Did he end up out in the cold?"

"It looks that way. This one won out because he's a practiced conniver."

"If the old woman leaves everything to the niece, it's not a bad match for him—"

"You said it! Why, didn't you know that her late husband was a man who traveled to India?"

They went on in the same tone until the carriages returned.

Let us now give the reader some explanation of José Manuel's triumph.

After the prayer master's good work, of which the readers have previously been informed, José Manuel became completely rehabilitated in Dona Maria's eyes. He once again frequented the house and little by little built a solid footing. One unexpected occurrence helped him most efficaciously. The executor of Dona Maria's late brother, Luisinha's father, who, as the readers have perhaps not forgotten, had once been engaged in a lawsuit with Dona Maria over the girl, suddenly came up with a new suit relative to some detail or other in the will, and Dona Maria had to enter into legal battle with him again. This coincided with the unexpected death of Dona Maria's lawyer. José Manuel offered to take charge of the case, and he orchestrated everything with such skill that in a short time—something no lawyer could have done—he had won the suit for Dona Maria.

Now the readers must be mindful of Dona Maria's mania for lawsuits. She would throw herself into them with a will, and such was the zeal she expended on the most insignificant judicial question, that she seemed to have her very life at stake in such cases. Hence may the satisfaction that she would have had on the day of her victory be appreciated—as well as the depth of her obligation to the man who had brought her that victory.

José Manuel took full advantage of this and, on the day he came to read Dona Maria the final decision in resolution of the case in her favor, he asked for her niece's hand, which was promised him without any great compunction.

On that occasion Luisinha was in one of the periods of depression so common in young people, and especially young women who are still moving along that flower-strewn path running from age thirteen to age twenty-five, when loneliness weighs heavily upon them.

Now, as all those reading me know, Leonardo had abandoned Luisinha; she therefore accepted her aunt's disposition with indifference.

XIII

Escape

Let us leave the newlyweds to the tranquil enjoyment of their honeymoon. Let us leave Dona Maria to overflow both with affection and counsel for her niece, who received them with indifference, and also with attentions to José Manuel, whose head had suddenly been changed into an entire arithmetical system—all figures, all sums, all multiplications. And let us return to find out what became of Leonardo, whom we left at the moment when he had been torn by Vidigal from the arms of love and luxury.

Vidigal had placed the youngster up in front of himself at the side of a grenadier, and he was marching a few paces behind. As they marched, the grenadier attempted to strike up a conversation, but he did not respond, seemingly engrossed in grave cogitation.

Someone very attentive might have noticed that Leonardo sometimes seemed to quicken the pace, albeit very slightly, while at other times he slowed it, that from time to time his eyes and his head turned, almost imperceptibly, to the left or to the right. Vidigal, whom none of this escaped, in all of those occasions found a pretext to give a sign of his presence; he would cough, tread more heavily, drag on the ground the parasol he always carried with him, like one who wished to say in response to Leonardo's innermost thoughts: "Take heed! I am here." And Leonardo thoroughly understood every bit of this; his lips contracted with anger and impatience. Yet for all that he had not abandoned his inclination: He was planning to make a break for it. He suspected that he was bound for the guardhouse, and in his mind he begged his gods to add many leagues to the length of the streets through which he would have to pass. When he glimpsed a street corner appear in the distance, he would say to himself: "This is it! I'll make a break up there and shag for it." But when the corner approached Vidigal would find something to say to the grenadier, and that corner would pass by. If a passageway opened up to the right or to the left, he would think to himself: "I'll head down into there and get away." But at the moment when he was going to make the final decision, he thought he could feel Vidigal's hand grab him by the jacket collar, and he shrank away from it. It was not the grenadiers that put fear into him; never in all the plans of escape that then passed through his head did he ever take them into account. But Vidigal, the cruel major, was the constant term in his calculations.

The poor youth, during those inner struggles, sweated more than he did on the day he made his first declaration of love to Luisinha. There had been only one other situation in his life that resembled the one in which he now found himself, and that was the one he went through as a child, that half-second that it took him to traverse the air on the wings of that formidable kick his father had fetched him.

Suddenly a circumstance came to his aid. We know not from what cause, a great outcry was heard along the street: shouts, whistles, and the sound of running. Leonardo experienced a kind of vertigo: His ears buzzed, his sight grew dim, and—giving the grenadier beside him a shove—he broke into flight. Vidigal gave a leap and reached his arm out to catch him but barely brushed his back with his fingertips. The youth had calculated well: Vidigal had been distracted by the noise on the street, and he had taken advantage of the occasion. Vidigal and the grenadiers immediately set out in pursuit. Leonardo hightailed it up the first open passageway he came across; his pursuers promptly turned in after him, and they ran up the first flight of stairs in a body. Hardly had they made the turn and begun climbing the second flight when the curtains of a sedan-chair, which had been standing at the entrance and which they had passed by, flew open, and Leonardo bolted out of it and gained the street in a bound. Upon entering and coming across that refuge, he had hidden inside; the grenadiers and Vidigal had not paid attention to it in the haste with which they had entered, and that had represented his salvation.

It is impossible to describe what Leonardo felt when he had peeked between the curtains of the sedan-chair and saw them pass by and begin to climb the stairs. It was a quick succession of cold and heat, of shaking and immobility, of fear and courage. That paternal kick came to his memory once again; it was the standard of comparison for all his sufferings.

While Vidigal and the grenadiers scoured the house they had entered, Leonardo was putting distance between them and in four jumps found himself back at Vidinha's house, where she greeted him with a hug saying, "Aww! Here he is!"

A ray of joy brightened all countenances save those of the two rival brothers, who were horribly disappointed. The two old women took back off the mantillas they had just put on to go out and see what they could do about the matter. Leonardo's presence was like a beneficent aura dispelling the clouds of a heavy storm that, having begun to roar with the words "he was betrayed" when Leonardo was arrested, had come to beat fully upon the house and promised to last for a good long time.

Vidinha, having first exchanged a few nasty remarks with her male cousins about Leonardo's arrest, had decided to leave off with half-measures and she went straight after them—with, as the saying goes, four rocks in her hand—blaming them for what had just occurred.

They denied any knowledge of it and got into an argument with her. At first the two old women both took Vidinha's side, but after the latter had hurled three or four exceedingly strong words at her cousins, her aunt took offense and moved to her two sons' side. The other woman, Vidinha's mother, protested her sister's partiality and, accompanied by the rest of the group, reinforced Vidinha's position. With the two camps thus divided up and set in opposition to each other, with formidable champions on each part, it is easy to foresee what would have happened had Leonardo not arrived so precisely in time to calm the whole matter down.

Overcome with the joy of seeing himself free, he did not even take the time to remonstrate against his enemies; he knew with certainty who had instigated what had been done to him, for he had found that out from the conversation that the grenadier had tried to strike up with him.

Major Vidigal hit the ceiling about the case: Never before had a lone miscreant upon whom he had laid hands ever escaped, and then this individual had come along to give him a comeuppance, to offend him in his vanity as a good police commandant, and to demean him in the eyes of his own grenadiers. Anyone who put something over on Major Vidigal, by whatever means, would end up under his protection and would find him always on his side. If Leonardo had not run away but had fanagled his release some other way, Vidigal might even have become his friend in the end. But having been left in a bad light, the major would now regard him as his inveterate enemy until he could get completely even with him.

It is clear, then, that Leonardo's fortunes always redounded to his harm. It was really a considerable handicap in those days to have Major Vidigal as an enemy, especially when, like Leonardo, one led so "normal" and so "upright" a life.

We shall now see what took place in the house that Vidigal entered with his grenadiers in search of Leonardo.

X I V

Vidigal Baffled

Major Vidigal, seeing that he had been bested, let out a bellow, and, as we have previously intimated to the readers, promised himself that he would exact serious revenge from Leonardo.

"Now," he said to himself, "to think that I spend my time in this sort of life, wracking my brain thinking up ways to chase down every good-for-nothing idling around this city; succeeding—at the cost of many days' labor, many nights passed without shutting my eyes, much running, and a great deal of work—in making myself feared and respected by those who fear and respect no one else, the bums and the hoodlums. And now, after all that, to see a little ruffian show me up, shame me in front of these soldiers and all these people! Now there is no urchin around who, when he hears about this, isn't going to be laughing at me and isn't counting on being able to do the same thing to me!"

The major was right: He was in fact being laughed at, and the first to do it were the grenadiers. In spite of the fact that, slaves to discipline, they had expended the most sincere efforts to aid him, and also in spite of the fact that some of the fame from the major's deeds redounded upon them, they nonetheless found what had just happened rather funny, for they knew Vidigal's vanity well and saw the puzzled look left on his face in the end. Then, no sooner had the major set foot back across the threshold of the house at which Leonardo had escaped when a huge crowd that had witnessed it all broke into uproarious laughter.

"Well, Major," said one of those in the crowd, "this time

> The little bird has flown
> And left its feathers in my hand."

"Sir Major," said another, "why don't you check your pockets?"

"Inside your cap," added another.

"Behind the door," yet another chimed in.

And a chorus of laughter accompanied each of these pieces of advice.

"There's the pest, inside the sedan-chair!" someone suddenly called out.

Vidigal, as though instinctively, raced to the sedan-chair and threw back its curtains. On that occasion the laughter was Homeric. The major then understood the means Leonardo had used to escape him and he emitted a prolonged "ah." He finally withdrew, humiliated and ruminating plans for his own rehabilitation.

"If those young men from the Conceição," he said to himself, "who brought that scoundrel to my attention, had told me the sort of person he was, I wouldn't have gone through this kind of shame."

In these words the readers can see that the charges made by Vidinha against her cousins had more than considerable merit to them. In fact, what had happened was the result of the bargain that, for the reason that the reader well knows, the two rivals had struck on the day of the quarrel: They had betrayed Leonardo. They had gone to see Vidigal and, without needing to lie, made up a pretty bed for Leonardo to lie in: He was a man with no trade or training living at others' expense, having barged into a house headed by two old women who had not learned well enough the lessons of experience, and moreover was stealing the love of their cousin away from the two of them.

Vidigal's eyes had widened at that story and he had been very grateful to the two youths for the information that they had brought him. This was one more pennant he would add to the triumphs his police work had earned him. The first attempt, however, cost him dearly indeed.

Here, more or less, are the reflections in which the major was engrossed. Nothing would please him more than, on some day when it would be least expected, to go to the two old women's house with an escort of grenadiers, surround it, and catch Leonardo before he could escape. This, however, was repugnant to his wounded pride. It is true that he had often had recourse to such means, but that had been to catch inveterate criminals known to be such. He did not wish, therefore, to use that means to catch a novice who was just starting out in that calling. No, that he would not do; he wouldn't surround the house, and furthermore he did not want any aid whatsoever from the grenadiers. He swore to himself that he alone, with no one's assistance, would lay hands on Leonardo.

Vidigal was going into the guardhouse, which was his destination after his defeat, when he suddenly felt his legs being grabbed hold of. He saw at his feet a woman in a mantilla, crying, sobbing loudly, a handkerchief to her face.

"What is this, *senhora*? Leave me be. Today must really be my unlucky day."

The only response was a continuation of the sobbing.

"*Senhora*, are you going to turn loose my legs or not? I don't like wailers for hire . . . understand?"

Still sobbing.

"Now this is really fine. . . . If someone you know has died, go grieve over the bed; that's the warm spot."

The lament redoubled.

"May three hundred devils come to my aid! Where is this going to end? This woman will end up pulling me over!"

By now there were many people gathered round the doorway. After a little time was finally passed in silence, as the major was ready to use some harsh measure to get himself free of the weeper, she raised her head and, taking the handkerchief away from her face, exclaimed through her tears: "Major, sir, let him go, let my godson go; let him go, let the poor boy go; he hasn't a lick of sense, I know, but . . ."

And, very purposefully, the sobbing choked off her words.

It was the *comadre*, who, having heard about her godson's arrest, had come for the purpose of pouring out those tears on his behalf, unaware of the fact that he had escaped. The scene produced the expectable effect. The grenadiers, every time the *comadre* cried "let him go, let him go," dissolved in laughter. And, as they had explained everything out of the corners of their mouths to the other bystanders, the latter accompanied them in their laughter. The major took all of this as an ironic joke that the evil genius of crime and vagrancy was playing on him: in order for him to get free of the *comadre*, who would not release her hold on his knees, he would have to declare out of his own mouth in front of all these people that Leonardo had got away! He so declared—and then hurried away from all those eyes, in each of which he could descry an insult.

The *comadre*, as soon as she heard the declaration, attempted to withdraw, and she too could not help but find humor in the affair.

X V

Spilled Broth

The *comadre*, leaving the major given over to his shame, headed immediately for the house where Leonardo was to be found, to congratulate him and tell him of the despair into which his escape had plunged Vidigal. Leonardo was relying on that and was not surprised, but Vidinha and the two old women, amid many curses and imprecations, chuckled for a long time at the major's expense. The *comadre*, as was her wont, took advantage of the opportunity and, after wearing down of talk about the major, delivered a sermon to Leonardo in which, aside from a few exaggerations, there was a great fund of truth—so much so that even Vidinha admitted that she was right on many matters. The sermon's theme was the need for Leonardo to find some employment, to abandon the life he was leading which, pleasant though it might be, was nonetheless susceptible to such crises as the one that had just arisen. The sanction of all the laws that the preacher sought to impress upon her listener was to be found in the clutches of Vidigal. "In the final analysis," she said at the end of each thought, "you're going to fall into his grasp; and then you'll find a uniform across your back."

The notion of the uniform had a devastating effect on Leonardo's spirit; to be a soldier was at that time—and perhaps still is today—the worst thing that could befall a man. He thus promised sincerely that he would change his ways and try to find a position where he would be protected from any police whim coming from the terrible major. Nevertheless, finding a job for someone who had never given a thought to such a thing up to a certain age, and to do so right away, was not the easiest of tasks.

Meanwhile, the *comadre*'s energy translated into activity, and a few days later she returned very happy and informed Leonardo that she had found him an excellent position that would prepare him—as she thought—for a grand future and put him perfectly beyond the reach of Vidigal's ire. The position was that of servant in the royal pantries. Setting aside the noun "pantries" and concentrating only on the adjective "royal," all those concerned and Leonardo himself were enthralled with the *comadre*'s find. Employee of the royal household?! Oh, that was nothing to turn up one's nose at! And in the pantries! That inexhaustible source, so bountiful, so rich! . . . The *comadre*'s proposal was accepted without a single second thought on anyone's part.

How the *comadre* had been able to arrange such a thing for her godson is something that should be of little concern to us. Within a few days, Leonardo found himself installed in his post, very content and full of himself.

The major, who had not lost sight of him, learned of these steps and bit his lips in rage when he saw him so well quartered. Only by leaving the kind of life he had been living could Leonardo undercut the major's pretexts for laying his hands on him some day soon.

"I wonder if he is really changing," asked the major contemplatively. "If he does change I lose my revenge. But—and this hope heartened him—he doesn't have the look of one who is born to change."

The major was right: Leonardo did not seem born to change. During his first days of service everything went wonderfully; only someone with bad faith would have noticed a certain unaccustomed bounty in the pantry of Vidinha's house, but that was nothing to be concerned about.

Leonardo, however, had apparently received from his father the fate that misfortunes always came to him through the vagaries of his heart. In the patio of the royal pantries there lived a lackey in company with a girl who looked after his quarters. The girl was pretty and the lackey an absolute lout cut from the most grotesque of molds. The girl inspired the compassion of anyone who happened to see her in the hands of such a possessor. Leonardo, whose heart was full of compassion, felt for the girl, as did everyone. And let us hasten to add that that sentiment was so sincere that it could not fail to awaken the sincerest gratitude in its object as well. The person who receipted for the compassion of one and the gratitude of the other was the lackey.

Back home, Vidinha began to wonder at the new employee's dedication to his duty and to note that his behavior toward her had dwindled a touch in intensity.

One day the lackey had gone out in service; no one was expecting him back soon; it was eleven o'clock in the morning. Exiting through one of the thousands of passageways that exist in the royal pantries, Leonardo had gone to the lackey's quarters. Let no one, however, think for a moment that he went for illicit purposes. To the contrary, it was for the very laudable purpose of taking the poor girl a porringer of the broth a portion of which had just shortly before been sent up to the king. . . . A mere gift from an employee in the royal pantries. Nothing censurable there. It would, however, be censurable if the recipient of such a gift did not endeavor to repay it with some extreme of civility: the girl, therefore, invited Leonardo to help her drink the broth. And how rude would he have been if he had not accepted so kind an offer? He accepted.

Suddenly, the opening of a door was heard. The girl, who had the porringer in her hand, trembled and the broth spilled.

The lackey, who had arrived unexpectedly, was the cause of all this. Leonardo raced precipitously along the shortest route he could find, doubtless in search of another porringer of broth, since the first one had been spilled. The lackey was running too—after him—doubtless to ask him this time to bring enough so that a third might share as well.

The outcome of it all was that shortly thereafter there could be heard inside the noise of breaking crockery, furniture being thrown to the floor, yells, and general shouting. Then Leonardo was seen crossing the patio of the pantries at a run, and the lackey was seen going back to his quarters with the gold braid torn off his livery, which also had one tail missing.

The next day, Leonardo was dismissed from the royal pantries.

Jealousy

By the following day Vidigal knew every detail of all that had happened to Leonardo, and he put himself on the alert, since the opportunity was ripe.

Leonardo had entered the royal pantries with his left foot first. The storm he had weathered there was nothing in comparison with the one that came down upon his head when the true cause of his dismissal was learned at home.

It is a great misfortune when the woman whom we love does not return that love, but it is also no small mischance when we fall into the hands of a woman who takes it into her head to love us truly. Leonardo could provide testimony to the latter truth. Vidinha was jealous in the highest degree. Now women possess an infinite number of ways of manifesting that sentiment. Some go into a corner and cry, and they elegantly cry floods of tears there; this is quite comfortable for whoever has to tolerate them. Others resort to reprisals, and in this case they burst out uncontrolledly against whomever it might be; this method is, of course, more agreeable for themselves. Others neither resort to the slightest reprisal nor spill a tear, but for the period of a week or two, from the first light of dawn to the fall of night, they mutter an entire calendar of lamentations in which figure their father, their mother, their relatives and friends, their *compadre*, their *comadre*, their dowry, their sons and daughters, and everything else of that sort—this without stopping for a single instant, without a second of rest, in such a way as to leave inside the head of the wretch who has to listen an eternal gabbling capable of melting a brain of stone. Others decide that they should affect scorn and indifference; they become amusing, and it is funny to watch them. Finally, still others allow themselves to be overcome by an unbridled and irrepressible fury; they curse, they blaspheme, they break up household implements, tear their clothes, beat the slaves and the children, and torment the neighbors; this is the worst of all the manifestations, the one that drives us to the most thorough desperation, the least economical and also the most fruitless. Vidinha fit in this last category.

As we were just saying, then, scarcely had the true cause of Leonardo's dismissal been understood when a storm broke that will have its equal only in the cataclysm that is to precede the annihilation of the globe. After screaming, crying, cursing, blaspheming, threatening, ripping, breaking, and destroying, Vidinha paused for an instant, concentrated, meditated, and then, as though taking a major resolution: "Mother," she said to one of the old women, "I want your mantilla."

"My dear daughter," the old woman responded, "what kind of strangeness is this? Where could you be going with a mantilla on now?"

"I know where I'm going—I want your mantilla, I said—I want your mantilla."

They all gathered around Vidinha, perplexed by that resolution. Leonardo was seated—or, rather, huddled—in a corner, withdrawn and quiet.

"I want your mantilla, mother; I want it, and I want—"

"But where will you be going, girl? . . . My God! . . . Something's come over you . . ."

"I am going to the royal pantries."

"By the Heavens! . . ."

"I am going—What do I care if it's the king's house? I am going—I'm going to find that lackey—And I'm going to ask him a couple of questions—And either the Baby Jesus isn't the son of the Virgin or this day there's not going to be one thing left standing in those pantries."

"What foolishness, girl. . . . What lunacy! . . ."

The two male cousins laughed to themselves about what was going on.

There is nothing more eminently prosaic than a furious woman. Everything in Vidinha that was coyness, that was allure, that was voluptuousness had disappeared; she was ugly, even repugnant. No one could dissuade her from her purpose; she proceeded to put on the mantilla and was getting ready to leave; entreaties, tears, nothing could restrain her.

Leonardo saw that the situation was going from bad to worse and, having remained silent until then, decided to beg Vidinha as well not to go. But, as the saying goes, the revision was worse than the sonnet. "Aww," replied Vidinha, "that woman must really be pretty. Aww, you think I'm not going to go? It figures—just because you ask? Aww."

And she went.

Night was beginning to fall.

The members of the household were all greatly concerned; no one knew what ought to be done. Leonardo decided to go along with Vidinha, to see if he could dissuade her along the way.

Vidinha was walking so fast that at first Leonardo almost lost her from view. He finally caught up to her and started pleading with her to turn back, making the finest of promises to engage in better behavior from then on and give her no further reason for displeasure. Vidinha, however, paid no attention to anything and kept right on walking. Leonardo resorted to threats; Vidinha quickened her pace. He returned again to pleading; Vidinha kept right on walking.

They had now reached the Palace Square. Vidinha, almost at a run, left Leonardo a few yards behind, went in the entrance to the pantries well before him, and disappeared from view. Leonardo stopped for an instant to decide whether he should go in as well or not. He finally decided to go in. Just as he was crossing the threshold, he suddenly wheeled about and tried to run back the other way. A lean but strong hand latched on to him, securing him by the jacket collar. It was the hand of Major Vidigal, whom he had run up against as he entered and from whom he was trying to flee. Seeing that all efforts would be useless, since there were guards nearby, Leonardo resigned himself. The major looked at him, laughing a malign little laugh, and merely said to him, very deliberately and calmly, "Now let's go."

Leonardo understood very well the meaning of those three words, and off he marched, at the major's side, in the direction the latter indicated.

X V I I

Straw Fire

Let us leave Leonardo bound for his destiny in the company of Major Vidigal and see what took place in the royal pantries after his arrest. Vidinha inquired here, inquired there, and then rushed like a bolt of lightning to the lackey's quarters. The "broth" girl, caught unprepared on this occasion, was quite startled at the arrival of Vidinha, who, recognizing instinctively that here was the cause of her misfortunes, tossed her mantilla over a chair and began advancing upon the other. "I've come here," she said, "to tell you right to your face that you are a creature with no feelings—"

The girl, unable to grasp any meaning in all this, was dumbfounded, not knowing what to say in reply.

Vidinha went on, "You've no feelings, I say, and no one's going to tell me otherwise."

"What the . . . What the devil kind of a thing is this?" bellowed a stentorian voice. It was the lackey, who, home at the time and having heard Vidinha's first two diatribes, came in to see what was going on.

However arrogant the lackey's voice might have been and however intimidating his almost Herculean figure, Vidinha did not retreat a single step, did not undo a single wrinkle in her forehead. Instead, she seemed to signal that his presence there favored her intentions—so much so that, now addressing him in turn, she went on in the following manner: "You're a man I don't even know why wears a beard on his face—"

The shock and also the whole look of Vidinha, her face distorted with rage, somewhat disarmed him, and he responded more tamely, "Well, young lady, did you come here just to say all these pretty things, or what brought you here?"

"Now what do you suppose brought me here?" answered Vidinha in a mocking tone, shooting a meaningful glare at the third person in the scene. "Now what could it be? Aww! I just came to see if I could get a little broth to drink."

The lackey's girl turned pale. His eyes widened and he nodded his head as if to say "Now I understand!" And his anger immediately started to rise at the recollection of that event which his companion's docility and perhaps his own temperament had made him forget. Vidinha, however, in order to say those last words, had relaxed her own countenance a bit and had regained a great deal of the charms theretofore disfigured by rage. Moreover, on pronouncing the habitual "Aww!" she had disclosed a slight smile, revealing her magnificent teeth. The lackey apparently belonged to the Leonardo clan: He mellowed on the spot and was left with sense enough only to smile and to respond, in a disconcerted tone, "there, there."

"'There, there'," Vidinha repeated, "so he says 'there, there'? Aww! Must not need to have a drop of shame; these two creatures were made for each other. God made them and the devil brought them together. One drinks broth and the other says 'there, there'."

And she grabbed up her mantilla and prepared to leave.

It had all amounted to a straw fire. She had expected to encounter answers of conviction to her charges and under that presumption had thought of a thousand plans involving attack, defense, screaming, hitting, arrest, and so on. But nothing like that had taken place, and, without knowing exactly why, she found herself somewhat relieved, almost satisfied. She fired some more volleys at the two; she explained who she was; but she did not say what she wanted. At last, without doing anything more, she went out, saying "Ah! Did they imagine that it'd be left like this? At least I gave them a few words but good ones . . ."

A woman's heart is like that: It seems to be made of straw, flaming up so easily, producing a lot of smoke, but in five minutes it's all ash that the slightest breeze can pick up and scatter.

The lackey, as soon as Vidinha had gone, rather than break into a tirade against his companion as she, pale and trembling, expected, showed himself quite calm and, on the pretext of an errand, also exited posthaste. He was turning over in his mind a plan the realization of which would, as they say, take a good thing and make it even better. Vidinha had enchanted him; Leonardo had wronged him. To win even a tiny portion of Vidinha's affection would be simultaneously to avenge himself upon Leonardo and see his desires triumph. However impossible the matter might seem, he did not for all that shrink from it; he was a patient and tenacious person.

Reaching the entrance to the royal pantries, he inquired of the sentinel the direction Vidinha had taken, went off in the same direction, and soon caught up to her. He followed her at a distance to find out where she lived, and he saw her go into her house.

XVIII

Reprisals

When Vidinha arrived home she found the whole family still in great shock and confusion at the lunacy in which she had engaged. When they saw her come in, the two old women threw themselves upon her and covered her with hugs and kisses and tears. But she was still under the influence of the violent emotions through which she had just passed and was unable to respond to those demonstrations of affection: She dropped onto a bench and spent some time in silence, not giving answers to the thousand questions that were addressed to her. That silence further intensified the family's anxiety.

She finally made up her mind to break it, exclaiming: "They thought the whole business would just stay that way? They were wrong . . . Aww! . . . I want them to know what I'm about . . ."

"So, girl, you went and did something stupid . . ."

"Stupid? . . . Aww . . . I did what any woman with blood in her veins would do. . . . And now get him over here; we've still got an account to settle."

"That's true, but he still hasn't come back. . . . He's had time, since he left right after you did, trying to catch you . . ."

"That's right," seconded Vidinha with a certain fright in her voice. "He didn't come into the pantry basement, and when I came back out I didn't see him . . ."

"I hope nothing's happened to him! The major swore! . . ."

"The major!" they all repeated with signs of the most visible fright.

And confusion broke out anew in the house, because, as the readers will have noticed, despite the unsavory things that Leonardo had caused the family, everyone there, except the two rival male cousins, was in fact extremely fond of him. To ask either one of the male cousins to go out looking for him was something that no one even dreamed of, so sure were they that they would refuse. They therefore had to wait for that former sacristan of the Sé to come in from the street before the proper actions could be taken.

The readers are perhaps surprised that in all that has happened in the home of Vidinha's family we have not spoken of this last figure. We have done so purposely, to demonstrate that he had taken a part in none of it. The distant and primordial cause of all these occurrences—for it was as the result of his friendship that Leonardo joined the family—he had considered himself most fortunate that no inculpations had fallen upon his head, against which he could defend himself only with difficulty. A man of tact, he had preserved an absolutely neutral position for himself in all the squabbles. Such, then, was the cause of our silence about him.

Unfortunately, that night he came back later than usual, and when he arrived there was no longer time to do anything. The whole family had spent the night in the highest anxiety, their hopes of seeing Leonardo arrive at any moment having been completely banished after a certain hour. No one doubted any longer that something had happened to him, and, in the frightening pictures that each imagined, the figure of Major Vidigal always appeared in the foreground. Nor did anyone doubt that in whatever it was that had happened to Leonardo the major had perforce played an active and important, if not principal, role.

Thus at dawn the next day the first place they sent to in order to find out about him was the guardhouse. But to their general surprise, he was not to be found there, nor was there news of him from that quarter. They looked for him in various other places, but found out nothing: neither news nor messages.

It occurred to Vidinha that they should go get the *comadre* and inform her of all that had taken place. The poor woman, who knew nothing about any of it, put her hands to her head. "That boy was born on an ill-starred day," she said, "or it's something that's been cast upon him. There's no other answer . . ." And she soon set out to hunt for her godson.

All hopes were pinned on the *comadre*; no one doubted that once she set out on the streets Leonardo's whereabouts would soon be discovered. They were all mistaken, for not even the *comadre* was able to find him, so adroitly had the major covered his tracks. They spent many days in complete ignorance of his fate, and suspicions thus began to arise that he might himself have had an interest in hiding out and that that was the reason they had not yet discovered him. Those suspicions took shape, and a certain indignation at such a tactic began to surface within the family. That indignation grew and suddenly took on the proportions of an intense hatred, even on the part of the two old women.

If what they believed were indeed the case, there could be no blacker ingratitude than that of Leonardo toward those people who had so generously taken him in. In the invectives regularly launched against him, Vidinha always led off, and she had cause to do so: Besides having the same complaints against him as the others, she had as well the spite of love betrayed. In certain hearts love is like that: All its tenderness, its dedication, its faithfulness vanishes after certain revelations and is transformed into an implacable hatred.

One strange thing that Vidinha had noticed ever since she had gone to the pantries was that not a single day passed on which she did not see the lackey at least twice. She had pointed him out to the family, and all of them now knew him too. At first it bothered her, and all the more so because he never once passed by without taking off his hat with a smile on his face. It seemed to her outright proof of a glaring shamelessness. Later she began to suspect that the constant passing-by and the compliments must necessarily have an explanation.

It happened that that one of the old women who was Vidinha's mother confessed that she had not found the lackey bad-looking, and that opinion began to circulate through the family. One day when one of the old women was at the window with Vidinha as the lackey passed by, she said between her teeth and as though indifferent, "If I was the person involved, I know what I'd do—"

Vidinha, while she did not ask the old woman to explain her words, nonetheless did not fail to give them consideration and to mull them over for some time.

On the next day the same old woman called her to the window at the same time as the previous day, and the lackey went by and paid his compliment as always. On that occasion the old woman said, as a supplement to yesterday's thought, "Well, I'd leave that Leonardo out in the cold, and it'd be a good job too since it'd get two birds with one stone—him and her."

Reading the old woman's private thoughts with our storyteller's freedom, we can tell the reader who may not have guessed as much that the "her" referred to the girl with the broth. With that explanation, even the least perspicacious will doubtless understand what the old woman meant by leaving Leonardo "out in the cold."

Vidinha, who had been blessed with no little intelligence, understood it all exceedingly well—and with no less facility, let us inform the readers, as the old woman's way of thinking perchance corresponded to her own. Several more hints from the old woman followed thereafter, and Vidinha finally came to a decision.

We shall spare the readers certain of the details and merely report that the outcome of all of this was that a few days later the lackey was to be seen in Vidinha's house paying the family a visit! The visits continued, and soon there could be heard through the neighborhood a rumor that contained as much malevolence as it did truth.

Things settled down more or less as follows: Peace had been restored to the family. I know not who proposed that the reestablishment of calm and the "new fortunes" be solemnized by an outing into the country, but that idea was acted upon. By a curious twist of fate they chose as the location for their picnic the Cajueiros, the very place where the family had met Leonardo.

The lackey had been invited; he could not have been dealt with otherwise, since he was one of the reasons for the celebration. Unfortunately, however, he had one defect: Under normal circumstances he was able to drink moderately, but when he had reason to be happy he had the habit of doubling his dose; and when that happened he turned into a hell-raiser and a bully. Hence it came to pass that in the middle of the party, at mealtime, he took offense—at what we know not—and began by grabbing the corners of the mat that was serving as the table and sending dishes, bottles, glasses, and everything else flying over the guests' heads. The two male cousins tried to restrain him, but they were unable to do so; Vidinha broke into tears; the two old women swore; some people tried to restore the peace while others added to the disorder. As a result, an infernal uproar reigned.

When they least expected, out of the brush stepped Major Vidigal, closing a circle of grenadiers that flanked him on his left and on his right and surrounded the entire party.

"Seize that man, grenadier," said the major to one of his soldiers, pointing to the lackey, who, wobbling on his feet, held in one hand a basket in which the flour had been brought and in the other a bottle with which he was threatening all those around.

The grenadier hesitated at the major's order; the entire family, coming together in unison, let out a cry of alarm directed to the soldier.

"Well?" the major replied, seeing the hesitation.

The grenadier took a step toward the lackey.

"Take it easy with the crockery, buddy," the latter bellowed. "Remember that we still have a score to settle about that broth . . ." The lackey had recognized in the grenadier our friend Leonardo, just as had the family as soon as he appeared.

And it was indeed he.

X I X

The Grenadier

The score was, then, completely settled between Leonardo and the lackey: Each had had his vengeance upon the other. The last blow struck in the contest had been Leanardo's. He blessed his fate, and even Major Vidigal, for having provided him the opportunity to snatch fortune's cup from the lips of his rival. He was even almost happy that he had been conscripted. We have done well in observing that for him there was neither fortune that was not transformed into misfortune nor misfortune that did not end up as fortune.

The lackey, as we have said, had been taken away by Leonardo; and the readers, familiar with the fate that befell all Major Vidigal's prisoners, must now suppose that he was pointed to the road leading to the guardhouse in the Sé Square. But the condition that he was in did not allow his being led there. The vapors that had risen from his stomach to his head slowly condensed, and by the middle of the journey they were pressing upon his brain with the weight of a hundred pounds. His head, unable to hold itself up, fell down upon his trunk, which, finding that weight excessive, tried to appeal to his legs; they, however, were no stronger and, bending wobbly and tremulous, dropped the braggart of a short time before flat upon the sidewalk. The soldiers were unable to raise him, for, as we observed at the outset, he was of a colossal corpulence. It was thus necessary to abandon the prize altogether. The major had little difficulty with this, first because of the work that any other decision would have involved and second because, albeit of the lowest class, the lackey was still a member of the royal household and at the time such standing brought with it some not inconsiderable immunities.

Leonardo tried some additional measures so that the first prisoner he had taken would not escape without more definitive result, since that would be a bad sign for his future military career, but, that notwithstanding, his most beautiful revenge had already been exacted.

So the royal lackey was left abandoned on the pavement.

Let us now satisfy in a few words the curiosity that our readers doubtless harbor to know how Leonardo had acceded to the position in which he was now to be found. After, as we know, being captured by the major at the entranceway to the royal pantries, he had been conducted by his captor in person to a safe place, from which he exited only as an enlistee in the New Regiment. All the batallions in the city contained a company of grenadiers, and, as there was an opening in the New Regiment's grenadier company, Leonardo was selected to fill it. When he heard of this, the major chose him for his service (because it was from those grenadier companies that soldiers were selected for police duties), since, as someone experienced in such matters, he intuited that Leonardo would be a valuable aide. Up to a certain point the major was not mistaken. In fact Leonardo, being naturally cunning and having till now lived in a vast school of delinquency and chicanery, was probably acquainted with every trick of the trade. Nevertheless, there was one factor that kept him from giving good service, and that was that the major often had to waste on him and his misdeeds time that was necessary for the general discharge of duties. The force of the habits that he had acquired was so strong that not even the rigors of discipline could deter them.

Let us tell of the first villainy that he took it upon himself to practice after donning the uniform, which was all the more regrettable in that at the outset he had shown himself to be so earnest a soldier that he was almost beginning to gain a reputation for strictness.

The wags and the hoodlums of the city, who were Major Vidigal's constant prey, conceived the idea of immortalizing his deeds in some way, and they invented a fado with the following refrain between the chorusus:

Papa, lele, seculorum.

In this fado the central character was the major, who, represented as dead, was laid out in a winding sheet in the middle of the room. The rest of the characters stood around him in a circle singing suggestive songs that all ended in the refrain here set forth.

The major, when he learned of this, started looking for an opportune moment to get even with them for such a mockery, which made it clear what the composers wished for him. One day he received the tip that a full "Papa, lele" was being planned for that night in a house on Conceição Hill, and he made preparations to catch the perpetrators in the act.

At the opportune time he sent two or three grenadiers ahead, one at a time, to check out what was going on, having first arranged affirmative and negative signs so that they could signal each other whether or not there was opportunity and cause for an assault. The grenadier closest to the house would communicate the signs to the next one back, he would pass them on, the next would do the same until they reached the major's position. It was a regular system of advanced scouts, as though a full-scale campaign was involved. If the affirmative sign were given, they would all march up in a leisurely manner and then come together for the assault. If it was negative, they were to disperse in silence, for one of the major's great manias was never to show that he had been gotten the better of. It fell to Leonardo's lot to be the lookout closest to the enemy and to give the first sign. He therefore marched forward, and his companions took up their positions and waited. They waited for a long time. They grew tired of waiting. Finally, just when they were getting ready to contravene their orders and abandon their posts to search for Leonardo, a long whistle came three times in a row. That was the agreed-upon negative sign. By virtue of this they dispersed in frustration and went to join the major at the bottom of the slope, at the place overlooking the entrance to the Aljube. When they gathered there they waited a long time without Leonardo's appearing. The major began to turn the case over in his mind; he suddenly gave the order to ascend the hill. They did so and, now marching behind the major's lead, made for the house in question. To the surprise of all, as they approached they saw lights and heard the strumming of guitars and the singing of songs. A full-scale fado was in progress inside. Without need of great security pecautions, since everyone seemed engrossed, the major had the house surrounded and caught everyone with, as the saying goes, his finger in the pot. It was precisely at the ceremony's solemn climax. The person playing the part of "Papa" was laid out on the floor wound in a sheet, his head covered, and the entire company was singing and dancing around him.

When the major knocked and went in accompanied by his troops, everyone stopped, frozen with fear. The person in the sheet gave a great shudder and then became motionless, as though he were made of stone, playing the part of the cadaver perhaps more faithfully than he wished. As was his practice, the major ordered the festivities to go on a while longer in his presence. Then began the inquiry into the occupation of each one, and, in accord with what was discovered there, he started either sending them off or having them set aside to be given fuller disposition. During the entire scene, which took its own time, the man in the sheet lay motionless in the same position, his head covered.

When the entire circle had been accounted for, the major said to him, "Okay, comrade inside the winding sheet, do you really want them to carry you off right from here to the grave?"

Not a movement in response.

"Oh! He's dead, so naturally he's lost the power of speech!"

Profound silence.

The major gave a signal to one of the grenadiers, who poked the figure with the point of his light hook. Not even then did it move, however. At another signal from the major the grenadier fetched him a tremendous blow. At that the cadaver was resuscitated and got his feet under him in a bound. Even so, he tried to escape out a window keeping his head still covered. The grenadiers laid hold of him, and the major said, "Man, just because you're dead, don't hurry so to go to hell; talk to us first."

And pulling the cloth off his face, he added, "Now let us look upon the face of the deceased."

A cry of astonishment from the grenadiers, accompanied by a thunderous outburst of laughter, cut the major short. When the face of the dead man was uncovered, he was recognized to be our friend Leonardo!

New Deviltries

We know not if it availed Leonardo that this was the first time he had incurred punishment, having previously maintained the strictest observance of all his duties, or if the very audacity of the deed won him more of the major's sympathy. The upshot was that, aside from the laughter and mockery of his comrades and the anguished half hour he spent in the winding sheet, to the shock of everyone and especially of himself, nothing more happened. The major had thus held out a great proof of unusual benevolence. As a result, Leonardo went about for some days abashed and pensive, as though crushed by the weight of tremendous remorse. His comrades found this a great source of repartee with which to poke fun at him and did not give him a moment's peace in their midst.

"He's still not completely resuscitated," said one, passing near.

"What do you mean?" said another. "He is no longer of this world."

"Papa lele seculorum" intoned others in chorus.

To none of these provocations did he offer the slightest response, and he was wise in acting thus, for that way he did not supply his pitiless comrades with yet more material for mockery. When those events ended, all was forgotten and matters returned to their ordinary course.

One day, the major announced that he had a great and important mission to carry out. There was a convivial malefactor, absolute exemplar of the miscreants of the era, whom the major had had his eye on for months without finding any opportunity to lay his hand on him. A sort whose occupation was an unsolvable puzzle for many people, he nonetheless always seemed more or less well heeled. All that he possessed of real value was a cape, in which he went about constantly wrapped, and a guitar that he never let get far from him. He enjoyed a reputation as a clever and entertaining fellow, and there was no festivity of any kind to which he was not invited. He spent all his time corresponding to such invitations. Dawn regularly found him at a party that had begun the evening before, for example a birthday party; he would leave it for a baptismal dinner, and at night he had a wedding banquet. The fame that he had as an entertaining fellow, which provided him with so handsome a way to pass his time, he owed to certain abilities, in one of which in particular he knew no rival. He played the guitar and sang *modinhas* extremely well, he danced the fado with great perfection, he could speak black language and sing admirably well in it, he could act crippled in any part of his body with extreme naturalness, he could imitate perfectly the speech of the country folk, he knew thousands of riddles, and finally—and this was his rarest talent—he could with rare perfection make an infinite variety of faces that no one else could imitate. He was consequently the delight of the spirited society in which he found himself. Whoever put on a celebration in his or her house and wanted to have a big crowd and good company had only to announce to the invitees that Teotônio (for that was his name) would be attending.

Now as regards his occupation or means of livelihood, which for many was, as we have said, an impenetrable secret, Major Vidigal worked and worked until he unearthed it. On prescribed days of the week a certain number of individuals would come together in the attic where Teotônio lived and stay there until late at night: He was the banker for gamblers.

Knowing this, the major wanted greatly to catch him in the act. As he had been trying to do so for a considerable time without being able to accomplish it—because his vigilance was always being eluded by the continual changing of the days on which the circle would meet—he resolved to lay his hands on Teotônio at the first chance and then use him in the capture of his companions.

As the readers will recall, old Leonardo, that is, Leonardo-Pataca, was living with the *comadre*'s daughter and by her had an offspring, whose birth we asked you to attend. Well, the passage of some time notwithstanding, the little girl was still unbaptized. Leonardo-Pataca, at the importuning of the *comadre*, who was greatly bothered by the procrastination, finally determined the day when his daughter would become a Christian. In accordance with immutable custom, there was a celebration of that occasion, and, in accordance with current fashion, Teotônio was invited. The major had heard about it, and it was precisely there that he lay in wait, determined to catch Teotônio. It was for this that he had notified his soldiers in the manner of which we have spoken above.

It was the major's misfortune always to be ruining others' good times and an infelicity for us who write these lines to fall into the monotony of almost always repeating the same scenes with slight variations. Nevertheless, the faithfulness with which we keep true to the times, seeking to sketch a part of their customs, obligates us to do so.

At the appointed time the major arrived at Leonardo-Pataca's house. As there was not the least reason for violence, since everything was going on in the most perfect peace, the major entered alone, with Leonardo-Pataca's prior approval, and attended the festivities. Precisely when he arrived Teotônio was on stage with all his talents. Having already run through all the others, he was ready to go to the last one, which was the face-making. It must be noted that not only did he know how to make random faces but he also knew how to make them in such a way as more or less to impersonate a known figure. It was this that was now making the bystanders convulse with laughter.

They were all seated, and Teotônio, standing in the middle of the room, would look at one person and show the face of an old man, suddenly spin around toward another with the face of an idiot laughing inanely, and so on for a good long while, doing a new face each time. Finally, having now exhausted his repertoire, he ran to one side, located himself in a position where everyone could see him at the same time, and presented his last face. The company dissolved in a roar of laughter pointing to the major: He had just imitated, with great exactness, the long, lean face of Vidigal.

The major bit his lip as he recognized Teotônio's jest, and, if he had had good intentions with regard to him, at that moment better ones were formed.

The laughter went on for a great deal of time. Unable to confront it impassively and, as we have suggested, not having a just reason for breaking in, he found it preferable to withdraw and, taking up a suitable position, await the dispersal of the party so that he could then invite Teotônio to go do a few impersonations for the grenadiers at the guardhouse. He therefore exited, thoroughly abashed.

Meeting those of his grenadiers who had stationed themselves a short distance away, he spoke to Leonardo and made it clear to him that he wanted at all cost to detain Teotônio that night but was afraid that the people in the house might anticipate that and help him escape somehow. He therefore needed someone who could go stand watch up close without arousing suspicion; that person had to be Leonardo.

"I'm unwelcome in my father's house," the latter replied to the major's proposal.

"It's a fine day for reconciliation—"

"What if they won't receive me?"

"What about your godmother? She's in there."

"But how about her daughter, who's a real viper when it comes to me?"

"Viper or no viper, it's up to you; for when duty calls . . . I don't want that ne'er-do-well going around using me with impunity as a model for his impersonations."

The grenadiers, who knew Teotônio and were acquainted with his talents, immediately understood from the major's words what had taken place, and they dissolved in laughter in their turn. With that appeal to duty, something with which he had not exactly been in good standing since the night of the "Papa-lele," Leonardo succeeded in overcoming all the difficulties and repugnance that he had manifested at executing the mission that the major had charged him with and set out on the path to his father's house.

He arrived and knocked on the door. When those inside glimpsed the colors of his uniform and his shako there was a cry of alarm. And, in a movement that seemed prearranged (the major was indeed right!), all the candles in the front room were quickly extinguished and there set in a hubbub such that it seemed that everyone was fighting with everyone else.

Leonardo saw this as his first setback, but he did not, for all that, fail to think that the fright he caused was amusing. He decided then to call from outside to try to calm the fearful.

"A fine way for a son to be received in his father's house! All that's missing are the rattles for it to be Holy Wednesday—"

The *comadre*, who heard and recognized her godson's voice, burst out laughing and exclaimed, "Look at the trick he played on us! It's Leonardo. Bring out the candles everybody; there's nothing to worry about, for this corporal of the guard is family."

"That hooligan," old Leonardo grumbled, "always doing just what pleases him; look what a fright he gave to all these people. Oh Teotônio my friend, come on down; there's nothing to worry about . . ."

At the light of the first candle brought out, Teotônio could be seen climbing down through a trapdoor from the space above the front bedroom ceiling, where he had gone to hide.

As soon as he set foot on the floor he made a face of fright that was so expressive that there was a tremendous explosion of hilarity amongst them all. People began to emerge from various corners of the house, and the merrymaking recommenced with Leonardo's participation.

Some people could not restrain their distrust and fear at Leonardo's presence on this occasion and in that uniform right after the major's departure. But the *comadre* calmed them all saying that he had got permission at the barracks, because he was not on duty that day, to come attend his sister's baptism.

"He's a bit crazy," she said over and over, "but very loving, and he never forgets his family."

Leonardo confirmed these protestations on the part of the *comadre*, all the while participating in the festivities, now that, despite his expectations, they had all received him so well into the house. To the degree that he warmed to the pleasure of the fado and the *cantigas* Leonardo began to feel remorse at the Judas role he was playing. When he looked at Teotônio, who from the moment he had entered had made him laugh so much, his heart ached at the realization that it was he who would have to turn him over to the major. No few times did it pass through his head to help him escape by warning him, but then discipline, the Papa-lele, came to his mind, and he hesitated.

As he was being assailed by such thoughts he glanced repeatedly at Teotônio. The latter, who was nobody's fool, began to suspect something; by what instinct we know not, he read what Leonardo was thinking and put himself on guard.

Leonardo came quickly to a decision. "Okay; duty goodbye," he said to himself. "I'm going to get the man out of here somehow or other."

And from where he was standing he added, in a loud voice, "Oh, Mr. Teotônio, do you want to know something? If you put a foot through that door, the major is going to snatch you up. He's waiting for you outside and sent me in here for that very purpose—"

"The devil!" they all exclaimed.

"But let's not panic; it can all be worked out. I'm good at this kind of thing."

"But don't put yourself in a bad spot, boy," the *comadre* whispered in Leonardo's ear. "Keep in mind that the major is no soft touch; you could get into a lot of trouble."

"Aw, I feel sorry for him just because he can make those faces."

Then the two of them, Leonardo and Teotônio, sat down together and hatched a plan to enable the latter to get away from the major and the former to stay out of trouble.

The night was already quite far along when the two of them arranged for a large number of guests to leave at the same time. And Leonardo, leaving ahead of them, ran to meet the major.

"Here comes the weasel now, Major."

"Close in, close in!" said the major.

And each man went off to his assigned position. The major hid in a corridor doorway and kept his eye out.

There approached the major a figure calmly whistling the refrain of a *modinha*. When he was a short distance away the major leaped out at him and seized him.

A feeble "ay" was uttered, accompanied by a "Release me! What is this?"

The major looked more closely, since he had not recognized the voice of Teotônio, and saw that he had captured a poor hunchback, one who on top of that was crippled in the right leg and the left arm.

"Oh, go to hell," said the major. "Get out of here. I don't know what such figures are doing in the streets at this hour."

The cripple headed hastily off, free of his fear, continuing all the while to whistle his refrain. After that a most profound silence fell, and the major saw only the party guests pass by, Teotônio not figuring amongst them.

The major burned with a fury and, gathering together the grenadiers, said to Leonardo: "He didn't come out—"

"Yes he did," the latter replied; wearing a white jacket and a straw hat. I saw him turn down toward the door where you were posted."

"White jacket and straw hat?" asked the major.

"Yes, sir, and black breeches. I didn't grab him because I could see that he wasn't going to be able to escape you, Major sir."

"Oh the scoundrel, the scoundrel," he muttered. "I've never been so . . . It was the hunchback, the cripple . . ."

"He does a very good hunchback and a very good cripple," said one of the grenadiers. "I saw him do them once, and it was just like real life . . ."

The cripple the major had captured had indeed been Teotônio. Leonardo laughed up his sleeve at the trick that had been played on the major.

It was not long, however, before that pleasure turned sour, as the major came to find out that it had all been done with his connivance.

X X I

Revelation

It has been said many times that the only thing worse than an enemy is a bad friend. One of Leonardo-Pataca's guests called himself a close friend of Teotônio's and, in the light of the lengths to which Leonardo had gone to keep the latter free of the major's clutches, made great protestations of sharing thereafter a part of that friendship with him in such a way that neither of the two was diminished. A scant few moments after that protestation, he provided the first indication of how he was prepared to live up to it.

As the scenes we have described were taking place, dawn had begun to break. The major and his men withdrew but were still in the vicinity of the place where the attempt had been made to capture Teotônio when the so-called friend to whom we have referred, who was one of the last people to quit the area, running across the patrol and seeing that Teotônio was not to be seen in its midst, concluded that the plan had come out a success and that this time it was the major who had been outwitted. As a result, he experienced a paroxysm of delight and, forgetting about the major's presence, ran up to Leonardo and hugged him, exclaiming with impetuous enthusiasm, "Bravo! As long as you live you'll never pull off anything else quite so grand. It was a thing of beauty. He will be forever in your debt, and I along with him, because I'm his friend—and yours as well!"

Leonardo was flabbergasted by the imprudence of the act. The major, who had been crestfallen thinking about the trick by which he had just been victimized, suddenly wheeled about. The word "he" uttered by this horrible friend brought the light to his eyes. Leonardo was roused from the stupor into which he had fallen by the major's voice saying to him in no uncertain terms, "Repair to the barracks under arrest!"

At that sentence Leonardo brought up all the spite, all the rancor that he had in the depths of his being, and he glared at the imprudent figure who had brought this on and who, still oblivious, was pitilessly grasping his hand seemingly unprepared to loose it so soon.

Let us now leave Leonardo to march to the barracks under arrest, a victim to his own dedication, and go on to other matters. We have not spoken of Dona Maria and her people in some time. The readers should be informed that once the honeymoon—in which everything had been roses—was past, our friend José Manuel, as the saying goes, showed his true colors. He did such things that within a few months all was in a pitched battle: Along with his wife Luisinha he had moved out of Dona Maria's house and, over the matter of a dowry or not, an inheritence here or there, Dona Maria had launched an action against him that was so complex that it was doubtful whether the old lady would have enough days remaining in her life actually to see it through.

For Luisinha José Manuel had turned into a true dragon-husband of the sort that only those times could offer such perfect examples, constant scourges to their wives. After they had moved out of Dona Maria's house, never again had Luisinha seen the air of the street except in glances stolen through the slits of the shutters. Then she wept for the freedom she had previously enjoyed: The promenades, the conversations at the door on moonlit nights, Sunday Mass at the Sé in the company of her aunt with the entourage of slave-children behind them, the callers they used to receive, and Leonardo, whom she missed so much—in fine everything that she had not appreciated enough at the time but that now seemed so pleasant and so beautiful. Having married José Manuel in accordance with Dona Maria's wishes, she vowed an enormous indifference to her husband, which is perhaps the worst hatred of all.

Now Luisinha's married life faithfully represented the lives of the greater number of the young women being married in those days. It was for that reason that the Vidinhas were not rare and there were few families without cause to lament some little chagrin of the kind suffered by that poor family that had gone to the Stone Oratory only to return home diminished in number—whose story had provided the *comadre* with her plot's theme as she tried to disqualify José Manuel from the contest.

Well, it is clear that while Dona Maria had been put out with the *comadre* because of her machinations prior to José Manuel's marriage to her niece, now that she was butting heads with him instead the bonds of friendship that had loosened for a while might draw tight again. That is indeed what took place.

One day the two of them came across each other at Mass and started speaking again. Leonardo's misadventures, which provided the topic for that conversation, moved Dona Maria, who in her turn then told the *comadre* about everything that was now befalling poor Luisinha.

"Oh, *senhora!*" said the *comadre* in reference to José Manuel, "I think something inside of me rumbled whenever I saw that evil man; I curse the man, who is a downright blackguard. All this'll drag the poor girl down into her grave. Poor child! Well-raised but ill-fated."

"I never thought, my dear, I never thought that such a thing would happen. . . . But what a swindler he was! Such sweet words, such a saintly manner! Now, *senhora*, now I can really believe the story about the girl abducted at the Stone Oratory; he's completely capable of such a thing. . . . But I'll get my revenge—oh just you wait and see, just as sure as I'm standing here! The court justices are still there, and they're going to give me that pleasure. I trust in God for that."

Out of that conversation and the other things that followed was born the two women's reconciliation.

Once certain friendships are interrupted, or even undergo a minor setback, it is difficult for them then to return to their prior state. With other friendships, however, the reverse occurs; the setbacks are productive because the return of peace proves easy, and as a result they seem to grow even closer. The friendship existing between Dona Maria and the *comadre* was of this latter sort. Therefore, after the chat at Mass not only did relations between the two return to their prior state but they became more solid than ever before. From then on there was no secret between them that was not mutually communicated, and they made a pact to aid one another to effect remedies, one of them for the ills afflicting her niece, the other for her godson's deviltries.

Leonardo, as we have said, was under arrest. He had sent word of the fact to his *comadre*, who flew into a fit, not so much because of that fact in itself but because of the noble motive that had led to it. The first step that the two women, Dona Maria and the *comadre*, had to take as a result of their pact was to try to arrange Leonardo's release and free him from the whatever else (God only knows) was likely being prepared for him.

We shall see how they went about that task.

X X I I

Endeavors

The *comadre's* first step was to take herself to the major's house to intercede on Leonardo's behalf. The major , however, proved inflexible: The case was a serious one, discipline could not be challenged more than once with impunity, the punishment must be unfailing and great. The *comadre*, who had gone full of hopes, found out from the major something of which she was unaware and did not even suspect: Leonardo would not only remain a prisoner for a longer time but he also would be flogged. . . . As soon as the major told her this, the poor woman fell to her knees, wept, wailed—all, however, in vain. She left in despair and, her mantilla drooping, all disheveled, flew to Dona Maria's house. When she saw her enter in such a state, Dona Maria rose from her small bench and put down her lace cushion.

"What is the matter, my dear, what is it?" she exclaimed. "Good God, what is it? Speak to me!"

"Oh, dear, dear *senhora* Dona Maria, what a disaster!" the *comadre* answered. "What a star-crossed boy—Just look at what's happening to him for doing a good deed! . . . And I who suffer it and feel it as though he were my son!" And her sobs choked her.

"Tell me, *senhora*," Dona Maria said again; "speak, for you touch me deeply."

"Dona Maria, he's going to . . . he's going to . . . be flogged—Leonardo!"

"My Lord! Poor boy! Just look at what all this has finally led to! It's fate, that's what it is, poor child; the boy was born on a bad day. No, *comadre*, I'll swear to that on my soul's salvation. . . . But haven't you spoken to the major? What did he say?"

"Hard as a rock, *senhora*; nothing could move him. I entreated him in the name of the Five Wounds, of the Holy Lady . . . all in vain, to no avail."

"All right, don't despair, *comadre*; there's still one way that I suspect won't fail us. Let's go to her house, for that's the sure way. She and I get on very well; she'll intercede for the boy."

"That had occurred to me, but with the anguish I was in I forgot about it. If something can't be worked out through her . . . then there is no hope."

The readers are now curious to know who "she" is, and they are right in being so. We shall satisfy them. The major was himself an old sinner and in his own day had been amongst those who had not, as the saying goes, had the sense they were born with. Still today there remained one thing that at times brought his past back up; that one thing was Maria-Regalada, who lived in the Prainha. In her day Maria-Regalada had been, in the common parlance, a prime lady of the town. She was by nature a lover of good times, she lived in continuous merriment, laughed at everything, and every time she laughed she laughed for a long time and with great enjoyment: hence the nickname "regalada" that had been appended to her name.

This business of nicknames was a very common practice at the time of our story; the readers should therefore not be surprised that many of the characters that figure here have such an appendage added to their names.

It is often said, and the poets swear it over and over again, that the first love is the true love. We have been studying that question, and today's conclusion is that one should put little stock in what poets say. Through our investigations we have arrived at the conclusion that the true love is either all the loves together or else it is only one, in which case it is not the first but rather the last. The last is the one that is true because it is the only one that does not change. Let the female readers who disagree with this doctrine convince me to the contrary if they are able.

All this comes to say that Maria-Regalada had a true love for Major Vidigal and the major repaid it in the same coin. Now Dona Maria was one of Maria-Regalada's closest confidantes. That is why, in speaking of "her," Dona Maria and the *comadre* manifested such hopefulness about Leonardo's eventual fate.

In those times (and there are those who say it is a defect of ours) the use of influence, of connections among parents and godparents, constituted a true mainspring within the entire working of society.

"Go have the sedan-chair brought up," called Dona Maria to one of her slave women.

"Let's go, *senhora*, let's go, for this business afflicts me deeply."

Dona Maria hastily prepared and climbed into her sedan-chair. The godmother picked up her mantilla, and they set out for the Prainha.

Maria-Regalada received them with hearty good humor. "What a miracle of Santa Engrácia! What good luck! What a pleasure! What brings you here? This is a stroke of fortune!"

"It is indeed a stroke of fortune," replied Dona Maria, "but of bad fortune."

With the usual ceremony, which in those days was not elaborate, the *comadre* was introduced, as she was not an acquaintance of Maria-Regalada's. First Dona Maria and then the *comadre*, each on her own part, told Leonardo's story in all its detail. And after endless circumlocution that put the listener's patience to the test and nearly made her die of curiosity, they at last got to the important point, the reason that had brought them there: They wanted no less than Leonardo's release and pardon, and they were relying on Maria-Regalada's influence over the major to achieve that end.

"Now," said she, assuming an air of modesty, "I don't have much influence . . . those were really other times . . . the major . . . things are different now. Dona Maria . . . after he went into the police . . . it does seem like just yesterday . . . it's hard to tell what's what around here! . . . But Dona Maria, I still can't say no, it's just the way my heart is and always has been . . . in my time many people have taken advantage of that. I'll do what I can, I'll talk to him. Maybe he'll pay attention to me . . ."

"He will, he will," the *comadre* answered, "he's not so old as to have completely forgotten old times."

"We'll see, we'll see. You know what men are like, *senhora comadre*."

"You're telling me? Do I ever!" the latter quickly rejoined.

"But now," Dona Maria interrupted, "the business requires all possible haste because they could lay on the poor boy's back at any time, and after that not even Santo Antônio could take it back."

"Nothing to worry about: We can still get there on time, with the grace of God. To be absolutely certain, let's all three of us go right from here to the major's house, and we'll each do everything in our power to get the young man freed."

Maria-Regalada drsssed hurriedly, took up her mantilla, and, the two walking alongside the sedan-chair in which Dona Maria traveled, off they went to the major's house.

XXIII

Three Women on a Mission

The three, then, set out for the house of the major, who at that time lived on the Rua da Misericórdia, one of the oldest streets in the city. The major received them in a colored-print robe and sandals, not having initially gauged the caliber of the visit. As soon as he recognized the three women, however, he rushed to the adjacent bedroom and threw on his uniform tunic as quickly as possible. Since time was short and it was impolite to leave the ladies unattended, he did not don the rest of the uniform but returned to the parlor in the uniform top, informal breeches, sandals, and, as was his custom, an Alcobaça kerchief over his shoulder. The *comadre*, seeing him thus attired, could scarcely stifle a giggle that came to her lips despite the aggrieved state she was in. The salutations of greeting were carried out without incident. The *comadre* had discerned in the major's haste to enter a good sign for the outcome of their mission. The fact that in his old age he retained sweet remembrances of his own youth was also in their favor. As soon as he saw himself surrounded by women—in something other than a public place and in circumstances in which discipline would not be prejudiced—he would turn to mush in a manner to be rivaled only by the elder Leonardo. If the ladies were to tumble to this weak spot of his, if they flattered him, if they paid him compliments no matter how stupidly put on they might be, they could drag whatever they wanted out of him. He might himself spontaneously offer to help in what they desired and then be grateful to them on top of it. Nevertheless, even though the *comadre* was aware of this circumstance in advance—or inuited it from appearances—the gravity of the affair being dealt with was such that not even this sufficed to calm her. She poised for the attack, aided by her companions, who, albeit less directly concerned about Leonardo's fate, were not therefore less committed to his cause. There was a moment of confusion in deciding who would be the commission's orator. The major perceived that and had a burst of pride at seeing three women so clumsy and unsure in the presence of his high person. He made a gesture as though of encouragement, involuntarily scraping his sandals across the floor.

"Oh! Sandals and tunic, a fine thing. . . . An old man's way, my dear ladies; in my day I would never do such things . . ."

"Dona Maria should get in a word on that score," the *comadre* chimed in, referring to Maria-Regalada and trying to find a way to get into the subject, whatever it might be; "but that's not important; we have other concerns . . ."

"It's true, Major; the old times are gone forever."

"And God forgive the one who still yearns for them," replied the major, laughing the wrinkled laugh of old sensuality.

"Yes, yes," returned Maria-Regalada, "but leave all those things for another time."

"Oh, my dear," chimed in Dona Maria, who had been silent until then, perhaps fatigued by the prodigious number of bows she had made coming in, "let each recall his own old times; it's a consolation. For myself, I like it when I think . . ."

"You're like me," the major replied, "when I touch the old wounds . . ."

"Well, it's precisely because I do remember those old wounds," Maria-Regalada cut in, "that I've come here with these ladies, whom the major knows well. If it weren't for who they are, I wouldn't have come, for the matter is serious . . ."

The *comadre* considered this a well-formulated opportunity and nodded her head in a sign of approval.

"Then let's see what that serious matter has to do with," the major responded, intuiting from the *comadre*'s presence more or less what was up and therefore shaking his head dubiously, either to demonstrate his own importance or because he really did not want great hopes generated.

His interlocutor went on: "Your grenadier Leonardo is a fine young man."

The major arched his eyebrows and drew in his lips, like one who did not agree *in toto* with what was being said.

"Don't start at me like that, Major. He *is* in fact a very fine young man, and there's no reason for him to be punished for some little something he did. . . . No reason, sir, none at all for a young man who is no vagrant to be flogged. You know very well that when his godfather died he left him a little something, which could very well be in his hands right now and he, as a result, free of that cursed uniform that I've never liked (except for one case, as is well known), if his father, who has it . . . but let's leave the father out of this, for he doesn't add anything to the case . . ."

"I know all about it, all about it," the major cut in.

"Not yet, Major sir," the *comadre* observed. "You still don't know the most important part, which is that what he did on that occasion was almost beyond his control. You know, a son in his father's house . . ."

"But a son when he is a soldier," the major shot back with full disciplinary gravity.

"But even so he doesn't stop being a son," Dona Maria returned.

"I understand that, but what about the law?"

"Oh the law . . . what is the law, if the major would be so kind? . . ."

The major smiled in candid modesty. The discussion was thus growing animated. But the major would not yield an inch; indeed, he seemed more inflexible than ever. He even went so far as to stand up and speak very forcefully against Leonardo's deed and for the necessity of a severe punishment. It was funny to see him, in the lovely uniform we have described, standing and delivering a sermon on discipline before that three-person audience that was so incredulous as to resist his strongest arguments.

Moreover, the three had still not utilized their last recourse against him; they now brought it to bear.

When the major was at his most expansive, the three women all at once, as if by prior plan, burst into tears. . . . The major stopped . . . he looked at them for an instant; his visage visibly softened, wrinkled up, and finally, from the emotion, he burst into tears as well. No sooner did the three see this triumph than they charged the enemy. The result was an uproar, an indescribable wailing session that might well have moved stones.

The major was turning from being moved emotionally to being bewildered, almost as though he were ashamed of the tears that were rolling down his cheeks. He wiped them away and sought to reassume his prior gravity. "No," he said, disengaging himself from the three women and pacing the room in long strides. "No. What would they say about me if they saw me here bawling like a baby? I, Major Vidigal, crying in the company of three women! . . . Ladies, the case is a serious one and I see no way out of it. Example, discipline, military law . . . no way out; it can't be done . . ." And he turned his back to the three, continuing to pace, his sandles whacking heavily on the floor.

Maria-Regalada said very softly to the other two, upon whose countenances not the slightest glimmer of hope shone: "All is not lost yet . . ." And addressing herself to the major, she added, "Very well, Major, but water downstream doesn't turn the mill wheel . . ."

"What 'downstream,' my lady? You have to see that the case is a serious one . . ."

"Be that as it may, I'm sorry to have walked over here and not have been any use to my friend. I was, if truth be told, expecting this, so I didn't make any promises. . . . Nevertheless, in the last place I want to tell you something, but it has to be in private . . ."

"Come along then; I'm ready."

Anyone with some discernment would have recognized, though not easily, that the major had for some time been disposed to give in, but he wanted to be begged to do so.

Maria-Regalada took the major into a corner of the room and said some words into his ear. The major 's face cleared, he wriggled from head to toe, rubbed his head, swayed back and forth on his legs, bit his lips.

"You are something!" he said to his interlocutor in a low voice. "Did you have to bring that up? Well . . ."

"Well, thank God that all your entreaties have finally reached an end," answered Maria-Regalada aloud.

"Yes?" exclaimed the other two, smiling with hope.

"I said that the major was a man with a good heart . . ."

"I never doubted it, in spite of everything . . . but now, what's past is past; the case was a serious one, as he said, and it *is* a favor! . . ."

"Well, Dona Maria, once a king, always a gentleman . . ."

"Gentleman? Nonsense! I wasn't born for that."

The major cut short this explosion of gratitude that promised to go on for quite a time. "You're going to be even more pleased with me . . . I won't say why; you'll see . . ."

"What you've done just now is magnificent; we'll wait to see what the other could be . . ."

"I know, it's . . ."

"It's got to be . . ."

"I think I'd guess . . ."

"Do you know what else?" the major interrupted. "It is time for an appointment I cannot miss. . . . The boy is free of everything . . . provided," he added, looking over to Maria-Regalada, "what's said stays said."

"I've never gone back on my word," the latter replied.

The three withdrew filled with the greatest happiness, and the major then left as well, to carry out his promise.

XXIV

Death Is the Judge

Dona Maria set out directly for home in her sedan-chair. When she got there she noticed a great uproar and commotion and immediately tried to discover its cause. One of her niece's slave-men was waiting for her with a letter. As soon as she had read it Dona Maria was not so much saddened as set back on her heels.

"Don't remove the sedan-chair; just wait, for I'll be going out again." And indeed she climbed into it anew and ordered that she be taken to her niece's house.

The situation was as follows. José Manuel had had to be carried into the house after suffering a violent attack of apoplexy on the street as he was returning from the registry, where he had had a serious conflict with Dona Maria's lawyer about the suit in which they were engaged. Poor Luisinha, seeing herself in this situation and not knowing what to do, had immediately sent a messenger to her aunt.

As soon as she entered, Dona Maria had a doctor called. After he had examined the patient, the doctor declared that the case was beyond help. Some procedures were taken nonetheless, but they had no effect.

"You are a widow, my child," said Dona Maria, somewhat compunctious from the doctor's declaration. Luisinha broke into tears, but only in the way that she would cry for any creature, having, as she did, a tender heart.

Some people from the neighborhood were present, and one of the woman among them said quietly to another, "Those aren't widow's tears." And they were not, as we have said. Most of the time the world makes a crime of that. But what of antecedent factors? Had José Manuel perchance ever been Luisinha's husband in his heart? He had been such only as regards the proprieties, and for the proprieties those tears served equally well. Neither the doctor nor Dona Maria had been wrong: At nightfall José Manuel expired.

The next day they made arrangements for the funeral. The *comadre*, who had been informed of everything, came by in sympathy to lend her good offices and her consolations.

The funeral procession set out accompanied by the friends of the family; the household slaves raised a tremendous wail. All the neighborhood was at its windows, and everything was analyzed, from the handles and fixtures on the casket to the number and standing of the invitees. And on each of those points three or four different opinions were registered.

In those times funeral orations were not common practice, nor were obituaries, so much in fashion today. Thus we at least escape that. José Manuel sleeps in peace in his last resting place.

As the *comadre* had promised, someone arrived almost at nightfall. It was Leonardo. When he entered Dona Maria's drawing room, she could not restrain a cry of surprise. He came in wearing the complete uniform of a sergeant of the company of grenadiers!

"What! Look what the major did! How can it be?"

"It's true, ma'am," Leonardo answered. "I owe it all to him."

It was the object of general amazement. They would all have been satisfied with Leonardo's mere release, and he turned up not only released and free but even elevated to the rank of sergeant, which is no small thing in the army.

Leonardo began to seek with his eyes something or someone he was curious to see. He came upon it: It was Luisinha. The two had not seen each other for a long time; they could not hide the sense of awkwardness that came over them. And that emotion was all the greater for their both being surprised at the other. Luisinha found Leonardo a handsome, robust young man with a moustache and sideburns—elegant to the utmost, a grenadier soldier in his well-tailored sergeant's uniform. Leonardo found Luisinha a grown-up, even elegant, young lady, her eyes and hair black, completely devoid of her former physical timidity. Moreover, her eyes, reddened by tears, her face paled if not truly by the unpleasant happenings of that day then surely by their antecedents, had on this occasion a touch of melancholy beauty about them that as a general rule might not capture the attention of a sergeant of grenadiers but that certainly moved Sergeant Leonardo, who, after all, was not just any sergeant. And so much so that, during the mute scene that took place when their eyes met, Leonardo's thoughts swiftly returned to the events of his prior life and, going back over it event by event, he reached that ridiculous but ingenuous scene of the declaration of love he had made to Luisinha. It seemed to him that he had chosen the time badly back then and that now it would have a much more appropriate one.

The *comadre*, who paid a perspicacious attention to everything that was happening, all but read those thoughts in her godson's mind. She made an almost imperceptible gesture of delight; some radiant notion began to glow in her mind. She then began to retrace an old plan whose realization she had worked for over a long period of time and whose chance for success had been presented to her anew by what had just happened.

When her first emotions subsided, Luisinha rose and made Leonardo a cautious curtsy. He responded with something between an awkward bow and a military salute.

At that point the *comadre* broke into the conversation, endeavoring to engage Dona Maria and leave the two young people in each other's company. "Tell me," said she, addressing Dona Maria, "what about that lawsuit between yourself and the deceased?"

"Death was the judge this time. He has no heirs; he was alone in the world. . . . I didn't complete my objective, it's true, because I can't really say that I won; but neither did I lose. Now of course I take great pleasure in giving everything to the girl, but I didn't want to have things taken away from me other than by my own free will."

"That's just fine; let the past be over and done with. That is how God is: He writes straight with crooked lines."

And so they continued on in their conversation. The two young people, after some time in silence — as all the visitors had now departed — gradually, word by word, began a dialogue, and after a while they were as engrossed in conversation as were the *comadre* and Dona Maria, with the difference that the two women's conversation was carried out at full voice and with a lack of concern while theirs was quiet and reserved.

There is nothing that, if interrupted, is more quickly resumed than that familiarity in which the heart has an interest. Do not be surprised, therefore, that Luisinha and Leonardo had given themselves over to it.

And do you wish to see a peculiarity that sometimes occurs? Since reaching her majority and becoming a young lady, Luisinha had never had moments of real pleasure such as those she was enjoying in this conversation, on a mourning day, after the departure of the coffin that was taking to the cemetary the man who was supposed to have brought her happiness. Leonardo, for his part, had also never, amid all the vicissitudes of his exorbitant life, experienced moments that raced by as fast as these in which he observed the object of his first love under the weight of misfortune on a day of weeping.

It seems, then, that these very circumstances had brought the past back to life: The *comadre*, over there in her chair, was rejoicing in it all and, while seeming to pay full attention to Dona Maria, was not missing a single detail.

The time of leave-taking finally arrived, not for the *comadre*, who had offered to keep the widow company, but for Leonardo, whom the major was awaiting. It was, after all, a day in which he was on duty, and he had obtained permission to carry out the bipartite task of presenting his condolences to Dona Maria and thanking her for the interest she had shown in him by, through the intermediary of Maria-Regalada, causing the major to secure both his pardon from the punishment to which he had been destined and also the promotion in rank that he had so rapidly received.

Upon their leave-taking Luisinha involuntarily extended her hand to Leonardo, who pressed it forcefully. Now, in those times that itself was enough to set everyone's tongues awagging!

X X V

Happy Ending

The *comadre* passed almost the entire period of mourning with the widow and her aunt, and she accompanied them to Mass on the seventh day. Leonardo appeared on that occasion as well, and he took the family home after the service was over.

That handclasp that Luisinha had permitted Leonardo on the day of her husband's funeral had not gone unnoticed by Dona Maria either, just as many of the other facts deriving from that one had not escaped her.

The fact is that a certain idea that she had in her mind did not seem so extravagant to her. Often, at the Ave Maria, as the good matron sat down on her bench in a corner of her drawing room to pray, between one "Our Father" and another "Ave Maria" on her blessed rosary there would come to her the idea of marrying the recent widow anew, since she ran the risk of being left at any time unprotected in a world in which husbands like José Manuel can easily appear, especially to well-off widows.

At the same time that that idea occurred to her she would think of Leonardo, who had been in love with her niece when they were both children and who was, albeit wild, a good young man—and not completely unsupported either, thanks to the benevolence of his barber godfather. It is true that what his father had done in that respect was not exactly clear, but, as it was a matter of testimentary proceeds, Dona Maria saw nothing easier than instituting a suit, the outcome of which could not be in doubt.

There was, however, in the midst of all this one factor that confounded her plans. Leonardo was a soldier. Now in those times to be a soldier was an awful thing.

When Dona Maria reached this point in her meditations, she abandoned them and went on with her rosary.

The *comadre* engaged in almost exactly the same calculations on her part, and she too recognized that difficulty and that difficulty alone as a hindrance to her plans.

While these two were thinking, the other two were acting: Luisinha and Leonardo had recommenced their former courtship. And if anyone wants to see something that moves right along it's a widow's courtship. At the first opportunity, Leonardo tried to execute a new declaration; Luisinha, however, rendered that a summary endeavor by accepting the declaration proffered so many years ago. Without being seen, the two saw each other often and arranged their affairs.

Unfortunately, the same difficulty also presented itself to them: a line sergeant could not marry. There was perhaps a very simple way of resolving it all. Above all else, however, they loved each other quite sincerely, and the idea of an illegitimate union was repugnant to them. Love profoundly inspired them. The recourse of which we have spoken, that caricature of a family then very much in vogue, is surely one of the factors that has produced the sad moral state of our society.

That difficulty alone held the two back. One day, however, Leonardo found an expedient and came to tell Luisinha about the way that would resolve everything: He could remain a soldier and marry at the same time by resigning from the line troops and transferring to a similar position in the militia.

The difficulty, however, lay in arranging that resignation and that transfer; Luisinha took charge of solving the problem. One day when her aunt was praying on her rosary, precisely during one of those intervals between "Our Father" and "Ave Maria" of which we have already spoken, Luisinha went to her and told her the entire story in confidence, introducing her narrative with the following declaration, which cut right to the heart of the matter: "To obey you and make you happy I married once, and I was unhappy. I now want to see if I can do better making the choice myself."

Before long, however, she realized that her caution had been unnecessary, because Dona Maria confessed that she had been meditating on the same plan for some time. The two therefore struck a bargain.

The major 's goodwill inspired a great deal of confidence in him, and they therefore decided to have recourse to him once more. They went to meet with Maria-Regalada, who on the previous night had sent to inform them that she had moved from the Prainha and to tell them that they were always welcome at her new address.

The *comadre*, apprised of everything, was a part of the mission. When they entered Maria-Regalada's house, the first person to appear before them was Major Vidigal and, what was more, Major Vidigal in casual dress: robe and sandals.

"Oh," exclaimed the *comadre* in a malicious tone of voice as soon as Maria-Regalada appeared, "from what one can see, things are going well here . . ."

"You recall, don't you," replied Maria-Regalada, "that secret with which I obtained the young man's pardon? Well, this is it!"

Maria-Regalada had for a long time resisted the ardent desire that the major nourished of having her come to live with him once and for all. We attribute that resistance to caprice and nothing more, in order not to pass harsh judgment upon anyone. The fact is that the major had persisted mightily in the matter and must have had his reasons.

The secret that Maria-Regalada had whispered into the major's ear the day she, along with Dona Maria and the *comadre*, had gone to plead for Leonardo was the promise that, if the request were granted, she would accede to the major's fancy.

Thus is explained his benevolence toward Leonardo, which went so far as not only to conceal and pardon all of his transgressions but also to secure the rapid promotion for him. The major 's presence in Maria-Regalada's home is likewise explained.

After this they all entered into a conference. This time the major thought that the request was a just one in the light of its objective. Through his influence, it was achieved in its entirety, and in a week he handed Leonardo two papers. One was his discharge from the line troops, the other his appointment as a militia sergeant.

Beyond that Leonardo received at the same time a letter from his father, in which he summoned him to come take possession of all that his godfather had left him, which was found to have been kept religiously intact.

[space break OK?—comp.]

Once the indispensable mourning period was past, Leonardo, in the uniform of a militia sergeant, was married to Luisinha in the Sé, with the family as a whole in attendance.

From then on the other side of the coin shone. There followed the death of Dona Maria, that of Leonardo-Pataca, and a whole string of sad events that we shall spare the readers by putting our final period here.

THE END

The Novel and the *Crônica*

Especially after studies by Mário de Andrade, Darcy Damasceno, Antônio Cândido, and Walnice Nogueira Galvão, it is not hard to point out traits that make the novel *Memoirs of a Militia Sergeant* stand out in nineteenth century Brazilian prose. Mário de Andrade described the novel's characters as, for all intents and purposes, poor, free people: "lower middle class, Gypsies, mobsters, and grenadiers." Nogueira Galvão emphasized the novel's "faithful portrayal of low style," which is present in its dialogues, its narration, and in its "anti-literary world view." Damasceno maintained that *Memoirs* "goes against the literary taste of its time both because it counters sentimentalism with humor, and because it contains spontaneous, emotional language rather than mere rhetoric." Antônio Cândido argued that the novel created "a world which seems free from the burden of sin and error, . . . [different from] one in which the preference for repressive symbols capable of thwarting impulsive outbursts" predominates, as was true in Brazilian Romanticism. He also claimed that the book allows "a sort of give and take between good and evil, canceling out one another yet never appearing as entire entities."[1]

Memoirs of a Militia Sergeant was first published in serialized chapters alongside reviews of variety shows in the newspaper *Correio Mercantil* between 27 June 1852 and 31 July 1853. As I shall show below, in part because of this fact and in part despite it, one can consider Manuel Antônio de Almeida's novel to be the starting point for one of the most significant currents in nineteenth-century Brazilian fiction. This trend is rooted in the then close relationship between the novel and verbal and pictorial satire such as *crônicas* and cartoons published by newspapers during that time. Subsequent novels in the same vein include *O Garatuja* [The scrawl] by José de Alencar, *A Carteira do Meu Tio* [My uncle's wallet], *Memórias do Sobrinho do Meu Tio* [Memories of my uncle's nephew], and *A Luneta Mágica* [The magic telescope] by Joaquim Manuel de Macedo, and *A Família Agulha* [The needle family], by Luís Guimarães Júnior. On the other hand, as Antônio Cândido suggested, *Memoirs* was also similar to the "comic and satiric work during the Regency (1831–1840) and the early years of the Second Empire (1840–1889)" and cannot be considered to have arisen without antecedents.[2]

Uniforms and Packages

Among the many expressions typical of nineteenth century popular speech used by Almeida to create the colloquial Brazilian flavor of the language in his novel, a particular proclivity for images linked to tailoring or cloth merchandising stands out. In translation, of course, some of this disappears and I will have to refer here to the Portuguese original. The oft-repeated assertion that the mischievous Leonardo was not born for *emendas* (both "amendments" and "mending") is a prime example. Another example occurs in two different forms: At the end of the serialized version of the novel, the narrator suggests that the readers avail themselves of some good *ponto* (either a "point" or a "stitch"), whereas at the end of the book as published in Portuguese, he informs the reader that he has made his final "point [period]" or final "stitch." Consider also the sixteenth chapter of Part One, which reports the surprisingly rapid release of the Reverend. Major Vidigal, when he caught the reverend at the gypsy's party and took him to the guardhouse, only wanted to give him a "sample of the cloth [a taste of the medicine]."

These amendments/mendings, points/stitches, and samples of cloth are textile double entendres and lead the way to the final pun in Leonardo's adventures. The pun is based on the words *farda* ("uniform") and *fardo* ("package" or "burden"). The protagonist goes from being a homeless boy to a militia sergeant and acquires his own *fardamento* ("military dress"), and this appears juxtaposed to the task or threat of *en-*

fardamento ("packaging" or "burdening"), a word which was regularly printed in the advertisements that ran alongside the stories appearing in "Pacotilha," the variety section normally included in the *Correio Mercantil's* Sunday edition, where the serialized version of *Memoirs of a Militia Sergeant* first appeared. It is to this textual context that we must first attend if we are to expand our understanding of this novel.

Cecília de Lara, in the introduction to her 1978 critical edition of *Memórias* points out the extensive use of retail metaphors in the "Pacotilha" section of the paper.[3] This includes Almeida's regular use of the word "customer" instead of "reader." "Pacotilha's" letters section was known as the "office"; and the name of the supplement itself, in addition to meaning "trifle," also denotes the amount of duty-free cloth or goods a passenger or crew member could take on board a ship. The paper even used the name "Carijó and Company" as the byline for all the articles, to preserve the anonymity of its contributors (one of whom was, from 1852 on, as we now know, Almeida himself): "What sort of cloth has not been packaged by the great firm Carijó and Company? What breed of rational and even irrational being has not been packaged or burdened, or has not been skewered by Antônio's needle, or been the victim of Gregório's miraculous pen?" (27 July 1851).

The collaboration of social chroniclers and merchants can be seen in "Pacotilha's" insistence on "packaging" as the way to present both its subject matter and the staff's writing process. If one examines the "Pacotilhas" in the *Correio Mercantil*, one notices the repeated references to writing as packaging (6 July 1851): "We go on packaging as long as no one calls us to lunch, which is often late on days of so much work." The third number (23 February 1851) ends: "It's ten o'clock, I'm going to a costume ball. Boy, bring me my boots! Manuel, sew this package up and mail it!" The following complaint appears on 16 March 1851: "If I didn't pride myself in being a good Christian, I would have quit packaging the Pacotilha." A few days later (23 March 1851) the following threat appeared: "If I find that you're getting angry, just take a gander at Antônio's needle. This man, whether you like it or not, will sew it [the "Pacotilha"] up and package it once a week, come rain or shine." One could in fact quote any issue of "Pacotilha" and come up with a number of "orders" and "goods" in the process of being packaged.

These "goods" appear in the weekly supplement and address different subjects: domestic help, illegal slave trade, theaters, border disputes, *carnaval*, balls, support for the immigration of free settlers, Parliament, freedom of the press, and the contrast between the written constitution and the absolutist practices of the government. The articles in "Pacotilha" dealt with this wide range of subject matter almost always using retail metaphors. As the first "Pacotilha" (9 February 1851) explains: "Everyone knows that a pacotilha normally contains merchandise of many different types, thus it should be understood that a wide range of subject matter will fall within the compass of our writers' pens. They humbly beg your indulgence even to soar to great heights, though these may have been already touched by others." In the issue for 27 July 1851 one finds a series of comparisons used to underscore the heterogeneity and miscellany found in the Sunday supplement:

> Sometimes Pacotilha looked like a pharmacy where one could find all sorts of medicine. Other times it looked like a dragnet used to catch different types of fish, big or small. On other occasions, a bazaar or a huge showroom for different products of human ingenuity. And finally a vast, sumptuous banquet, where the delicacies were jumbled owing to their great number.

But whether or not we are confronted with a bazaar, a business, or a pharmacy, it is not primarily the variety of material addressed in this supplement's articles that interests us or even these retail analogies. Nor is it merely because the *Correio Mercantil*, was, as Lara reminds us, "a newspaper which specialized in business."[4] What is especially of interest here as we try to understand *Memoirs of a Militia Sergeant* is the very nature of these supplements dealing simultaneously with entertainment and commercial endeavors during a time when more people began to write about business. This juxtaposition is precisely why the supplement seems to emphasize orders, packages, and the firm Carijó and Company. In this respect "Pacotilha" is similar to earlier satiric publications such as *A loja de Belchior* [The second-hand store] of 1833. This publication satirized the "moderate whorehouse scum" and also referred to its readers as "customers" and to its articles as "odds and ends or junk of all types"—or as an exposition of "robberies done by cautious thieves." Another magazine of this sort was the 1863 *Bazar Volante* [Flying bazaar]. Here the purported commercial establishment acquires a winged character suggesting both the variety of issues dealt with as well as a great mobility (in tone, subject matter, and scale).

Now, as Davi Arrigucci Jr. has emphasized, it was not just in Sunday supplements and miscellanies but in a most popular genre closely linked to them in the Brazilian press since the 1830s—the *crônica*, or short, semi-fictional account—that "writers seemed to prepare themselves for a clearly fictional form": the novel.[5] If, in addition to their proximity in *Correio Mercantil*'s Sunday supplement, tailoring and cloth trade images point towards a link between *Memoirs of a Militia Sergeant* and the articles in "Pacotilha", they also share other features, which, when examined, will help us understand the importance of the interchange between the novel and the *crônica* in nineteenth-century Brazilian prose.

One factor is the term *pacotilha* itself, which, as noted above, designates a small package and was chosen as the title of the section for weekly *crônicas* and the serial publication of Almeida's novel. Besides suggesting the wide variety of subject matter and the supposedly commercial nature of the pieces it published, the name also implies that each issue was relatively autonomous and self-contained, as was each installment of the adventures of Leonardo Junior. Each *crônica* in "Pacotilha" stood alone and contained some comment concerning events of the previous week. True, authors eventually began to make suggestions about topics which would appear in subsequent columns, or they alluded to earlier stories. The pieces nonetheless ended with complimentary closings such as: "Until the next one, dear customers"; "Until tomorrow"; or something similar. Even though there were unifying elements in the series of "packages," e.g., the origin of the article (the firm's office), the byline "Carijó," the people regularly mentioned (the boss, Antônio, Gregório, and Manuel), an identical network of retail images, and a uniformly somewhat theatrical textual format which dealt playfully with the news of the week, all the *crônica*s can be read independently, without needing to consult another.

This discontinuity among the weekly variety supplements, however, contrasts directly with the narrative sequentiality generally based on a plot that organizes the episodic but continuous serialized novel. And if the *crônicas* and novels in "Pacotilha" share a similar fractionating process in their serialization, given that they are published weekly, and given that they are a product of an incipient literary industry, there is, nonetheless, a perceptible difference between them because there is an essential discontinuity in a Sunday variety supplement but a necessary continuity in a serialized novel.

Pacotilha Way

Serialization is not the only similar yet differentiating point of contact between the "packages" and *Memoirs of a Militia Sergeant*, as well as between other nineteenth-century serialized novels and satiric pieces. There are also themes, dialogic formulas, oscillations, prosaisms, and sources of humor that clearly seem to link the two genres.

In both "Pacotilha's" articles and in the *Memoirs* one sees similar motifs. One of them is the feast of Pentecost or the Holy Spirit, which appears in number 70 (6 June 1852) and in the first part of the novel. The theme of the illicit slave trade also appears in the serialized version of Chapter IX, "The *Compadre's* `I've Done Pretty Well'," where the apparently easygoing barber is shown to have a lack of scruples, a quality that is linked to his having been for a time, a "doctor" on a slave ship. This theme was also common in the "packages." In the 23 February 1851 issue the "Pacotilha" contains critiques of the nominal "Constitution" which is belied by the real-life "absolutism" of those whose "backs are . . . protected by Dom Basílio or Dom Simão." These critiques appear right next to "Well now, the law . . . what is the law if you so desire, Major?" which Dona Maria says to Major Vidigal in an episode of the *Memoirs*. Throughout the novel the author takes potshots at mutual obligations (*compadresco*) and "pull" (*empenho*), claiming that they are "the real forces behind the entire social mechanism." In another issue of "Pacotilha" (16 March 1851), a satiric piece concerning "bad neighbors" mirrors the friction Leonardo's godfather experiences with his neighbor on his godson's behalf as well as the novel's constant comments concerning the habit of "snooping in other people's lives and asking slaves for information about what goes on behind closed doors." In addition, there was a curious case outlined in another issue (30 May 1852) of a veteran "sergeant, and Inspector in the second block of the Santa Rita Parish," whose presence "at those wild parties" at the firm of Carijó and Company had provoked numerous complaints. This sergeant seems to presage the protagonist of the serialized novel, the first installment of which would appear in less than a month's time.

In both genres it is likewise not hard to discern the frequent use of a dialogue between narrator and reader: A fictitious interlocutor appears to emphasize particular motives, to summarize what has happened, and to set up a point of view for the readers. This was a strategic move since neither genre, but especially not the novel, was entirely fixed at that time. "Dear customers, I have begun," says Carijó on 27 July 1851. "Dear customers, today I'm upset and angry," reads the *crônica* for 15 March 1851. "The customers will have to make do with the facts of the old story from the 25th, 26th, and 27th of June of bygone eras," declares the author in his introduction, where he apparently ignores the topics of the previous week on 27 June 1852, when the *Memoirs* began to appear. This interchange was obligatory in "Pacotilha's" *crônicas* and was often accompanied by an internal dramatization as in Carijó's orders and his dialogues with the packager, the "boy," and whoever was responsible for the firm's accounts. If in this novel the narrator fails to mention "customers," there nevertheless continues to be constant interchange between him and the reader: it is a sort of protracted pointless chatter, similar to that of the *crônica*. One reads phrases such as: "The readers surely remember"; "perhaps some readers may have a notion"; "as most readers know by heart from A to Z"; "the reader should not be surprised by this"; "if the reader thought about what we said a while ago"; "as everyone who reads me knows"; and "lest the readers wonder."

One also finds attempts at drawing the public in by invoking them. In the case of a genre such as the *crônica*, which is notable for its variety of motifs and of venues (as one issue notes when it contrasts "The war in the River Plate" with the "internal war" against the boss), as well as for its varied language (now descriptive, now satiric, now moralizing), this invocation works as a necessary means of situating the reader in these shifting tides. In the case of a serialized novel, it also works to bring possibly forgotten elements into the foreground or to foreshadow future developments and to try, as others have already noted, to maintain the reader's "interest in the story . . . [and a] consistent affective link between the story-teller and the listener."[6]

And, considering the heterogeneous material itself and the need to review the issues of the week, as well as the need to be brief and to record daily life and particular forces in the fictional sense, it is not surprising that chroniclers and novelists working alongside each other might find themselves forced to create a self-image; that they might experiment with self-satire in the midst of their obligatory changes. On 23 March 1853 an author asked:

> And how about that? Aren't I in a pickle? I've bundled myself up here in Pacotilha! And why not? If I try to talk about everything and everybody, it's natural, logical, and consequential that I tell you some of the moves I've made, the ups and downs I've suffered.

As another quotation will suggest, such self-packaging does not exactly produce a hero. After addressing a hypothetical demand to sign the articles with their real names, one author (23 February 1853) says, "While I don't consider myself a coward or a fighter, could I possibly sign my own name every time I sent out a package?" Sometimes, citing or complaining about someone else's affront, Carijó ends up repeating it in a sort of purposeful self-disqualification and in this way links the writer himself to the events and news that were the standard butts of jokes in "Pacotilha." On 16 March 1851 an author refers to a journalistic "bad neighbor" who had stolen both his "cashier" (editor) and "cloth" (news). He says: "He even went so far as to say that I'm no painter, just a cartoon hack."

In *Memoirs of a Militia Sergeant*, if the first person narrator appears to be a chronicler when describing customs, parties, and processions, he does not seem quite as enmeshed in his material as "Pacotilha's" chroniclers were. In addition, the author's anonymity is preserved in a much more abstract fashion since the installments were signed "A Brazilian," rather than "Carijó." At times, however, there are certain attempts at familiarity, as in the case of Part One, Chapter XIX, "Pentecost Sunday." The first paragraph says: "In his childhood, the writer of these memoirs had the opportunity to witness the *Folias*, although they were then in their last stages of decadence." Another gesture aimed at putting the narrator on a par with the reader occurs at the end of Chapter XXI (Part Two), "Revelation," where the author adds the expression "God only knows" and pretends to know as little about the protagonist's future as the reader does.

There was one passage in the serialized version (later excised from the book) in which the author gives a veritable self-portrait. At the end of the that version he says:

> The author does not have the stomach to deal with (sad) things like this, and this is why he ends this story asking the readers to forget this book and not to blame him for its defects, because it was only an attempt. If someone says that it is bad practice for an apprentice barber to learn his trade on silly customers, that person will realize that the readers will profit only from some good point that this attempt may have made. So, please be tolerant of a mere beginner.

Beginner, apprentice barber, incapability of dealing with sad events—if the self-portrait of the chronicler-narrator is not exactly flattering, it is not quite as devastating as the one mentioned above, where the chronicler suggests he is a coward or a cartoon hack for Carijó. This does not, however, mean that the narrator of *Memoirs* does not become, from time to time, a particular type of caricaturist, similar to the Sunday "packagers."

The Cartoon Hack

In this novel there is, however, no dearth of instances in which its author makes frequent incursions into the terrain of caricature. One of them is the protagonist, Leonardo, who, as a child, in his godfather's barbershop, "would amuse himself by making faces at the customers." As an adult, he played the supposedly dead Major Vidigal in a satirical folk ceremony. The other mocker was Teotônio, a guitarist, gambler, and consummate imitator and face-maker. He often mimicked stereotypes: the backwoods boy, the old man, the simpleton; or he took on people who were easily recognized, as in the case of his humorous imitation of Vidigal's "long, shriveled face."

Alongside these internal satiric models, the novel seems to be in direct dialogue, as far as its principal processes of character construction are concerned, not only with the habitual comic resources typical of variety supplements, but also with caricature itself, which spread throughout Brazil starting in the 1830s and 1840s.[7] (Precisely in the period during which the *crônica* began to take hold.)

Caricatures appeared in flyers, in different loose etchings, and, beginning in 1844, when the magazine known as *Lanterna Mágica* first appeared, in magazines and illustrated pamphlets. Indeed, the character descriptions in *Memoirs* seems to be modeled on pictorial satire and on two of its theoretical sources, basic to the times: physiognomy and phrenology, with their common belief that one could discern people's character by observing their outward appearance. "But physical characteristics never fail," the narrator declares at a certain point. And, for readers interested in discerning characters' affects, he goes so far as to mention, in Part One, Chapter XIX, "Pentecost Sunday," the "keen observer," who is capable of detecting rapid lifting of eyelids or fugitive glances.

Characterization of the main personages in *Memoirs* is, in fact, based mainly on physical descriptions and outward appearance. They are sometimes disproportionate, as in the case of Leonardo's father, who is "rotund and excessively fat." The godmother is "a short and excessively fat woman." The school master is "an entire man built on infinitesimal proportions: very short, very thin, with a narrow, shriveled face, and excessively bald." Other times the author exaggerates, as in the case of the several "veries" used to describe Dona Maria: "very fat, very short-wasted, [with a] very starched handkerchief." Contrast is used, as in the case of Vidigal, who inspires fear from his position of authority, but who appears at home sloppily dressed in his underwear, a calico coat, and clogs. Or in the case of the "meek, flute-like voice" of the Capuchine and the "thundering, hoarse voice" of the master of ceremonies in Chapter XIV (Part One), "Further Vengeance and Its Result." Difference of scale also appears: Consider the "short, fat matron," who is one more "whose shape was the complete antithesis of . . . [a] teeny tiny" man present at Leonardo's baptism. Doubles recur: the similar and outlandish dresses worn by Luisinha and Dona Maria; the bride's and groom's identical, ancient carriages in Chapter XII (Part Two); or the pair of ladies, "both widows, both fat, and both excessively similar," in whose house Leonardo lives as a boarder once he meets Vidinha.

Even when other details, beyond physical peculiarities, are added to characterizations, they are also unique yet similar to one another, or juxtaposed to distorted descriptions. Examples include Dona Maria's "mania for lawsuits" and Leonardo Junior's series of "pranks," or in Vidinha's overuse of the expression "Qual!" (Good grief!), which becomes a verbal tick. These are cases of one-note characterization using physiques, behavior, or speech. A single word, mania, behavioral or physical trait is caricatured as in pictorial humor and used to define the characters in *Memoirs*. This helps the reader remember characters (which is important in a serialized publication) as well as advancing the plot—or at least the progress of the narrative—since personages do not have to be reintroduced each time they appear.

It is not by chance that, in one of the exercises in caricature present in *Memoirs* (where José Manuel is described), the author defines his object as "a living *crônica*." That immediately links *crônica* and caricature, which, while they have been transformed by Almeida as well as by much of nineteenth-century Brazilian literature, became fundamental to the writing of Brazilian novels. The type of characterization coming from these descriptions based on specific, schematic, and rapidly detected traits suggests a static image of the individual, of a "painting" that can be reproduced fully or in part at any point in the story. And José Manuel is not the only victim of verbal and visual caricature in *Memoirs of a Militia Sergeant*. When one looks at the book's overall composition, other "paintings" work in a similar fashion. They deal with customs, parties, and typical sites "in the time of the king." They occur mainly as introductions to the chapters in the first part of the book.

As Nogueira Galvão has said about the first half of *Memoirs*, "there is an imbalance, an enlargement of the sketches to the detriment of the plot." This, according to her, is rectified in the second part, where the narrative can be seen to pick up and "the plot takes over."[8] The text seems in fact to go from being a series of *crônicas* to being a novel, and from being a historical narrative to being social analysis while maintaining nonetheless its ties to variety magazines and caricatures around which Brazilian prose fiction tested its wings during the nineteenth century.

These ties are particularly necessary if one goes back to the image of a "package" and remembers the wide range of material dealt with in nineteenth-century fiction during its formative period (1830-1850) and especially when it came to be increasingly accepted by the public sometime halfway through the 1840s. Within the obligatory nativistic approach to literature entailing local nature scenes, historical leaps, and caricature, it is not at all strange that novelists assumed the especially mobile perspective of the social chronicler as their favored model. Likewise it is not strange that, to define characters, they borrowed resources from pictorial humor and from the "physiologies" that were so popular then. Indeed, Almeida went so far as to outline a "physiology of voice."[9] A unique trait kept a character constant in the midst of suspense and turnabouts, in historical and other less direct circumstances, in issues of the day, and in these narratives which answered the needs of variety magazines as well as those of serialized novels.

Especially in the second part of *Memoirs*, the reader is faced with a so-called "continuous movement" or "narrative flux," which, according to Alfredo Bosi, portrays one of the marks of life in poverty—the perpetual subjection to material needs and the constant effort to juggle the whims of adverse conditions—as well as the relish with which one savors periods of good fortune.[10] As Cândido and Roberto Schwartz have maintained (taking their cue from a brief observation by Mário de Andrade), what distinguishes this novel are its characters and the privileges these free, unremarkable, propertyless men enjoyed in a slave-holding society such as nineteenth-century Brazil.[11] This can be seen not only in the feints they perform and minor blows they suffer to survive and avoid violence in a precarious milieu; it can also be seen in the book's narrative, which, as Nogueira Galvão has pointed out, consists of pendular oscillations between description and action. Cândido maintains that this oscillation consists of a give and take between order and chaos, legality and illegality, popular types, archetypes, and the concrete social rhythm of the times.

But if this glimpse into society, this purposeful toning down of then current romantic language, and these oscillations which define the narrative rhythm make *Memoirs of a Militia Sergeant* stand out in nineteenth-century Brazilian literature, they also point to a satiric current in that literature. Included in that current are several works alluded to at the beginning of this Afterword, such as Joaquim Manuel de Macedo's *My Uncle's Wallet, Memories of my Uncle's Nephew,* and *The Magic Telescope;* José de Alencar's *The Scrawl;* and Luís Guimarães Júnior's *The Needle Family.* This satiric bent is similarly marked by a link among *crônicas,* caricatures, and the novel. Examples include not only The *Needle Family's* caricatured individuals and its pace, which is reminiscent of an illustrated novelette, but also the activity of Ivo do Val in *The Scrawl.* This character even painted caricatures on walls. These novels' subject matter and tone were purposefully low rather than "elevated." In addition and especially, Macedo's novels often contained self-satire that mocked the chronicler-narrator, a device Almeida used in a more distanced way.

There is another aspect that links this series of works and sets their peculiar protagonists apart from other novels of the time. Leonardo from *Memoirs,* Simplício from *The Magic Telescope,* Ivo from *The Scrawl,* Anastácio and Bernardino Agulha from Guimarães Júnior's humoristic pamphlet, and Macedo's "uncle's nephew" are all half rascals, half dupes. Sometimes they get away with insignificant tricks and receive unexpected boons or hard blows—the latter are always portrayed with humor and ignominy. They are also quite earthy, just as are the descriptive passages and the novels' language itself. As Cândido has pointed out, this turn also gives these early novelistic protagonists a major role in the development of Brazilian fiction, clearing the way, as they seem to do, both for *Macunaíma* and *Serafim Ponte Grande* (two protagonists in twentieth-century Brazilian modernist fiction). These characters may even be said to have opened the road for Rubião in Machado de Assis' *Quincas Borba* (1891) and, to a point, but in this case without the earlier characters' naïveté, for Machado's protagonist-narrator of *Memórias Póstumas de Brás Cubas* (1881).

The mixture of naïveté, foolishness, and knavery that characterizes not only Leonardo, but the entire lot of Simplícios, Needles, Scrawls, and uncle's nephews also brings them back once more, through a different route, to nineteenth-century satiric journalism, which is the fundamental interlocutor in the creation of chronicler-narrators and caricature-characters. For these simple but wily protagonists, who are often called "mischievous" and "devilish" or are infantilized by parents, uncles, and godparents, and similar figures—mischievous children— begin to appear in all sorts of periodicals. Cases include the "Vida do relator" [The Writer's Life Story] included in *O Nicodemos* (1851) and the

magazine *O Menino Travesso* [Mischievous child] (1842), "a comic, critical, and always moral periodical" that defined its own name by asking,
"If their innocence allows children to say whatever they want, how can
one foresee that a mischievous child will not say everything he feels,
since there is so much material that will make him burst at the seams?"
All topics would now be fair game for the fiction writer.

Add to this a brief commentary included in *Bazar Volante* (21 Octo-
ber 1866). Here Brazil itself becomes the mischievous child:

> Brazil thought a moment. The unreflective and inexperienced youth run-
> ning toward his ruin hesitated at the top of the inclined plane where false
> advisors had impelled him. He surveyed the abyss that was about to swal-
> low him, and, fearlessly forcing himself, he made his way through the
> throng that in gleeful anticipation had gathered to applaud the downfall
> of the American colossus.

Although ending with hopeful rhetoric, this excerpt begins by belit-
tling the "unreflective and inexperienced" country. One should remember that earlier in the nineteenth century, when Emperor Dom Pedro II
was still a minor, the country was wracked by political instability. And
this seems to suggest one more meaning for the satiric character called
the mischievous child—even in the fictional world of Leonardo.

* * *

There is, however, an obvious difference. These fictional characters'
"pranks" and "turnabouts" are not exactly allegorical; they are, instead and
especially, ways of underscoring the action, rhythm, movement, and oscillations typical of satiric novels during their early days. This subgenre
took its earliest steps at the same time authors of other books dealt with
epic matters or produced grandiloquent historical sketches. It became a
sort of critical and destabilizing twin of a literary model in the process of
establishing itself. This novel, just like the duty-free packages, seems destined by its very humoristic purpose, to "package itself up" and burden itself as well. And this is how Leonardo's *Memoirs* and the supplement's
"packages," the novel and the *crônica*, as well as Leonardo's ultimate burden of uniforms (grenadier and militia man) all come together.

—Flora Süssekind
Translated by Arthur Brakel

NOTES

1. Mário de Andrade, "Introdução," in *Memórias de um sargento de milícias* by Manuel Antônio de Almeida, ed. Cecília de Lara (Rio de Janeiro: Livros Técnicos e Científicos, 1978) 306; Walnice Nogueira Galvão, "No tempo do rei," in *Saco de gatos* (São Paulo: Livraria Duas Cidades/Secretaria de Cultura, Ciências e Tecnologia, 1976) 30; Darcy Damasceno, "Afetividade lingüística nas *Memórias de um sargento de milícias*," *Revista Brasileira de Filologia*, 2:2 (Dezembro 1956) 159; Antônio Cândido, "Dialéctica da malandragem," in *O discurso e a cidade* (São Paulo: Duas Cidades, 1993) 48, 49.

2. Cândido, "Dialéctica da malandragem," 29.

3. See the note by Cecília de Lara in *Memórias de um sargento de milícias* (edition cited in note 1) xvi–xxii. The "Pacotilha" series can be found on microfilm at the National Library in Rio de Janeiro.

4. Ibid., xviii. See also Richard Graham, *Britain and the Onset of Modernization in Brazil, 1850–1914* (São Paulo: Brasiliense, 1973). Graham points out that the 1850s heralded the beginning of Brazil's modernization with an increase in exports, the appearance of new firms, and regularization of business practices owing to the 1850 Commercial Code. For information on the market and means of production in Rio de Janeiro during the period in which this novel is set ("the time of the king"), see João Luís Ribeiro Fragoso, *Homens de Grossa Aventura: Acumulação e hierarquia na praça mercantil do Rio de Janeiro, 1790–1830* (Rio de Janeiro: Arquivo Nacional, 1992).

5. Davi Arrigucci Jr., "Fragmentos sobre a crônica," in *Enigma e comentário* (São Paulo: Companhia das Letras, 1987) 58.

6. Damasceno, "Afetividade lingüística," 170. For more on the Brazilian feuilleton see Marlyse Meyer, *Folhetim: Uma história* (São Paulo: Companhia das Letras, 1996).

7. For more on the use of visual material in the supplement, see Lara, xvi. See also Herman Lima, *História da caricatura no Brasil*, 4 vols. (Rio de Janeiro: José Olympio Editora, 1963).

8. Nogueira Galvão, "No tempo do rei," 28.

9. "Fisiologia da Voz," *Correio Mercantil*, 9 July 1854. This can also be found in Manuel Antônio de Almeida, *Obra Dispersa* (Rio de Janeiro: Graphia Editorial, 1991) 19–23.

10. Alfredo Bosi, *História concisa da literatura brasileira* (São Paulo: Cultrix, 1974) 147.

11. For more on this subject see Roberto Schwartz, "Outra Capitu," in *Duas Meninas* (São Paulo: Companhia das Letras, 1997) 132ff.